Commonwealth
or Empire?

Russia, Central Asia, and
the Transcaucasus

Commonwealth or Empire?
Russia, Central Asia, and the Transcaucasus

William E. Odom
Robert Dujarric

Hudson Institute
Indianapolis, Indiana

Hudson Institute
Indianapolis, Indiana

ISBN 1-55813-050-0
Copyright © 1995 Hudson Institute, Inc.

Printed in the United States of America.
This book may be ordered from:
Hudson Institute
Herman Kahn Center
P.O. Box 26-919
Indianapolis, Indiana 46226
(317) 545-1000

Contents

Map 1   The Caucasus and Central Asia

The Caucasus and Central Asia

Map 2 Ethnic Groups in Southern CIS and Neighboring Middle Eastern Countries

Ethnic Groups in Southern Soviet Union and Neighboring Middle Eastern Countries

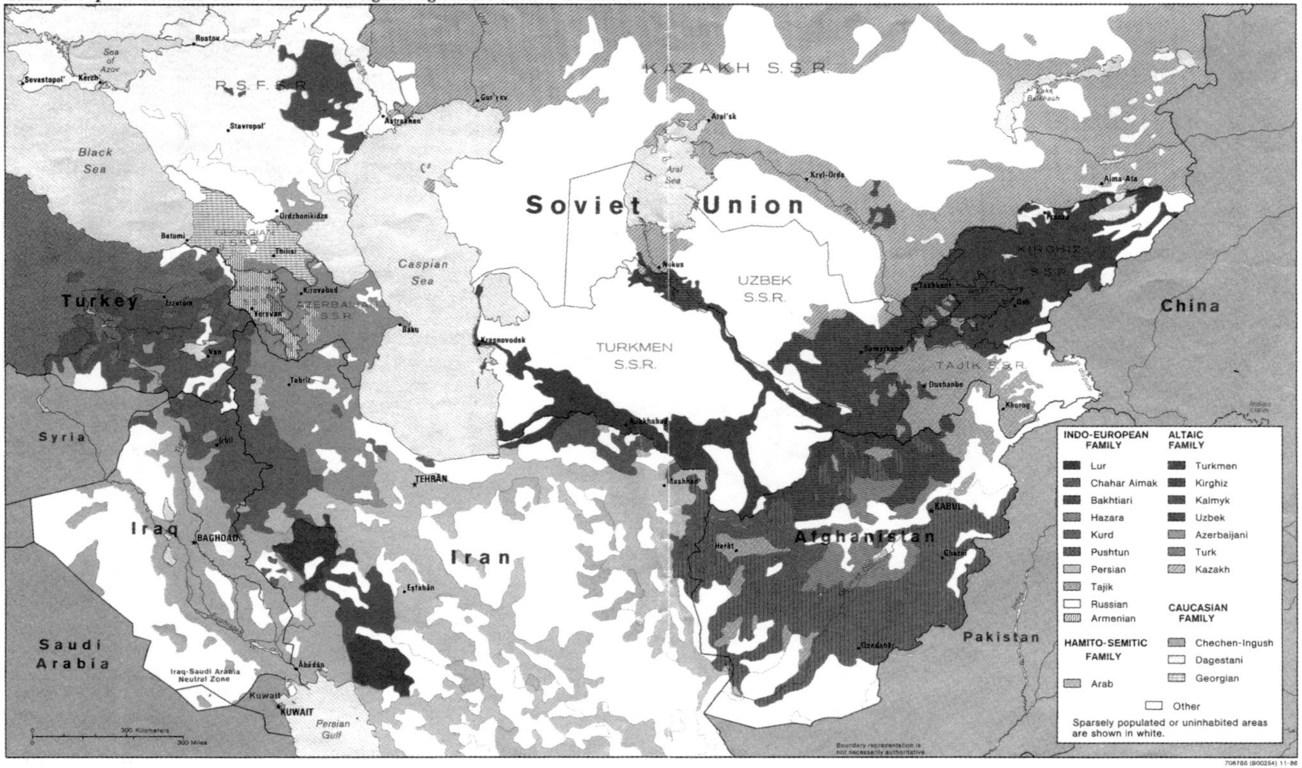

Map 3 Major Ethnic Groups in Central Asia

Major Ethnic Groups in Central Asia

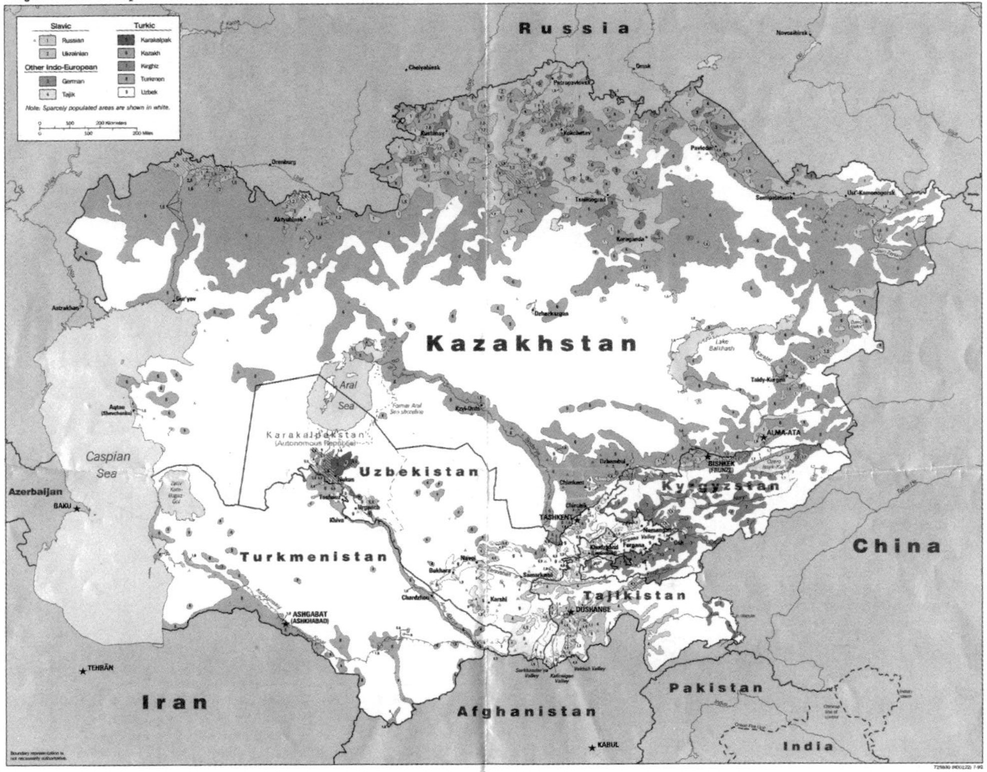

Map 4 Ethnolinguistic Groups in the Caucasus Region

Ethnolinguistic Groups in the Caucasus Region

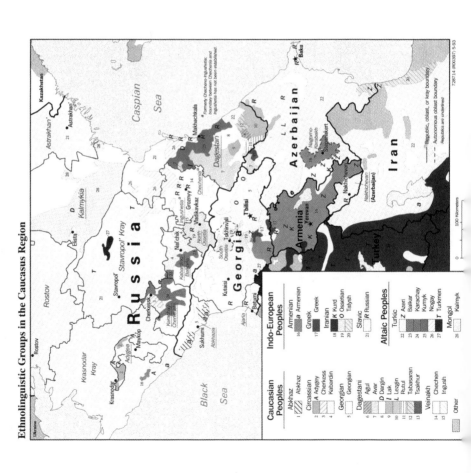

Map 5 Kurdistan

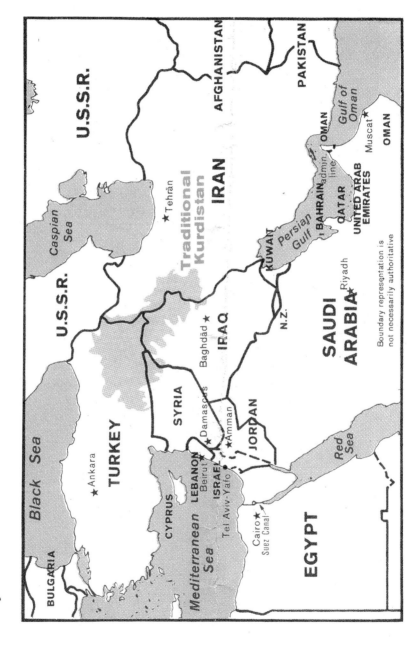

Map 6 Tajikistan

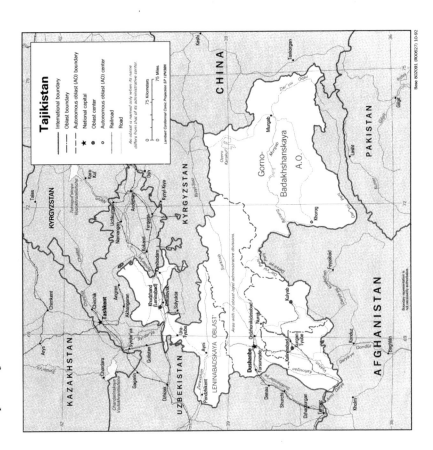

Map 7   Energy to the World

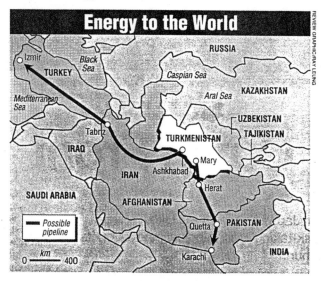

Map 8   Kazakhstan Oil Export Options

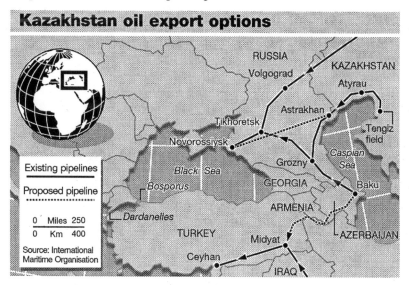

Acknowledgments

This book was made possible by the Office of the Assistant Secretary of Defense for International Security Policy, which provided funding for Hudson Institute's initial study of *Regional Stability After the Soviet Breakup: Central Asia and the Transcaucasus.* We would also like to express our gratitude to the Smith Richardson Foundation, which funded a research trip to Kazakhstan, Kyrgyzstan, Uzbekistan, and Georgia, and to Peter Richardson and Arvid Nelson in particular. In Almaty, Bishkek, Tashkent, Samarkand, and Tbilisi we were warmly welcomed by government officials and researchers and would like to express our thanks to all of them for their hospitality.

At Hudson Institute's Washington office, Matt Garber provided invaluable assistance in research, organizing our massive files, and sorting publications and reports. Debora Hansen also helped us greatly in the management of the project. At Hudson's headquarters in Indianapolis, Deborah Jones and Gwen Rosen in the library provided us promptly with all the books and journals we required. Neil Pickett read the entire study and gave us useful comments and suggestions. Anne Himmelfarb and Sam Karnick edited the manuscript with great speed and quality, and Sam supervised the production process.

Obviously, we are responsible for all the errors and imperfections which may remain, and the views expressed in this book do not necessarily reflect the opinion of the Department of Defense or any of its agencies.

William E. Odom
Robert Dujarric
Washington, D.C.
December 1994

Preface

The conventional wisdom holds that the dissolution of the Soviet Union "changed the world." So far, so good. But the initial hopeful notion that the end of the cold war would bring on an era of unprecedented peace and tranquillity was far too optimistic. Instead, we have encountered an extremely fluid and unpredictable international situation. Solid information and insights about what is really going on have been hard to come by.

To help remedy this, during the past three years Hudson Institute's national security program has completed a number of studies that look closely at rapidly changing areas of the world. These have focused on regions of longstanding U.S. policy concern, such as Europe and East Asia, as well as on countries in South America, South Asia, and the South Pacific. Various government agencies have supported these studies, primarily the Navy, the Defense Nuclear Agency, and the Agency for International Development.

In 1992, the Office of the Secretary of Defense, International Security Affairs, supported an additional set of studies which allowed Hudson to examine two regions whose growing importance to the U.S. was accompanied by relatively little knowledge of the circumstances likely to contribute to (or detract from) their stability. *Commonwealth or Empire? Russia, Central Asia, and the Transcaucasus* is an outgrowth of that research.

One of the most important questions of the post-Cold War era has been whether Russia will be able to establish a viable democracy or will relapse into authoritarianism and a passion for empire-building. The regions under examination in *Commonwealth or Empire?* will be crucial to that outcome. Of the fifteen successor states created by the breakup of the Soviet Union, five are in Central Asia and three are in the Transcaucasus. These countries are now open again to influences from their traditional neighbors in the Middle East, South Asia, and East Asia. But if these new nations forge closer relationships with their neighbors, how will Russia react?

The authors of *Commonwealth or Empire?*, Hudson Director of National Security Studies William E. Odom and Research Fellow Robert Dujarric, conclude that, in fact, no outside state is making a significant effort to replace Russian influence in either region, and that the cultural ties of both regions to the Middle East through languages and religion have not reasserted themselves with the vigor many experts anticipated. The more important question, they believe, is whether Russia will move into the power vacuum. The answer will carry tremendous implications not only for U.S. national security but also for Russia's own domestic political development. If the relationship between Moscow and the two regions again becomes one of empire, the prospects for Russian democracy will be considerably dimmed. Hence Central Asia and the Transcaucasus may have a significant effect on U.S. strategic interests through the rest of the decade.

Commonwealth or Empire? refrains from making specific policy recommendations, preferring to sort out what is happening and what is likely to happen, not how to make a particular outcome more likely. The magnitude of the topic and the brief period since the end of Soviet rule make a truly comprehensive and definitive study impossible. Before that can be done, studies such as *Commonwealth or Empire?* must break new trails, explore new terrain, and discover new vistas. It is, therefore, an essential exploratory endeavor.

The study was particularly helped by private support from the Smith Richardson Foundation. The foundation's director, Peter Richardson, made possible a trip to both regions during which the authors engaged in discussions with the heads of four of the states, as well as many of their subordinate officials. Arvid Nelson of the Smith Richardson Foundation deserves a special word of gratitude for his organization and management of the trip, as well as his substantive participation. Although the Smith Richardson Foundation and the U.S. government agencies that provided support bear no responsibility for the conclusions of the study, Hudson Institute gratefully acknowledges their assistance.

Leslie Lenkowsky
President
Hudson Institute

Introduction

The Soviet Union covered one-sixth of the earth's land surface, and its empire included several other nations in Central Europe, Asia, and Latin America. The repercussions from its breakup and the fall of communism will continue to be felt for many years, possibly decades.

Much has been written on Russia and on Central Europe, but very little about the southern rim of the former USSR. The eight new nations in this region—Kazakhstan, Kyrgyzstan, Tajikistan, Uzbekistan, Turkmenistan, Azerbaijan, Armenia, and Georgia—were the least-known regions of the Soviet empire. Few Westerners visited them, and even fewer were familiar with their cultures and languages. For most analysts, to study the Soviet Union was to focus on Soviet Russia, a Russian-speaking realm governed by Russians.

Consequently, when the southern republics attained independence, they were *terrae incognitae.* To this day, our body of knowledge about these republics remains limited compared to our understanding of Russia. Yet it is important for students of world politics to grasp the new realities of this southern tier, for several reasons. First, an analysis of Russian policy toward these countries reveals much about Russia's goals and ambitions throughout the former Soviet Union. Second, if Russia successfully executes its policy of imperial reassertion described in the first chapter of this book, Russian democracy will have little or no prospect of survival. Thus Russia's future is partly being written in its "near abroad." Third, the end of the Soviet Union has allowed half a dozen countries to deepen their relations with the new nations of the Transcaucasus and Central Asia. Although as of late 1994 Russia remained the key outside power in the region, nations such as Turkey, Iran, and China could see their roles in the region grow considerably, especially if Russia's presence diminishes. It is therefore important to analyze the development of new international linkages, such as China's with Central Asia, that could alter regional diplomacy in the late 1990s and beyond.

After the breakup of the Soviet Union, the dropping of the Iron Curtain along the southern Soviet border exposed two regions on the periphery of that empire—Central Asia and the Transcaucasus—to neighboring regions with which they had long been close before Soviet rule. Central Asia's khanates of Kokand, Samarkand, Bukhara, Khiva, and others were centers of power in the 15th and 16th centuries. Persian cultural influences ran deep, and Islam connected these regions to the Turkish and Arab worlds as well. The famous "Silk Road" between Europe and China had traversed Central Asia and brought the region cultural, economic, and political influences from the Orient. The region also provided a home for migrant herdsmen from groups left over from the age of the Mongol invasions, people who were forcibly settled by the Russians only during the 19th and 20th centuries.

Persians and Turks fought over the Transcaucasus for centuries. Whereas the Armenians and Georgians were Christians, many other groups were Muslim, including the Azeri (the largest such group) and a large number of small ethnic groups in the North Caucasus. Greek settlements on the eastern and northern shores of the Black Sea brought still other outside influences to the region.

Both these regions figured in the 19th century "great game" of imperial competition between Britain and Russia. Looking on with nervousness while Russia colonized Central Asia in the late 19th century, Britain attempted to check Russian progress and pose obstacles to it. In the Caucasus, the discovery of oil deposits near Baku brought British, Russian, and other oil companies into competition for access.

The late 19th century also witnessed the emergence of what Marxists would classify as an inchoate "national intelligentsia" in most countries of both regions. European ideas of national identity made their way into the thinking of the few educated elites in several of the major ethic groups. These elites began to publish newspapers and journals in which they developed their thoughts on their own "nationalisms," seeking to tie them to their histories, cultures, and distinctive experiences and traditions. None of these small movements got very far, but they made sufficient progress in the early 20th century to become a matter of interest to the Russian revolutionaries, especially the Marxists. Some members of these nationalistic movements became revolutionaries; others did not. Yet they created the beginnings of local nationalisms which were highly incomplete in their synthesis of their political, cultural, and religious heritages with European ideas of nationalism. The cataclysmic events of the Russian Revolution seemed to offer them an opportunity to make the transition from merely writing and thinking to exercising sovereign political power. Instead, these events devoured them.

The advent of Soviet power and the Bolshevik victory in the Russian civil war propelled both regions into the embryonic "socialist camp" and cut them off from outside influences other than Soviet power. For the next seven decades they remained largely isolated and subject to the great Marxist-Leninist experiment in trying to transform more than one-hundred ethnic groups into one great clan of homogeneous new "Soviet" citizens devoid of their previous "bourgeois" inclination to hold strong ethnic and national identities. The regime characterized Islam and Christianity as "opiates" of the masses, to be discarded as mere reminders of a bygone epoch in their historical development toward a socialist society with no private ownership of the means of production and possessing a new "scientifically" grounded "class consciousness" for fighting their way to a classless communist society.

To say the least, neighboring societies that had similar religious, ethnic, and cultural legacies but were outside the Soviet Union had dramatically different experiences during these seven decades. But with the removal of the Soviet border and the creation of new possibilities for extensive economic, cultural, and political intercourse with those neighboring societies, what was likely to happen in Central Asia and the Transcaucasus? Would the states of these regions cast off the Soviet experience like a bad dream and rapidly return to their old social and political patterns? Would they seek to restore their ties to the Middle East, Turkey, Iran, and China? Would other countries rush into Central Asia and the Transcaucasus? Affirmative answers to these questions, based more on hunches than analysis, tended to inform most Western opinion in the early 1990s.

A second set of questions about these two regions concerned political and military stability. Would the new situation involve a high degree of instability? Would internal wars over political and economic succession flare up? Would the old borders drawn by Stalin to demarcate these states be thrown into serious dispute? Would outside forces become involved in such disputes? If so, which outside countries would become involved? And would they promote stability or try to exploit instability? In this last connection, of course, to what extent would competition over these regions evoke a new version of the 19th century's "great game"?

A third set of questions, related closely to the first and second sets, concerned religious and cultural identities. The Iranian revolution and the rise of a theocratic regime with proclivities toward expansionism and international troublemaking posed the prospect of that kind of theocratic revolution spreading to Central Asia and into some of the Muslim societies of the Caucasus. What would be the implications of that? Is such a revolution a serious prospect, likely to materialize?

A fourth set of questions concerned the nature and degree of Russian influence likely to remain or be restored in both regions. The formal dissolution of the Soviet Union took place rapidly, with little or no broad discussion about successor entities. The Commonwealth of Independent States (CIS) was at best a vague concept with which to replace the excessively centralized Soviet system. Would it soon become merely a new name for the old Soviet system? Could it become something like the European Union? Would Russian influence through the CIS and other channels increase stability or undercut it? What would happen to the individual states in Central Asia and the Transcaucasus? These states had only inchoate traditions of "nationalism" compared to Europe and the European parts of the old Soviet Union. What kind of political systems would their political cultures support? Were their elites sufficiently able and consolidated to maintain their new independence? Did they really want that independence?

These questions cannot be answered in full today. Such answers would fill several volumes, and our knowledge of the domestic affairs of the states and societies of these two regions is still too limited. Their dynamics will undoubtedly surprise even those few Western scholars who have good knowledge of these countries. This does not mean that we should not attempt to find answers. On the contrary, the West requires even tentative answers to understand what is at stake in the great transition underway in both regions and in the rest of the former Soviet Union.

This volume is intended to provide tentative answers to some of these questions. Because the challenge is so large, it is difficult to decide where to begin and how to divide up the many tasks for analysis. To guide our main focus and provide a starting point, we have taken a cue from Machiavelli, who observed in *The Prince* that all stable states have in common good laws and strong armies, and that because there are no good laws without strong armies, he would set aside the discussion of laws and speak of armies.[1] Machiavelli's contribution to our understanding of the former Soviet Union is not mere chance or a small quotation taken out of context. Northern Italy in his day was rent asunder by quarreling factions and armed groups, and political order was practically nonexistent. He focused, therefore, on instructing political leaders on how to achieve political stability. Today the collapse of the Soviet system has left vast territories and many states and groups without political stability, especially in parts of Central Asia and the Transcaucasus. In such situations, military power has an enormous effect on political stability; some kinds of militaries, as Machiavelli was careful to explain, undermine stability whereas others sustain it.

Accordingly, the primary focus of this study is on military developments during and after the dissolution of the Soviet Union. It begins with Russia's attempts to make the Commonwealth of Independent States something more than a fig leaf intended to conceal the political, military, and economic vacuum created by the dissolution of Soviet institutions. That analysis must treat all the former Soviet republics to some degree, but the emphasis is on those in Central Asia and the Transcaucasus. Economic affairs in the CIS are treated briefly. Finally, we offer a short look at the internal dynamics of each state in the two regions.

The focus on the CIS, of course, raises the role of Russia and its efforts to reassert its hegemony or forebear. The second part of the study, therefore, examines the development of the Russian military. Western students have disagreed deeply over whether a new Russian imperialism is emerging. Rather than simply enter that debate, this analysis looks at what the Russian military did between 1992 and 1994; how it assembled itself out of the pieces of the Soviet Armed Forces; how it related to the CIS military; how it developed a "military doctrine" that implied a great deal about Russian foreign policy goals; and how its demands for resources competed with other demands on the state budget.

This review of the new Russian military provides considerable new evidence for inferences about the imperial character of Moscow's policies toward Central Asia and the Transcaucasus. No other aspect of Russia's relations with other CIS countries involves the degree of institutional entanglement and political involvement the Russian military does. The varying political attitudes among the leaders of Central Asian and Transcaucasus states are thrown into more revealing light when seen in the context of their military relations with Moscow. It reveals their sense of dependence or independence, the resulting limits they perceive on their autonomy in other areas, and sometimes a clue to their strategies for longer-term political survival.

These two studies, of course, do not treat the issues of new external relations for Central Asia and the Transcaucasus. Are these new states rapidly moving into new orbits outside the old Soviet boundaries? The next section of this book, therefore, deals with the countries outside the former Soviet Union, both the ones contiguous to Central Asia (China, Afghanistan, and Iran) and a few that are not (Turkey, Pakistan, and India). Then we examine the policies of Turkey and Iran toward the Transcaucasus.

Conclusions from these sections of the study cast doubt on two points of conventional wisdom about these external influences on Central Asia and the Transcaucasus. First, neighboring Asian and Middle Eastern states are certainly more involved in both regions than during the Soviet period, but they do not begin to match the residual Russian influence. Second, and related, is a finding concerning radical Islam. After the breakup of the Soviet Union, many Western students of the region expressed great expectations of radical Islamic influence in the newly independent republics, especially in Central Asia. And Russian and Central Asian leaders have complained loudly and repeatedly about the dangers of Islamic radical movements destabilizing the region. The available evidence, however, supports precisely the opposite conclusion: although the Islamic cultural foundation is alive and gaining strength in the social lives of these states, radical Islamic political movements show no serious prospects of taking power. Only in Tajikistan in the short run and perhaps in Uzbekistan after a longer period might such movements arise, and even then they will originate only because of the highly repressive policies of the incumbent regimes, not because of an inherent popular demand.

Both these conclusions apply to the Transcaucasus as well, although the relations of Iran and Turkey with this region are quite different from and driven by strategic and political factors different from those behind the outside influences in Central Asia. The Christian countries of Armenia and Georgia account in part for this difference, but animosities between Iran and Turkey also play a role, as does geography.

The conclusions of this study go beyond a mere summing up of the main findings, to provide some thoughts about Russia's political future. Russia's connection to these regions may be more important for Russian domestic political development than it is for the regions themselves. The more deeply entangled Russia becomes in these regions, the more difficult it will be for Russian leaders to implement liberal economic and political reforms at home. The dilemma for U.S. policy is as follows: will we see an antiliberal, imperial Russia maintain stability in both regions, or will we watch these regions fall into internal chaos and disorder as Russia withdraws and devotes its political and economic resources to domestic reform? Russia cannot do both.

Notes

[1]See Niccolo Machiavelli, *The Prince* (New York: Alfred Knopf, 1992), 55, for this observation. The subsequent chapter deals with alternative kinds of military establishment and their impact on domestic politics. Machiavelli's conclusions remain remarkably relevant even today for countries such as those of Central Asia and the Transcaucasus.

ONE

The Commonwealth of Independent States: Central Asia and the Transcaucasus

Introduction

The formal dissolution of the Soviet Union at the end of 1991 abruptly gave the Soviet republics of Central Asia a status of political independence none of their leaders had sought. In the last years of Gorbachev's *perestroika* they had fought for and won more autonomy in economic affairs and a freer hand in appointment of local officials, but, unlike the Baltic republics and the republics of the Transcaucasus, none of the Central Asian republics had a strong political movement for full independence from the Soviet Union. Certainly there were deep-seated resentments against the privileged and fairly large Slavic populations in these republics, but the old communist leaders had remained firmly in control and supportive of Soviet power. Gorbachev's *glasnost* policy had not stimulated well-articulated nationalist movements in Central Asia as it had in the Baltic republics.

In the Transcaucasus the situation was different. Soviet military forces had violently repressed political demonstrations in Georgia and Azerbaijan. The bloody events in Tbilisi in April 1989 and in Baku in January 1990 inspired hostile political reactions against Soviet authority in both countries. Communist party officials were losing control, caught between new but poorly organized nationalist forces and Moscow's heavy-handed policies. Armenians also held huge public demonstrations for independence, but the crisis in the Nagorno-Karabakh autonomous oblast lent ambiguity to Armenian sentiments because Moscow was seen at times as a partner for forcing Azerbaijan to make concessions to the predominantly Armenian population of Nagorno-Karabakh.

The dissolution of the Soviet Union, therefore, came as a surprise to the states in both regions and at a time when none of them was well prepared for it. Moreover, the massive bureaucratic institutions of the Soviet political system were designed to insure a highly centralized state. The new de jure independence, therefore, coexisted with the old de facto subordination to Soviet institutions. The Commonwealth of Independent States (CIS) was conceived as the successor institution to the Soviet Union because those Russian leaders seeking to abolish the Soviet Union realized that some new institutional arrangement was essential to replace it.

In January 1992, therefore, the future status of all the states in both Central Asia and the Transcaucasus depended to a large degree on the nature of the CIS. Was it to be merely a new name for the old Soviet system? Would it be only a loose affiliation of the former Soviet republics? Or were there alternatives between those two extremities? Was political independence to be real or merely apparent? To the degree that it was real, would these new states be stable? Or would they fall into civil and regional wars?

The emerging patterns of power and institutional relations in the CIS during its first three years of development offer the best, although not the final, answers to these questions.

The motivation for creating the Commonwealth of Independent States (CIS) is to be found in Boris Yeltsin's need to complete the removal of Gorbachev after the events of 19-23 August 1991. Although this episode has been called a failed coup attempt against Gorbachev by his colleagues in the Soviet government, it was in fact a successful coup against Gorbachev by Yeltsin and the Russian government. By forcing the so-called "Emergency Committee" of the government to yield to Gorbachev, Yeltsin effectively took political power even though he restored Gorbachev to formal authority. That step, however, left Yeltsin in a wholly unsatisfactory situation. His old rival still held the formal trappings of power. The very act of saving Gorbachev had made it awkward for Yeltsin simply to replace him. After all, that was what he had just opposed, Gorbachev's arbitrary removal. He needed to find a way to sweep aside this inconvenient arrangement.

Yeltsin found the answer in a simple but sweeping bureaucratic maneuver: dissolving the Soviet Union. It was quite logical. During the last two years of Gorbachev's *perestroika,* leaders of the fifteen republics had fought—with considerable success—to acquire new powers, especially over economic policy, at the expense of the Soviet central government. Since mid-1990 when Yeltsin had become the chairman of the Russian Federation's[1] Supreme Soviet, he had followed a similar course, staking his political future on Russia against the Soviet Union. Gorbachev had reacted by proposing a new union treaty among the republics, and it was to be signed on 19 August, the day the so-called "Emergency Committee" attempted to assert its control. By completing the dissolution of the union, Yeltsin would leave Gorbachev without a formal post and thereby dispose of his old rival. In retrospect, it appears that Yeltsin followed this course with little advance planning, apparently having only the vaguest view of the larger outcomes he sought when he began his struggle in the summer of 1990.

Corroboration for this interpretation is found in the hasty and improvised creation of the CIS. It was originally intended to include only the Slavic republics of Russia, Ukraine, and Belarus; that is, those with a common legitimacy basis, Slavic ethnicity, and leaders equally hostile to Gorbachev. The Central Asian leaders, most notably Nursultan Nazarbayev of Kazakhstan, were not anxious to break up the Soviet Union and were furious at being excluded. Thus the deal worked out in Belovezhskaya Pushcha near Minsk on 8 December 1991 was quickly adapted to include eight additional republics, which signed an agreement in Alma Ata in Kazakhstan on 21 December. The Baltic republics and Georgia declined to join.[2] Only the skimpiest thought and planning for CIS institutional arrangements were evident before the CIS came into existence. Admittedly, the Soviet Union was already in a state of rapid political decay, but its precipitous collapse in late 1991 appears to have been as much the result of Yeltsin's tactical political convenience as anything else.

Even cursory consideration of the ramifications of dissolving the Soviet Union shows that it had to present dramatic challenges for building new institutional arrangements. The highly centralized Soviet economic system and military structures could not be quickly replaced by new ones. Moreover, because the decision was made by a very narrow section of the political elite, it did not reflect the preferences of large political groupings in Russia and several other CIS member states. Azerbaijan's parliament refused to ratify the agreement, and Moldova's parliament was not even asked to ratify it at first because rejection was certain. Apparently some Russians— particularly senior Soviet military officers—initially thought that creation of the CIS comprised merely a name change rather than a commitment to fundamental political and institutional restructuring.[3] Others, particularly Russian liberal democratic reformers, saw it as a way to cast off the more conservative regions of the USSR and expedite the transformation of Russia alone. Probably very few if any grasped the full implications of the step they were taking.

Thus Russian policy within the CIS was initially ambivalent— some officials in the Russian government were determined to retain as much of the Soviet empire as possible, while others resisted that goal. The story of post-Soviet Russian policy, therefore, is the story of the shifting balance between antireform and neoimperialist forces and liberal reform forces. Throughout 1992 and early 1993, the reformers retained considerable influence, particularly through Andrei Kozyrev in the ministry of foreign affairs and Yegor Gaidar on economic policy. By mid-1993, however, the defense ministry, factions in the parliament, and reactionary opinion-making circles became dominant. Yeltsin and Kozyrev increasingly shifted their positions to make them unobjectionable to those who decried the loss of Russian superpower status. That change breathed new life into the CIS after it had earlier appeared terminally moribund.

Turning to Central Asia and the Transcaucasus in particular, the CIS became central to Russian policy toward those regions after the breakup of the Soviet Union. Initially the CIS was the primary instrument, but it failed to take an institutional shape that could ensure Russian military and economic hegemony over the states of these regions. Moscow responded to the failure of CIS institutionalization by resorting to numerous bilateral arrangements with most of the newly independent republics. Yet it never completely gave up on the CIS in the course of 1992-94. By the fall of 1993, the CIS began to show signs of new life, as Georgia and Azerbaijan were coerced into joining it, which they had initially refused to do. Yet bilateral ties continued to provide the most important means for securing Russian influence, if not direct rule, in both regions.

A similar ambivalence characterized the policy of most Central Asian countries toward Russia and the CIS. The old communist rulers who remained in power in all states but Kyrgyzstan were reluctant to break fully with the Russian-dominated organization. They were not anxious to see the old command economic arrangements of the Soviet system collapse. Nor did they want to see the expansion of popular participation in their own countries. Like their conservative counterparts in Moscow, they sought to slow down or even stop the transition to liberal democracy and market economies. They maintained their interministerial ties in the police and intelligence areas, determined to prevent the kind of political upheaval that was occurring in Russia from spreading to their own societies. President Nazarbayev of Kazakhstan was the most articulate in suggesting CIS arrangements for preserving most of the old Soviet institutions while retaining the sovereign status of all member states. President Akayev of Kyrgyzstan was the exception, a former scholar brought to office by a wave of democratic reform, but he was disinclined to get out of step with Nazarbayev and others over CIS relations. Thus the Central Asian leaders largely sought to make the CIS simply a new Soviet Union that permitted them vastly expanded local autonomy, particularly for putting their ethnic compatriots into all the best government positions at the expense of Russians and other privileged ethnic groups.

In the Transcaucasus, experiences from the Gorbachev period prompted quite different attitudes toward the CIS. Only Armenia consistently maintained the CIS tie, because it needed Russian military support in the war over Nagorno-Karabakh. Georgians, angered by the Tbilisi massacre by Soviet military and police forces in April 1989, rallied behind Zviad Gamsakhurdia's policy of breaking all ties with Moscow. Although the Georgian government maintained observer status at most CIS meetings, it refused to join. The events in Baku in January 1990, when Soviet forces killed numerous people while dispersing a demonstration there and were believed by most Azeris to have created the disorders, inspired extremely hostile views toward Moscow. Thus, Azerbaijan initially remained outside the CIS.[4]

None of these republics, however, could retain independence from Moscow. Armenia, the single state in either Transcaucasia or Central Asia with sufficient ethnic homogeneity and political cohesion to have good prospects of consolidating internal stability and solidarity, was trapped by its dependency on the Russian military in its war with Azerbaijan. In both Georgia and Azerbaijan, although most Russian military units rapidly decayed and virtually disappeared after selling off their equipment to local buyers, greatly reducing Moscow's instruments for retaining control, local political cohesion was absent. The weakened residual Russian military and intelligence units at once began to play off regional separatists in Georgia against the government. Eduard Shevardnadze's return to Georgia hardly pleased the Russian military, which actually stepped up the conflicts, especially in Abkhazia in the spring of 1993. For a brief period in 1992-93, Azerbaijan proved able to elect a new president—who infuriated Moscow by his overtures to Turkey and his attempts to cut Russia out of Azerbaijan's oil industry through deals with Western firms. By backing a dissident Azeri military leader in his forcible overthrow of the Baku government, Moscow facilitated the installation of former Politburo member and Azerbaijan party chief Gaidar Aliyev as Azerbaijan's president. Not surprisingly, both Shevardnadze and Aliyev submitted to Russian pressure and made their countries members of the CIS. The alternative was continued civil war in which Russian military units backing the antigovernment groups would destroy them.

By 1994, Russia's CIS links with the Transcaucasus states superficially resembled those with Central Asia: old communist party elites were in charge in these countries and more sympathetic toward some kind of CIS union than toward pursuing democratic and market reforms as independent states. Shevardnadze was an exception in his own preferences, but he had been forced to play the Russian game. At the same time, Central Asia's Tajikistan—where the ruling communist elites had fallen into a civil war among themselves and with opposition groups—looked more like the Transcaucasus, where internal disorders were providing Moscow levers of control. Yet Tajikistan's old communists shared none of the stature and desire for genuine sovereignty that Shevardnadze and (to a lesser degree) Aliyev possessed.

This brief survey of the dynamics of the CIS and Russian relations with Central Asia and the Transcaucasus in the first two and a half years of the CIS's existence leaves a mixed picture. The CIS was hardly a stable and thriving institution, and relations between Moscow and the two regions were anything but regular. Russia was deeply involved in both regions in a fashion that looked much like a reassertion of imperial domination. At the same time, local leaders and factions facilitated—sometimes intentionally, sometimes unintentionally—the return of Russian hegemony. Moreover, in several states in these regions the governments were unable to maintain order, political cohesion, economic well-being, and popular support. Moscow insisted that it was merely maintaining stability in both regions and preventing the spread of civil war into Russia. Russian leaders also declared that the large number of ethnic Russians living in these regions endowed Moscow with a responsibility to look after their rights and well-being. Finally, Russia justified its policies by insisting that states outside the former Soviet Union were contributing to the instability in both regions and that these states would fill the vacuum with anti-Russian influences if Russia withdrew.

Exploring CIS developments in more detail during its first two years of existence reveals extremely complex dynamics in these regions, making both of their futures look highly indeterminate. At the same time, a few observable major trends provide some sense of the more probable future directions they will take. Exposing the complexities without losing sight of the major trends can best be done by following several threads of development individually. The first and perhaps most important thread concerns military institutions. The creation of the CIS forced these institutions into first place on the CIS agenda in early 1992, and they have held that position consistently ever since. The second thread concerns economic policy. Although this policy was more complex than the treatment here will reveal, a summary examination of Russian macroeconomic and industrial policies exposes the paradoxes and inconsistencies in Russian policy, particularly toward Central Asia. The third thread concerns dynamics within the individual states of both regions. They are sufficiently different to demand a modicum of individual treatment for understanding both CIS and regional dynamics. Finally, the mosaic suggests answers to the larger questions of Russian intentions toward these regions.

CIS Military Developments

Creating CIS Armed Forces posed, in principle, the same kind of difficulties creating a standing military under the United Nations has always presented. The permanent members of the Security Council are sovereign powers. A military organization depends on clarity about precisely what political authority controls it, and it requires moral support from the society (or societies) it defends. Persuading soldiers to risk their lives for anything less than a clearly defined and legitimate political authority is difficult. Moreover, military leaders without clear political subordination are inexorably drawn into politics, usually over resource issues. For example, because the UN Security Council has never been able to provide either foundation, moral or political, creation of a standing military force has proven beyond its capability.

To Build or Not to Build CIS Armed Forces?

To the extent that the CIS was indeed a group of sovereign states, the creation of a CIS Armed Forces comprised an analogous predicament. Most senior Russian officers did not take the sovereignty of the CIS member states seriously at first, nor did many Russian civilian officials. At the same time, some CIS state leaders became ambivalent about their own sovereignty when they recognized the institutional and economic implications of such independence. By mid-March of 1992, however, their predicament was becoming clear even to the most ardent proponents of a CIS—they were not part of an organization that was just another name for the old Soviet Union. Summit meetings of CIS heads of state were rapidly making the reality obvious.

After the Central Asian reaction to the all-Slavic concept of a CIS, as expressed at the 8 December 1991 meeting near Minsk in Belarus, a second meeting convened in Almaty, Kazakhstan, on 21 December. The meeting place undoubtedly was chosen in deference to the bruised feelings of Central Asian leaders. This time, all the former Soviet republics except the three Baltic states were expected to attend, but Georgia ultimately refused. All the remaining eleven heads of state showed up.[5] The summit leaders decided that the main political institution of the CIS would be a conference comprising the heads of state and heads of government of each member. To address the multitude of institutional issues involved in dismantling the Soviet Union, six interministerial committees were set up: for foreign affairs, defense, economics and finance, transportation and communications, social security, and internal affairs. With these hasty actions complete, providing the illusion of institutional continuity, Yeltsin could move on to the formal step of dissolving the Soviet state.

Accordingly, all eleven heads of state convened on 30 December in Minsk. Although the Soviet Union was dissolved, major problems were already surfacing. Key military and economic issues could not be resolved. Marshal Yevgenii Shaposhnikov was appointed commander of the CIS Armed Forces for two months, and agreement was ostensibly reached on command arrangements for strategic nuclear forces, but no agreement was reached on command of conventional forces. The far more troublesome question of creating armed forces in each of the republics was simply put off.[6]

Although participants signed nine basic documents—including ones on strategic forces, border troops, joint space programs, and the status of property of the former Soviet Union abroad—they could not conceal their serious disagreements even in those areas. For example, Russia and Ukraine contested the disposition of the Soviet Navy, centering on the Black Sea Fleet, and most republics showed a determination to build independent armies. Participants could not agree on a new oath of allegiance for all military personnel. Marshal Shaposhnikov's proposal that they swear allegiance to the "peoples of the CIS" provoked strong objections from Ukraine, which countered by demanding that servicemen take an oath to the republic on whose territory they serve,[7] a portent of disagreements soon to arise between Shaposhnikov and Ukrainian leaders. Future trouble for the Border Troops was apparent in the instruction to their commander to conclude an agreement with each member state within two months.[8] No common understanding existed on who should control borders, or even which borders were to be controlled, making such a short deadline for resolving such issues unrealistic.

Behind Moscow's lack of preparation for the military transformation within the CIS was a competition among views about the structure and shape of new command arrangements.[9] Marshal

Shaposhnikov convened a meeting of future CIS ministers of defense in Moscow on 26-27 December 1991, where he presented the concept. It envisioned all ministries of defense and their forces directly under the commander of the CIS Combined Armed Forces (see fig. 1.1). The concept was immediately seen as a Trojan horse designed to maintain Russian supremacy. Thus, it got nowhere, although Shaposhnikov advertised it as only a transition arrangement to prevent administrative chaos in the interim. Colonel General Konstantin Kobets offered a structure based largely on the ideas of Russian civilian reformers and junior officers, ideas developed over the previous year or so (see fig. 1.2). His plan differed from Shaposhnikov's mainly in recognizing wholly independent national armed forces for each state, forces not subordinate to the CIS military command. Yet it retained the concept of two CIS commands, one for strategic forces--extremely broadly defined to include the Soviet navy and other forces tangentially related to purely strategic nuclear forces--and another for conventional "strategic mobile" forces. On the complicated issues of personnel, budgets, weapons procurement, supply, etc., the plan recognized the need for CIS interstate coordination through a series of commissions. Because it allowed for an independent armed force for each CIS member, the plan carried the day, despite the complexities it involved for administration and support functions and the reality that most CIS states could not possibly create independent armed forces without great expense and several years of preparation.

On these difficult issues rested another set of troubles—how to implement the Strategic Arms Reduction Talks (START) and Conventional Forces in Europe (CFE) treaties.[10] The geographic allocations of conventional forces under CFE made little sense if all the formerly Soviet territory was no longer to be a single military space.[11] In fact, the CFE allocations gave Ukraine a significant edge over Russia in tanks, artillery, and armored vehicles, and Belarus, being closer to Central Europe, also enjoyed advantages. Complicating matters further, the most modern models of tanks and artillery were in the western Soviet military districts, another loss to Russia under CFE, although some compensation would be provided by Russia's retention of the groups of forces in the former Warsaw Pact states.

Difficulties in implementing the START agreements proved no

Fig. 1.1
Ministry of Defense Plan

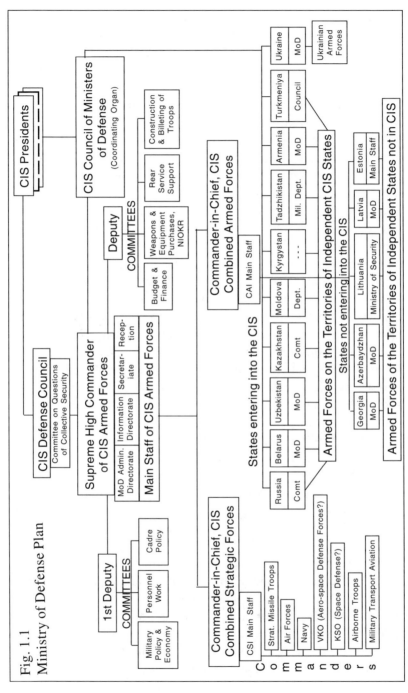

Source: FBIS-SOV-92-009, 14 January 1992, 11

less challenging, because of Ukraine's reluctance to give up all of its strategic nuclear weapons. This issue, of course, took on a life of its own outside the CIS arrangements, intensively involving U.S. officials in what was primarily a bilateral quarrel between Russia and Ukraine.[12] Belarus, by contrast, never raised serious objections to putting the strategic nuclear forces on its soil under Moscow's control. Likewise, President Nazarbayev of Kazakhstan remained cooperative despite occasional hints that he would use the nuclear missiles in Kazakhstan as a bargaining chip.

After the inauspicious beginning in Minsk on 30-31 December, much work remained; therefore, another CIS summit was convened, in Moscow on 16 January 1992. Ukraine and Marshal Shaposhnikov were already deeply involved in the quarrel over the appropriate oath for CIS servicemen, and Ukraine lost no time in forcing all military personnel on its territory to swear an oath to Ukraine or leave. The Black Sea Fleet had also become a bone of contention between Moscow and Kiev. Although other issues also concerned the CIS heads of state, the centrality of defense affairs was evident from the agenda for the Moscow summit, which contained ten items, eight of them concerning military matters.[13] Little progress was achieved, however, and a subsequent summit was scheduled to convene in Minsk on 14 February, providing time for more preparatory work.

On the face of it, the second Minsk summit appeared to accomplish much. Of the twelve agreements signed, seven concerned military issues, two concerned economic affairs, two diplomatic affairs with non-CIS states, and one was political, concerning CIS principles.[14] The military agreements in particular looked impressive, both for their titles and for their detail, but the trouble becomes evident when one observes who actually signed them. With the Baltic republics refusing to join, the CIS potentially had twelve member states, but Georgia did not formally join although it normally sent observer representation. That left a total of eleven formal participants; among these, Moldova's parliament did not ratify its membership until 1994. Moreover, signatures obtained at a summit meeting often required parliamentary ratification for the signatories before coming into force. The following list of agreements signed at Minsk in February 1992 shows the scope of military issues that had to be faced as well as the lack of consensus on how to resolve them:

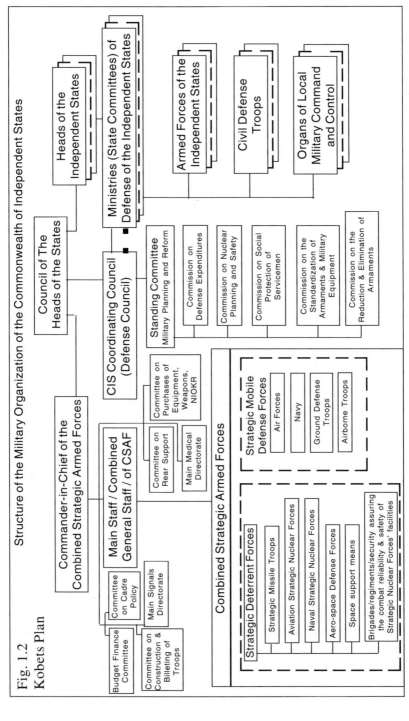

Fig. 1.2
Kobets Plan

Structure of the Military Organization of the Commonwealth of Independent States

Source: FBIS-SOV-92-009, 14 January 1992, 12

- Strategic Forces Agreement, signed by all but Moldova.
- General Purpose Forces Agreement, signed by eight members but not by Ukraine, Moldova, and Azerbaijan.
- Appointment of Marshal Shaposhnikov as Commander in Chief of CIS Armed Forces, signed by all but Moldova and Turkmenistan.
- Agreement on Supplying the Armed Forces, signed by seven but not by Ukraine, Kazakhstan, Azerbaijan, and Russia.
- Agreement on Safeguards of Servicemen, signed by all but Moldova.
- Decision to establish a Defense Ministers Council, signed by only five: Russia, Armenia, Tajikistan, Uzbekistan, and Kazakhstan.
- Protocol on Military Issues, signed by all eleven. (This was an instruction to the defense ministers to prepare a block of military agreements for the next summit.)

As the final document reveals, at Minsk more work was left undone than was completed. Noticeably absent was any effort to reach a formal agreement on a general CIS military budget, the bedrock on which any significant CIS military structure would have to stand. A few days later, on 21 February, the urgent finance issue was addressed in an agreement, but Georgia refused to sign it, and Ukraine insisted that it would participate only in a single budget for strategic forces, not for the whole CIS armed forces. Some of the other signatories also expressed reservations, leaving the document with little or no force.[15] Moreover, the definition and financing of strategic and general-purpose forces decided at the February summit proved anything but fully agreed in practice over the coming months.

When the CIS heads of states convened again, in Kiev on 20 March 1992, they initially faced an agenda of ten pressing military issues.[16] Another eighteen political and economic items were also scheduled for attention, but Yeltsin succeeded in removing three—succession of ownership of property broadly defined, financial liabilities between the Soviet state bank and central banks of the republics, and the status of the old Soviet Border Troops.[17] Not only were military issues piling up but also economic and political questions.

The heads of state reached agreement on the appointment of

commanders immediately subordinate to Marshal Shaposhnikov. General Yurii Maksimov was given command of the CIS Strategic Forces, and Colonel General Vladimir Semyonov received command of the CIS General Purpose Forces.[18] Shaposhnikov was also assigned a chief of staff for the CIS Unified Armed Forces, Colonel General Viktor Samsonov. Three agreements were also signed, providing a legal basis for the CIS Armed Forces, the General Purpose Forces, and the powers for the CIS "defense bodies," that is, the Council of Heads of State, the Council of Heads of Governments, and the Council of Defense Ministers, respectively.[19]

On the crucial issues of a unified budget and a unified logistics system to support the CIS Armed Forces, the documents in Kiev apparently were merely revised versions of those presented earlier in Minsk. All but Azerbaijan and Turkmenistan signed the agreement "Maintaining Supplies to the CIS Armed Forces," including Russia, which had not signed the Minsk version because it was too loose and was insufficiently specific and binding. Moldova, not a party to the agreements on the CIS Armed Forces and their strategic and general purpose components, stipulated that it would "resolve the issues expounded in the present treaty only on a bilateral basis."[20] In fact, the agreement merely committed the members to "plan" a unified budget and did not commit them to live by it.

War in Nagorno-Karabakh, instability in Georgia, and strife in the "Dniester Republic" in Moldova intruded "peacekeeping" (or "peacemaking"[21]) onto the agenda in Kiev. Surprisingly, all CIS members but Turkmenistan signed an agreement to establish a CIS "group of peace maintenance forces." Restrictive conditions for use of these forces probably accounted for the broad support. They could be employed only after a request from all sides to the conflict and only after a cease-fire had been reached. They were to be constituted on a voluntary basis, drawing troops from member states not engaged in the conflict.[22]

In all, participants signed eleven documents on military matters, including two concerning Border Troops that were initially stricken from the agenda.[23] As in Minsk, few of the agreements were signed by all heads of state. Ukraine, Azerbaijan, Moldova, and Turkmenistan refused to sign agreements assigning particular powers to CIS military bodies as well as the "Agreement on the Joint

Armed Forces for a Transitional Period." Ukraine in particular opposed anything that would essentially provide for the continuation of
the Soviet Armed Forces, fearing the implications for Ukrainian sovereignty. Four of the states that had agreed to a CIS General Pur-
poses Forces at Minsk withdrew their support in Kiev—leaving only
Russia, Armenia, Kazakhstan, and Kyrgyzstan as signatories. As
noted, only Turkmenistan refused to sign the agreement for a new
group of peace-maintenance forces.[24]

Marshal Shaposhnikov tried to put a good face on the outcome
in Kiev, but his optimism was at odds with the facts. He and his staff
had struggled from the beginning to accomplish two fundamental
things. First, they wanted a legal basis on which to set the creation of
command and force structure arrangements, starting at the top. Indeed, they got four agreements, including the appointment of commanders and a chief of staff and legal status for the CIS Armed
Forces and the higher CIS defense bodies. Holdouts and reservations by member states on these agreements, however, left
Shaposhnikov with anything but a finished solution. Second, he ur-
gently wanted a common CIS military budget. Russia was carrying
the costs of virtually the whole residual Soviet Armed Forces, although carrying them very poorly by failing to provide regular pay
and supplies. On paper, it appeared that progress had been made, at
least toward planning a unified budget. Still, two states refused to
sign, and Moldova signed conditionally. In reality, neither a political
consensus nor adequate economic means underpinned the budget
agreement. Candidly assessed, the creation of a CIS combined armed
forces was going nowhere, and in the meantime the readiness conditions of the old Soviet forces throughout the CIS were rapidly declining as the Russian financial coffers became depleted.

Several senior Russian officers, most notably General Pavel
Grachev and Colonel General Konstantin Kobets, were agitating for
the creation of a Russian ministry of defense and a separate Russian
armed forces. Shaposhnikov enjoyed very little respect among his
Russian peers,[25] perhaps because the ground force officers had always dominated the top ranks of the Soviet military and Shaposhnikov
was an air force officer and pilot. Or it might have been caused by
his support for Yeltsin during the August coup crisis and his subsequent efforts to help Yeltsin purge the senior ranks of politically un-

reliable officers, a problem that plagued Grachev and Kobets as well. Precisely why no separate Russian defense ministry was created from the start is unclear. Belief in the upper circles of the Soviet officer corps that a CIS military would be a Russian instrument was undoubtedly an initial reason, but demonstrating full commitment to a combined military was also mentioned occasionally. As the wretched state of affairs throughout the armed forces worsened through the winter, however, the argument for a Russian ministry of defense became compelling. In April 1992, Yeltsin conceded that such a ministry would have to be created, and in May he appointed Grachev to head it. This decision indicated that Russia was beginning to give up on the idea of a unified CIS military establishment. The necessary political cooperation was clearly not forthcoming at the CIS summit meetings during the winter, and the Kiev meeting revealed that it would not be offered soon, if ever, voluntarily (see the following chapter on the Russian military).

Two days before the next summit meeting, held in Tashkent on 15-16 May, Shaposhnikov said, "a search for a civilized way to divide up the arms, equipment, and property of the former Soviet army, to create national armed forces, and to form a unified defense budget is under way."[26] He was not sanguine, however, regarding progress on the budget issue. The Belarus defense minister, Pavel Kozlovskii, also warned against expecting to achieve a unified budget, and the Russian delegation head, Aleksandr Kotenkov, complained that all attempts to deal with finances had come to a dead end.[27]

The agenda concerned almost thirty issues, including ten military items, but a new element was introduced by Russia, one that would mark a departure from the near-term goal of a genuinely unified CIS military. While continuing to battle for resolution of technical issues such as finance, supply, and manpower, Russia proposed a collective security treaty for the CIS. At previous summits there had been debate over whether the CIS military structure should follow the Warsaw Pact pattern or the NATO model, the former requiring great centralization, the latter comprising a much looser structure with emphasis on members' sovereignty. A collective security treaty was more in line with the NATO model and quite at odds with the centralizing efforts by Shaposhnikov and his staff. It was also more compatible with

Russia's plans to establish its own separate armed forces.

The treaty gambit, however, initially achieved only partial success, for a number of reasons. First, four heads of state did not attend. Ukraine, Kyrgyzstan, Moldova, and Tajikistan sent lower-level delegations. Second, only six states signed the treaty—Russia, Kazakhstan, Uzbekistan, Tajikistan, Turkmenistan, and Armenia. Third, considerable confusion arose about precisely which states did sign. Fourth, Ukraine declared the treaty incompatible with other CIS agreements, and Belarus, while supporting it, declared the treaty against its constitution. Nonetheless, a treaty did result, with six signatories and the opportunity for others to join later.[28]

The next CIS summit did not convene until October 1992 in Bishkek (known as Frunze in Soviet days), the capital of Kyrgyzstan. The agenda and the results reflected the same trends as the Tashkent meeting—continuing failure at creating a unified CIS military, more Russian pressure for collective security arrangements through an agreed collective security concept, some progress on bringing strategic nuclear forces under Russian control, and more bilateral agreements between Russia and individual states on military and border-control issues. The Russians tried to secure CIS agreements on an economic union for common monetary, credit, and currency policies, but they managed only to establish a CIS consultative committee for discussing economic issues, which Ukraine did not approve.[29]

Five CIS heads of state meetings were held in 1993: in Minsk in January and April, in Moscow in May and September, and in Ashgabat (formerly Askhabad), the capital of Turkmenistan, in late December. The participants largely hashed over the same old issues, but economic concerns—namely, another try at an economic union treaty—got more attention.[30] They did make modest progress in regularization. For example, the CIS Charter was adopted at a January meeting in Minsk, declaring seven CIS objectives and seven areas of mutual activity.[31] While emphasizing that the CIS is not a state and does not possess supranational authority, the charter spells out goals and cooperative activities—political, military, and economic—that require supranational authority to implement. An institutional structure continued to develop, at least on paper, giving a formal appearance of far more order and agreement than in fact existed. (See figs. 1.3 and 1.4.)

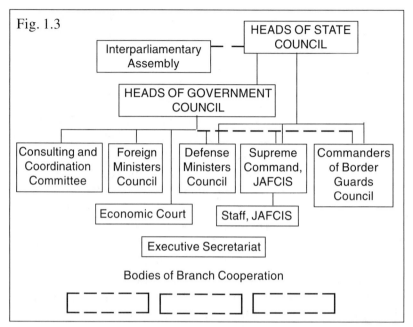

Fig. 1.3

Source: *Security Through Cooperation—93* (Moscow: Center for Information and Analytical Support of the Commonwealth, 1993), 50

The Councils of Defense and Foreign Ministers remained active, holding meetings between summits and jointly with them. So too did the CIS Interparliamentary Assembly (based on an agreement signed in Alma Ata [Almaty], 12 March 1992[32]) and the interior ministries (especially for handling Border Troop issues). But until the CIS Council of Heads of State implemented more solid agreements backed by all eleven members, these bodies could only work within the spotty CIS agreements reached during the first half of 1992. Substantive military policymaking shifted away from the CIS in two new directions, toward a national basis and toward bilateralism. On 15 June 1993 the Council of Defense Ministers abolished Shaposhnikov's post—commander in chief of CIS Armed Forces[33]—and it dissolved the CIS Armed Forces Command in December.[34] Russia in particular but also most other states were preoccupied with the construction of their own military institutions.

Shaposhnikov trudged along, still trying to make progress with a CIS military structure through the winter and spring of 1992-93, but

Fig. 1.4

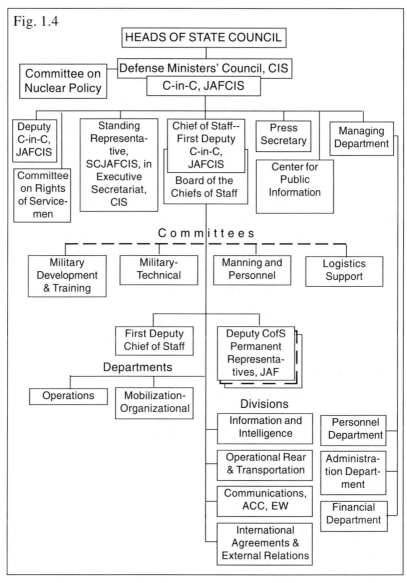

Source: *Security Through Cooperation—93* (Moscow: Center for Information and Analytical Support of the Commonwealth, 1993), 54

substantive authority shifted to Grachev, the Russian defense minister. The abolition of Shaposhnikov's post in June 1993 occurred primarily because Russia withdrew support, especially money to pay for it. Working parallel to Shaposhnikov's multilateral endeavors, the Russian defense ministry had more success in signing bilateral agreements with most of the CIS republican militaries, each dealing with the particular problems concerning Russian forces on other states' territory. Turkmenistan had preferred a bilateral tie all along; the government of Tajikistan, as it fell into civil war, desperately needed Russian military support and eagerly accepted bilateral arrangements in exchange for it.

The other Central Asian republics soon conformed to the same pattern. In the Transcaucasus, Armenia, like Tajikistan, sorely needed Russian military support and was eager to receive it from either the CIS military or Russia alone. Georgia resisted both multilateral and bilateral arrangements until early 1994. Azerbaijan followed a similar path with occasional exceptions. Moldova and Ukraine strongly resisted CIS and bilateral entanglements. Belarus was ambivalent, being generally cooperative but torn internally between a faction that wanted to maintain clear independence and one that regretted the breakup of the Soviet Union and preferred very close ties to Russia.

Finally, Ukraine proved the major stumbling block for all of Moscow's efforts to give the CIS institutional substance and authority over resources. Alone among the member states, Ukraine had the potential to create a significant national military establishment. Unlike the states of Central Asia and the Transcaucasus, Ukraine had a large number of native officers, and it inherited a large share of the Soviet ground forces and frontal aviation, not to mention significant nuclear forces. Most important, it had a strong nationalist political movement, especially in its western region. The last feature was lacking in Belarus, the only other non-Russian state with a sufficient native officer cadre and enough weaponry for an effective military.

Although the Ukrainian leadership squandered time by not pursuing economic and political reforms that were essential to provide a foundation for an effective military, it used its geographic position and size and its large hold on military capabilities to resist virtually all Russian initiatives within the CIS. The military oath issue signaled Kiev's determination to put its independence above all else, and the nuclear issue and the Black Sea Fleet dispute waxed and waned throughout 1992, 1993, and early 1994, occasionally requiring Presidents Kravchuk and Yeltsin to meet and keep the disagreements from exceeding the limits of diplomacy. Had Ukraine cooperated with Russia in establishing a CIS system of institutions and a unified military, most of the other states would probably have gone along as well. As it turned out, the Russian-Ukrainian bilateral disagreements provided these states with cover for exercising their own independent policies.

The Russian ministries of interior (MVD) and security (MO) also resorted to bilateral arrangements, although the early CIS committee on internal affairs did develop a series of multilateral meetings which occurred periodically among the police and intelligence chiefs of several member states. The MO, of course (while it lasted; it was reorganized and renamed in the late fall of 1993), had control of the Border Troops, and this responsibility required it to work out bilateral arrangements with other CIS members because the heads of state never reached an adequate CIS agreement on them.

The full story of all the bilateral arrangements is complex, and far from all the evidence about them is in the public domain. Many arrangements were made in secret, and their details, if not their existence, were kept from the public. Their larger significance for CIS developments, however, is clear enough. By the summer of 1992, CIS military development appeared to have collapsed almost entirely. Shaposhnikov, now evicted from the comfortable offices of the old Soviet defense ministry and exiled to the austere and empty headquarters of the former Warsaw Pact in Moscow, trudged on, periodically making media appearances and speaking optimistically, but the CIS military looked terminally ill. It was being rapidly displaced by the bilateral arrangements between Russia and other CIS states.

In its original conception, the CIS military had failed to materialize, but the legal shell of the CIS remained, awaiting content, and the embryo of that new content was the collective security treaty underpinned by the dense net of bilateral military ties. The civil strife and warfare in Tajikistan, the Transcaucasus, and the "Dniester Republic" in Moldova provided the nurturing womb for this embryo.

The CIS Between Two Russian Foreign Policies

Throughout 1992 and the first half of 1993, President Yeltsin more or less successfully backed his foreign minister, Andrei Kozyrev, in pursuit of a highly cooperative policy toward the United States and Europe. Western leaders reciprocated, placing their bets on a liberal transformation of Russia's domestic economy and political system. As Kozyrev warned at the CSCE (Conference on Security and Cooperation in Europe) in December 1992, he and Yeltsin were following this course against great internal resistance.[35] In addition to reactionary deputies in the parliament and their proponents in the media, the real center of resistance was in the defense ministry.

Although the CIS had initially failed to restore Moscow's control over most of the former Soviet republics, General Grachev and his staff were making progress in other ways, primarily two. First, bilateral agreements on military matters were providing an expanding legal basis for maintaining Russian forces in other republics and entangling their militaries in dependence on Russia for officer training and supplies of weapons and logistical support. Second, civil war in Georgia, the Armenian-Azerbaijani war, strife in the Transdniester region, and civil war in Tajikistan provided numerous opportunities for the defense ministry to become involved, both to hold down violence and to incite it when that suited Russian needs for political influence.

The failure of Yegor Gaidar, Yeltsin's leading economic reformer and, for a time, prime minister, to achieve significant economic improvement made it easier for the opposition to attack Yeltsin's policies, both domestic and foreign. Accusations of selling out to the West, of letting the International Monetary Fund and the World Bank govern Russia, and of aiding aggressive NATO policies in East Europe and against Serbia struck chords of sufficient domestic popular appeal to cause Yeltsin and Kozyrev to begin to reverse course.

From Ambivalence to Divide and Conquer

The most visible sign of Russia's change of course came in connection with the war in Tajikistan in July 1993. The ministry of defense (through its control of a Russian motor rifle division in

Dushanbe) and the ministry of security (through its Border Troops on the Afghan frontier) had essentially managed Russian policy toward the civil war there, but when 23 Russian Border Troops were killed in a skirmish on 13 July, Yeltsin took charge himself. The Russian Security Council swung into action, notifying the UN Security Council that Russia would help Tajikistan defend itself.[36] A few days later, Yeltsin appointed Kozyrev as Russia's "special representative" on Tajikistan, delegated to coordinate all of Russia's operations there.[37] Thereafter, Kozyrev became trenchantly assertive about Russia's role as the guarantor of peace in the CIS states. Most notably, in his address to the UN General Assembly in September, he defended a special peacekeeping role for Russia in the CIS and demanded that Russian peacekeeping forces be given the status of UN peacekeepers.

Russia tried to use a joint CIS military force in Tajikistan much earlier, getting the CIS Heads of State to agree to it in January 1993, but apparently only Kyrgyzstan sent a small force—one battalion—to reinforce the Afghan border.[38] (The force proved operationally incompetent, however, and was soon withdrawn.) After the July crisis, Yeltsin obtained agreements from Uzbekistan, Kyrgyzstan, and Kazakhstan to provide more diplomatic and military assistance.[39] Only Turkmenistan refused.[40] Kozyrev launched a major diplomatic offensive, seeking support from the CSCE, moderate Arab states, the United Nations, Washington, and Western Europe.[41]

This effort met no success, but it did signal a fundamental turn in Russian policy toward its "near abroad." Henceforth Kozyrev would defend Russia's special role for peacekeeping and military involvement within the CIS. Although he remained careful not to let this new approach destroy Russia's cooperative efforts with the West, he trod cautiously, pulled in opposite directions by the reactionary domestic forces and Russia's desperate need for economic assistance from the West.

The events of 3-4 October 1993, when Yeltsin had to use force to disperse the old parliament, gave this new foreign policy direction yet another push. Able to claim some credit for putting down the violence initiated by leaders in the old parliament, General Grachev apparently felt freer to press ahead with schemes for bringing Georgia and Azerbaijan under Moscow's hegemony; Armenia was already among the strongest supporters of Moscow's military policies in the CIS.

Armenia, of course, was at war with Azerbaijan when the Soviet Union dissolved, and it eagerly signed the collective security treaty at Tashkent during the 16 May 1992 CIS summit. Immediately thereafter, Armenian forces stepped up their operations and captured a land bridge between Armenia and Nagorno-Karabakh. On 21 May, Russia and Armenia signed an agreement for the continued stationing of the Russian 7th Army on Armenian territory.[42] Russian military bases in Georgia also provided training assistance for Armenian military personnel, tilting Russia quite strongly to Armenia's side in the conflict.[43]

Azerbaijan, meanwhile, held an election, and Abulfez Elchibey, leader of the nationalist Popular Front, won the presidency largely because he promised to turn the tide in the war with Armenia.[44] Elchibey pursued a stronger anti-CIS policy than his predecessor, successfully persuading the parliament to refuse to ratify CIS documents already signed by Azerbaijan. Moreover, he pressed for the withdrawal of all Russian military units still on Azeri soil, and he initiated active relations with Turkey and Western oil companies. This set of new policies deeply angered hard-liners in Moscow, but it took a year for the Russian military to bring Baku to heel; by the following summer, Elchibey's government had exhausted its military capabilities and faced growing public dissatisfaction. Russian operatives armed the forces of dissident Azeri major Surat Huseinov with sufficient means to carry out a successful insurrection. Gaidar Aliyev—a former communist party chief in Azerbaijan, KGB general, and alternate member of the Politburo—was able to exploit the crisis, apparently without resistance (and perhaps with covert support) from Russia. The parliament promptly elected him its chairman, effectively head of state, on 16 June.[45] Huseinov settled for head of the government, as prime minister.

For a time, Aliyev appeared to try to retain some autonomy for Azerbaijan, but by the end of 1993 he had agreed to make Azerbaijan a member of the CIS, and he cooperated fully with Moscow by ceasing the cooperative relationship with Turkey and bringing Russia back into the oil business in Baku. By early 1994, therefore, Russia had succeeded in reasserting considerable influence on this former Soviet republic. The process was not cost-free, because Russia had been working with the United States and Turkey for a settlement in Nagorno-Karabakh in May 1993, and according to a high-level Azeri official in Elchibey's government, an agreement was at hand when Russia abruptly backed Surat Huseinov's military insurrection.[46] Russian duplicity in this affair was not lost on Turkey, although it had little effect on U.S.-Russian relations. It did, however, achieve what Russia had been denied by Elchibey, the exclusive introduction of Russian forces into Azerbaijan as "peacekeepers." More troublesome was that it complicated relations with Armenia.

Armenian forces intensified operations during the summer of 1993, reaching close to the Azeri border with Iran and causing concern in Teheran. Now Russia was faced with restraining rather than encouraging the Armenian offensive, and by November, Kozyrev was threatening "something more than persuasion" to force Armenia to cut off support to its Karabakh forces. As two students of this Russian policy concluded in January 1994, Moscow abandoned real prospects for a settlement, apparently preferring a continuing state of war.[47]

Russia employed a similarly duplicitous strategy during 1993. Although in a state of decay, Russian forces remained in Georgia after the demise of the Soviet Union. With the overthrow of Gamsakhurdia's regime and the emergence of numerous factions and two separatist movements (in Abkhazia and South Ossetia), the opportunities for Russia to divide and conquer were enormously enhanced. General Grachev consistently denied that Russia was supporting the Abkhaz separatists. At the same time, however, he acted as though Russia owned Georgia. For example, during the spring of 1993 he affronted Shevardnadze several times by visiting Georgia and Abkhazia without even the courtesy of asking permission.[48]

By late September the Russian-aided Abkhaz forces had essentially routed the Georgian forces, and Georgia was forced to confront the reality of losing both its control over Abkhazia and its independence from Moscow. Chastened by defeat in Abkhazia and facing Gamsakhurdia's rebel forces in western Georgia, Shevardnadze had little choice but to ask for Russian support to save him and his government. To receive it, he would have to agree to make Georgia a member of the CIS, a step that would incite domestic opposition against him. Grachev and the Russian military were not impressed, and they rejected his plea. In desperation, Shevardnadze made a trip to Moscow on 8 October; he agreed not only to join the CIS but also to permit permanent stationing of Russian troops in Georgia and to lease Georgia's Black Sea port of Poti to Russia.[49]

Shortly thereafter, General Grachev went to Tbilisi to begin collecting the spoils of victory. Russian and Georgian military officials drew up protocols to legalize the basing of Russian forces in Georgia through 1995, something Georgia had stubbornly resisted.[50] In February 1994, Grachev moved to make these arrangements permanent within the CIS arrangements. Although a treaty for this purpose was signed, members of the Russian parliament criticized it as premature and stated that it might not be ratified.[51] Some deputies feared that such an agreement would imply that Russia was siding with the Georgian government too thoroughly, especially in its plans to reconstruct Georgia's military forces. They feared that these actions would incite anger in Ossetia and perhaps Abkhazia and possibly lead to separatist activity against Russia in North Ossetia. Grachev nonetheless disregarded such protests; indeed, in March 1994 Russia signed agreements with Georgia and Armenia for Russian Border Troops to maintain the frontier with Turkey, a conspicuous sign of Moscow's long-term policy intentions toward both countries.[52]

These conquests in Central Asia and the Transcaucasus were accompanied by an intensified campaign for UN peacekeeping authority and financial assistance for Russian forces deployed in both regions. Kozyrev, Grachev, one of his deputy ministers, and the Russian permanent representative to the UN all demanded such authority during the first three months of 1994.[53] During his April 1994 visit to Moscow, UN Secretary General Boutros Boutros-Ghali made it clear that Russia's request would not be met and that UN peacekeeping operations would be under the UN banner from beginning to end, replete with UN commanders and restrictions on the number of non-neutral troops involved. Nor would the UN provide Russia with the financial assistance it was seeking.[54] Russia reacted angrily. The foreign and defense ministries issued a joint statement expressing not only disappointment but also some indignation at the implication that Russian peacekeeping efforts in the CIS constituted interference in the internal affairs of sovereign states.[55]

The other region of periodic violence, of course, was the "Dniester Republic" a subunit of Moldova. Comprising a small strip of
land on the east bank of the Dniester River, populated by about
equal numbers of Russians, Ukrainians, and Moldovans, it was put
into the Moldovan Republic when the Nazi-Soviet Pact of 1939 allowed Stalin to absorb the Moldovan province of Romania in 1939-
40. After the breakup of the Soviet Union in 1992, the local government of the Transdniester declared independence from Moldova and
formed its own army, a militia organization supported by the Soviet
14th Army, the military unit long deployed in that region. During the
perestroika years, the KGB was suspected of fostering independence movements in the Transdniester and another subregion of
Moldova, Gagauz (where a Turkicized minority lives), as a tactic for
frightening and controlling Moldovan leaders who favored Moldovan independence (and possibly union with Romania).

Although Ukraine has as strong a claim to the Transdniester as
Russia does, local Russian military and political leaders refused to
accept it as part of Moldova and insisted that it was part of Russia.
And as long as the 14th Army remained there, Russia retained the
power to enforce their demands. In early April 1992 Yeltsin decreed
that the 14th Army belonged to the Russian Federation,[56] and in late
May he promised that the 14th Army would be withdrawn.[57] General Grachev acknowledged that policy decision but insisted that it
could not be implemented until peace was restored.[58] Accordingly,
no serious withdrawal effort was made, and the 14th Army commanders—first, Major General Yurii Netkachev and then Lt. General Aleksandr Lebed (who replaced Netkachev in late June 1992)—
were allowed to support a local autonomous militia which was fighting with the Moldovan police and backed the "Dniester Republic's"
Russian-dominated government in its demand for making the
Transdniester Autonomous Republic part of the Russian Federation.
The 14th Army could hardly have survived without supplies from
Russia; yet pretenses were maintained that Russia was providing
nothing.

Moldovan leaders, of course, believed that Russia was using its
foothold in the Transdniester to force Moldova back under Moscow's
hegemony. The Moldovan foreign minister made precisely this charge
in an address to the UN in October 1993, in reaction to Kozyrev's

recent insistence to the General Assembly that Russian troops in the
CIS were performing only a peacekeeping role. The foreign minister
asked the UN to help Moldova secure the withdrawal of the 14th
Army.[59] Although Moldova's president, Mircea Snegur, had signed
some of the CIS documents, the parliament refused to ratify CIS
membership. In the fall of 1993, under increasing pressure from
Moscow because of the new Yeltsin-Kozyrev policy toward the "near
abroad," Snegur attempted to obtain ratification but failed. Military
and economic pressure was taking its toll on Snegur and Moldova.
During fall and winter 1993-94, Russia tried to seduce Snegur with
an offer of territorial integrity which would allow Moldova to keep
the Transdniester in exchange for Moldova's agreement to the permanent stationing of the 14th Army in that country.[60]

Belarus, of course, presented no opportunity for the kind of violent divide-and-rule strategy Moscow had been able to apply in the
three regions discussed previously, but the Belarus leadership was
divided internally. This allowed Russia to play Prime Minister
Vyacheslav Kebich against the chairman of the parliament, Stanilau
Shuchkevich. Kebich favored a full military union with Russia, primarily because he wanted to keep Belarus's large military-industrial
sector tied to the Russian military-industrial structure. Schuchkevich
consistently hid behind the Belarus constitution in trying to limit the
binding character of most of the CIS agreements signed by Belarus.[61]
By April 1993, Kebich had prevailed, and the parliament voted to
sign and ratify the CIS collective security agreements.

Still, Schuchkevich continued to speak out against conceding so
much to Russia in the security area. Other political figures had also
expressed doubts, but the key issue for Belarus was not military but
economic. In January 1994, Belarus and Russia signed an agreement
of intent to unify their economies, a step that would amount to
Russia's annexation of Belarus.[62] Voices in both countries challenged
the agreement, and as of late 1994 its status remained unclear. Regardless of how the economic connection worked out, however,
Belarus had developed inextricable military ties to Russia. It was the
most cooperative with Moscow on the nuclear issue, and disputes
over loyalty oaths, the status of Russian officers in Belarus units,
and other such technical matters were never serious issues.

Finally, Ukraine stood apart from virtually all integration efforts, even as Yeltsin and Kozyrev began backing CIS policies long quietly pursued by General Grachev. By summer 1994, the nuclear issue, although apparently resolved through the mediation of U.S. Secretary of Defense William Perry, had hit snags over U.S. payments to Russia and Ukraine and delivery of nuclear materials by Russia to Ukraine for power plants. The Black Sea fleet dispute had also erupted several times during the first half of that year. Ukraine's political capacity to resist Russian pressure, however, was seriously undermined by the elections in April 1994 which left Kiev with a seriously polarized parliament.

In sum, on the military front Russia had achieved a great deal by late 1994. After abjectly failing to gain a CIS consensus for a unified military establishment during the first six months of the organization's existence, Moscow changed course. It created its own defense ministry and separate armed forces, and convinced five other parties to sign a collective security treaty. It then began a long process of rounding up wayward former Soviet republics and using divide-and-rule tactics to compel them to join the CIS security system. Ukraine retained a large degree of independence, but its internal political fissures were offering Moscow more opportunities to wedge Ukraine into a closer military arrangement with the CIS. This is a risky game, however, because Ukraine has the means to fight a war of resistance if it chooses or if Russia miscalculates and provokes a conflict. Crimean separatists and the Black Sea Fleet might provide the impetus for such an outcome in 1994-95.

CIS Economic Developments

The Structural Conditions

Dissolving the Soviet Union bequeathed the CIS even more economic disorder and institutional disruption than military disruption. The parallels are instructive because the Soviet economy was centrally planned, controlled, and directed, just as were the armed forces. Huge economic ministry structures, like large corporate monopolies, were headquartered in Moscow but managed firms spread over several republics, just as the Soviet air defense forces, navy, strategic forces, and air forces were centralized institutions deployed

USSR-wide and not easy to break into coherent operational suborganizations.

If all the CIS members had shifted to market economies, of course, reintegration through trade and transnational business firms could have proceeded without a new central directing apparatus and without seriously diminishing the sovereignty of member states. (This was not true of military relations, of course, because military operations cannot be run on a decentralized market basis. They could, of course, have been reestablished within a collective security arrangement analogous to NATO, but even that solution, as NATO's experience demonstrates, would have required coping with the constant tension between the needs of central coordination and direction on the one hand and maintenance of national sovereignty on the other, a tension most vividly demonstrated in France's arm's-length relationship with the NATO military command structure.)

Initially, only Russia took serious steps toward creating a market economy, and even Russian elites remained deeply divided about how to proceed and how far and how fast to go. Belarus and Ukraine essentially stood still and let their economies worsen. The economies in the Transcaucasus and Tajikistan fell into deep chaos as the imperatives of local wars and violent factional struggles pushed economic policy far down on the agenda. In Central Asia, no serious market reformers had arisen during Gorbachev's *perestroika* policy, and the two largest post-breakup economies, Kazakhstan and Uzbekistan, were headed by leaders not at all disposed toward market reforms. (When he realized that his country possessed significant natural gas reserves, Turkmenistan's president, Saparmurad Niyazov, chose the Persian Gulf oil-producing states as his economic development model, hoping to thrive on oil and gas exports while keeping his economy as one large state operation detached, of course, from the CIS economies.) Only President Akayev of Kyrgyzstan pursued a serious policy of transition to a market system, but his progress remained modest because of parliamentary opposition.

These leadership attitudes and a growing determination to defend some of their political sovereignty put Belarus, Ukraine, Kazakhstan, and Uzbekistan in a dilemma. President Nazarbayev of Kazakhstan in particular wanted CIS economic organs to maintain much of the old Soviet economic system. President Islam Karimov of Uzbekistan held a similar position but was less consistently outspoken in support of an economic union. Politics and war in the Transcaucasus largely removed the states in this region from the debate. Georgia and Azerbaijan, of course, did not want to be in the CIS, and Armenia wanted to win the war over Nagorno-Karabakh more than it wanted to take the lead in creating a CIS economic union.

Economic structures and regional specialization dating from the Soviet period made the transition to markets all the more difficult. Kazakhstan, for example, was extensively linked to the Russian economy. Its oil fields exported oil from western Kazakhstan to Russia and imported oil from Russia to the more populated regions of eastern and southern Kazakhstan.[63] The highly industrialized northern region of Kazakhstan is not only heavily populated with Russians but is linked more fully with the Russian economy than with the Kazakh economy. Moreover, some Russian factories such as the large Magnitogorsk Metallurgical Kombinat depend wholly on raw materials from Kazakhstan.[64] The southern Central Asian republics remain highly dependent on the former Soviet market for exports. Uzbekistan, for example, having been transformed into a "monocultural economy," exports its unprocessed cotton to plants in the European regions of the former USSR.[65]

In the Transcaucasus, Azerbaijan's oil industry was an important supplier of oil production equipment to the former USSR.[66] Georgia remains dependent on oil and other energy imports, and Armenia is highly dependent on nuclear energy, a local industry that requires cooperation with the Russian nuclear energy industry. All three Transcaucasus states exported agricultural products to Russia, Ukraine, and elsewhere in the former Soviet Union. Although their agricultural production base makes it easier to provide a subsistence income locally, foreign markets other than Russia are not easily accessible.

These economic linkages were further strengthened by transportation networks that limited ties between the Soviet periphery and the outside world. Moreover, the quality of local industrial goods—such as those in northern Kazakhstan, Azerbaijan's oil production equipment, and Uzbekistan's aviation industry—has been too low for competition in international markets.

Establishing the actual benefit-cost relationship of the Russian-Central Asia economic connection is difficult. It is widely asserted that Russia pays a high price for which it does not earn a fair return, amounting to more than $15 billion in subsidies to Central Asia.[67] Other analyses, however, conclude that Central Asia has paid heavily for the relationship, falling behind the per capita investment rate for the rest of the Soviet Union since the mid-1970s.[68] Because we lack market prices with which to make the calculations, the truth cannot be firmly established, but it would be a rare phenomenon if the pattern of Soviet investment, without scarcity prices to guide it, created a significant mutual economic advantage. One can say with considerable confidence, therefore, that both parties suffer economically because of the old planned-economy linkages.

Economic Impact of the Breakup

Economic transitions impose severe costs even in the best of circumstances; thus it is not surprising that the demise of the Soviet Union harmed the economies of the southern republics. No longer able to depend on the Soviet State Planning Commission (GOSPLAN) to direct deliveries of intermediate and finished products and to handle finance and credit issues for the old far-flung economic linkages among firms, republican economic ministries and plant managers have had to build informal communications and arrangements to substitute for GOSPLAN's role. Their success has been mixed at best: some plants resorted to market relations outside the old planned market links, and others closed down. Nonetheless, a considerable network of the old economic bureaucrats persisted. Kazakhstan, in particular, struggled to keep it vital. Nazarbayev repeatedly pleaded within the CIS councils for a CIS economic structure sustaining much of the old system.[69]

As the economic performance of the old system declined, the new nations failed to pursue structural reforms designed to facilitate market development. Akayev's policies in Kyrgyzstan were an exception, and even they met stubborn resistance in his parliament. Instead of reform, Central Asian and Azeri leaders sought salvation in foreign investment. Foreign businessmen, however, did not respond with the alacrity expected, and not surprisingly. Without internal legal and economic reforms, they could not expect to turn a profit on their capital.

The exception has been in mineral commodities—oil, gas, and some metals, especially gold. Turkmenistan attracted considerable foreign oil and gas interest, and Chevron showed strong interest in Kazakhstan's vast oil reserves.[70] Kyrgyzstan and Uzbekistan drew little attention, except from foreign gold-mining interests.[71] Civil war in Tajikistan, of course, discouraged foreign business entirely. Azerbaijan, under Elchibey's leadership and with British and Turkish assistance, signed contracts with foreign oil interests.[72] Armenia and Georgia, like Tajikistan, had no prospects for attracting foreign capital.

These kinds of foreign business deals appeared feasible largely because foreign firms could deal with local governments as economic corporations, much as Western oil firms deal with Middle East oil-producing states. They did not depend on internal markets, as investments in local manufacturing and commerce would. They were, however, largely expressions of interest, not delivery of capital. The latter depended on at least a modicum of internal reform so that contracts could be enforced and law and order adequate to permit production operations. Western financial institutions and political risk assessment experts consistently forecast gloomy prospects for successful foreign investment, even in mineral commodities.[73]

Russia added to the difficulties facing these states by insisting that oil pipelines pass through Russia. Moscow opposed a Georgian Black Sea terminal for Azeri oil, demanding that the terminal be in Novorossisk, a Russian Black Sea port.[74] Kazakhstan, because of its geographic location, could not avoid passing oil through Russia unless it could make arrangements for a pipeline southward through other Central Asian countries or Azerbaijan into Iran and Turkey. Moreover, Russia maneuvered both Azerbaijan and Kazakhstan into giving Russia shares in their oil projects without contributing any equity for them.[75]

Thus, the scenario of foreign investment saving the economies of Central Asia and Azerbaijan proved ephemeral and illusory. The internal conditions of these economies created major obstacles, but Russia added to them at every turn in the most promising business ventures, oil and gas exports. As their leaders attempted to save much of the old economic institutional structure, and as its performance declined, they faced requirements of genuine internal reform with great reluctance, timidity, and a faulty understanding of what precisely had to be done.[76]

Currency Reform and CIS Economic Relations

Devising a new monetary policy must be a major problem for any planned economy making a transition to a market, but in the CIS the complications were dramatically greater than for a single country. All members began by using the ruble, and they continued to do so during the first year. Even if they had agreed to a strong central political institution for the CIS and a uniform economic reform plan, monetary policy would have entailed a continuing political storm. In the event, however, they chose to follow an even more divisive course.

Transition to a market requires currency stabilization and (eventually) international convertibility. In the CIS, however, disciplined control of emission of currency and credits by the central bank would have rapidly driven most of the industrial sector into bankruptcy. Because of these concerns, Russia experienced very high inflation after Gaidar's monetary stabilization course because the head of the State Bank exercised his discretion to create easy money and credit, playing to the antireform forces in the parliament and industrial sector. Nonetheless, Russia avoided hyperinflation, and by the spring of 1994 inflation was actually declining, confounding all predictions after Gaidar's reform team left the government.

Most other CIS states, however, were not at all committed to currency stabilization. Especially in Central Asia (except for Kyrgyzstan) the aim was to protect the old industrial and collective-farm structures. That required expansive credit and easy monetary policy. Thus these countries, like the antireform groups in Russia, were immediately at odds with Gaidar's monetary policy. (More specifically, this policy was developed by finance minister Boris Fedorov with the close advice of Western economists, most notably Jeffrey Sachs of Harvard University, a specialist in such matters with experience in many other countries.)

Getting all or even several of the CIS states in step on monetary policy proved predictably impossible. By May of 1993 Kyrgyzstan made the decision to leave the ruble zone, introducing the "som" as its new currency unit.[77] This move angered the other Central Asian republics, especially Uzbekistan, which feared a flood of rubles from Kyrgyzstan. (The voided rubles from Kyrgyzstan were being used to buy scarce products in Uzbekistan, which was creating an outflow of goods and causing problems for consumers in Uzbekistan). Kyrgyzstan's president, Akayev, responded to Karimov's wrath by insisting that he had no other way to escape ruble inflation. That did not calm Karimov, and he closed all commercial relations with Kyrgyzstan. After his temper cooled, however, Karimov met with Akayev, in June, to sign agreements regulating their economic relations in dollars and to accept Akayev's admission that Kyrgyzstan owed Uzbekistan for gas deliveries.[78] Akayev had precipitated the unraveling of the ruble zone in the region, but Uzbekistan and Kazakhstan were not ready to leave it. In August, their representatives met with Russian representatives to establish a "ruble zone of a new type" for the entire CIS.[79]

Their efforts soon came to naught, largely because of Russian monetary developments. By November both Kazakhstan and Uzbekistan issued their own currencies.[80] The catalyst was Russia's unilateral decision to void all pre-1993 ruble notes. This immediately increased inflation in Central Asia and created shortages of new currency. Karimov insisted that he had been provoked into introducing his own currency, and Nazarbayev was no less upset with the Russian central bank.

Ironically, Viktor Gerashchenko, the head of the Russian bank, apparently took this decision to undermine the Gaidar and Fedorov policies of stabilizing the currency and restricting credits. In other words, he agreed with the Central Asians who wanted to retain much of the old economic system. Central Asians, however, saw his action as having quite the opposite effect, of continuing the destruction of the old system. Equally provoking to Kazakhstani and Uzbekistani antireformers was Russia's currency stabilization policy. The Russians wanted these countries to deposit hard currency and gold to back the Russian rubles they were using as their currencies.[81] To avoid having to make these deposits, the central Asian countries introduced their own currencies. Turkmenistan also intro-

duced its own currency, in the fall of 1993, but Tajikistan retained
the ruble, remaining the lone holdout; its war-torn economy was so
dependent on Russia it had no viable alternative.

The Transcaucasus states followed suit. The withdrawal of pre-
1993 ruble notes caused them the same difficulties as experienced in
Central Asia: inflation and shortages of new rubles. Accordingly,
Azerbaijan and Armenia introduced new currencies, and Georgia
resorted to a coupon system.

None of these countries was prepared for the sudden shift to a
domestically administered currency system. Even printing quality was
a high hurdle, which Uzbekistan did not manage to vault in producing its temporary coupon. Moreover, these nations had no expertise
in managing a monetary system; their industrial and agricultural credit
policies were highly inflationary; and they could only hope to settle
external accounts in dollars or some other convertible currency which
none held in adequate quantity. The consequences were predictable.
All these currencies rapidly depreciated.

Russian Economic Policy

Russia cannot be said to have had a single economic policy toward the CIS in 1992-94. The antireform central bank, industrialists, and collective-farm bureaucrats wanted a single ruble zone. As
mentioned earlier, they moved to take Belarus into the Russian
economy as an integral unit on terms that would allow the Belarus
central bank to create rubles at its own discretion. That caused a
public backlash when reformers such as Boris Fedorov estimated
the costs to Russia and the inflationary impact of the change. The
fate of the economic union was in limbo in the spring of 1994. As
noted, the Russian bank's voidance of pre-1993 rubles and the demand for hard currency and gold deposits in the fall of 1993 gave
the CIS single-currency system a destructive jolt. Moreover, during
1993 Russia intensified its practice of trying to force other CIS states
to settle trading accounts in hard currencies, which further shattered
the old economic institutional linkages.

In monetary policy and trade policy, therefore, Russia exacerbated the economic divisions among CIS states. If Russia continues
to pursue its fight with inflation by making credits tighter and money

emissions more disciplined, restoring the old planned economic system within the CIS will become an increasingly impractical alternative. (That pressure also affected the Russian military's capacity to hang on to its gains in Central Asia and the Transcaucasus.) In the spring of 1994, Grachev's defense ministry asked the new government for 80 trillion rubles, and later 87 trillion. The prime minister's budget allocated only 37.1 trillion.[82] The collective-farm lobby and the coal miners were also making large claims on the Russian budget. Russian domestic politics within its shaky but creeping economic transition were thus genuinely hindering the policy of restoring Russian hegemony over the CIS in general and Central Asia and the Transcaucasus in particular.

At the same time, Russian efforts to control and exploit foreign capital investment in Central Asian and Transcaucasus oil and other commodities ventures were effectively preventing these opportunities from materializing. It is difficult to say whether these actions were part of a general policy for retaining economic control of these regions or merely the actions of self-interested officials trying to rake off as much commodity-export profit as possible. In any case, they kept both regions from finding an alternative to close economic ties to Russia and the rest of the CIS.

Another factor in Russian policy is the legacy of Marxist-Leninist economic theory and thought. Unlike other CIS members, Russia had a significant group of economists who had trained themselves in Western macro- and microeconomic theory. Gaidar and Fedorov were among the most influential. These economists could envision a period of economic transition during which all the CIS states would individually shift to market systems. Thereafter, transnational economic integration might well follow a pattern like the one in Western Europe, which allowed national sovereignty to coexist with economic integration. But this circle of thinkers was small and essentially limited to Russia, and most of the officials in positions to make and implement economic policy had no such vision because they had no understanding of Western economic principles. They were much more inclined to consider resources and economic potential in Central Asia in terms of Marx's labor theory of value: the wealth is there; only labor is needed to get it out. Such officials did not consider political, legal, and market pricing structures as critical determinants of Central

Asian and Transcaucasus economic potential.

When individuals limited by such theory occupy the institutional positions most likely to suffer collapse or abolition during a market transition, they have further reasons to try to hang onto the CIS as a single economic institution based on their Marxist economic images of what that entails.

The key issue for 1995 is the degree to which the Russian transition to a market economy is reversible. Those who understand Western economic theory do not have a sufficient political constituency to carry the day. Yet the antireformers have no clear alternative programs, only residual Marxist ideas about how economies work and how wealth is created. The resulting policies toward CIS economic affairs have been contradictory, confusing, and counterproductive both for market relations and a return to central planning for the CIS.

CIS military development provides an instructive contrast with its economic developments. In the military sphere, Moscow had made great progress toward restoring much of the CIS to its control by the spring of 1994. In the economic sphere, by contrast, Moscow had done much to surrender such hegemony, especially in monetary and credit policy. At the same time, Moscow significantly hindered efforts of countries in Central Asia and Azerbaijan to find economic relief through foreign capital investment. In addition, Russian control of oil and pipelines and the collapse of the nations' new currencies could help force these areas to submit to a new Russian hegemony.

The States of Central Asia and the Transcaucasus

The foregoing treatment of the military and economic dimensions of CIS developments has, by necessity, already revealed significant distinctions among the states of Central Asia and the Transcaucasus. Yet it is useful to review each at the cost of some redundancy. Each state plays its own distinct role in CIS development, dictated largely by its domestic political dynamics, legacies, and resources. Although they share several common traits, they differ enormously in others, which causes them to behave differently. Western understanding of these countries has been rather limited, although access to them has improved since the dissolution of the Soviet Union.[83] The limited Western understanding constrains this analysis to the more conspicuous distinctions and to tentative conclusions about where they are headed.

Kazakhstan

Political development. As of the 1989 Soviet census, the Kazakhs comprised only 38 percent of the country's 17 million people, and Russians were about 37 percent. Ukrainians, Germans, Tatars, and other small groups such as Koreans compose the remainder. Since 1989, Slavic emigration and higher Kazakh birth rates have somewhat increased the percentage of Kazakhs in Kazakhstan, but the fact remains that the republic has by far the largest percentage of Slavs of any Central Asian nation. The politics of the country are very much determined by Kazakh-Russian relations, deriving not only from their numbers but from three additional factors.

First, a section of northern Kazakhstan was originally within the boundaries of the Russian empire, and Russians colonized the region heavily in the 19th century. Most Russians, particularly strong nationalists and some of the literary intelligentsia, consider Kazakhstan to be as clearly Russian territory as Moscow Oblast. Industrial development during the Soviet period reinforced this integral connection between northern Kazakhstan and the Russian Federation. Thus it will be difficult for Kazakhstan to remain independent for the indefinite future and be fully recognized as such by Russians while keeping the northern territories within its boundaries. At the same time, to surrender that region to Russia would be to open up endless demands for other border adjustments. This territorial legacy, therefore, ties Kazakhstan and Russia together like Siamese twins. Separating them runs the risk of death to Kazakhstan, probably through war.

Second, the Kazakhs were nomadic herdsmen well into the 19th century, only settling completely when forced by Soviet authorities. Although Kazakhs are nominally Muslim, Islam was never as strong a cultural factor there as in other parts of Central Asia, especially in Uzbekistan and Tajikistan. The Kazakhs were not converted until the 18th century. Thus Russification proceeded much farther among

the Kazakhs than in the rest of the region. Creating a Kazakh national and cultural identity today, therefore, is not merely a matter of
proclaiming liberation from Soviet rule. It also requires rolling back
Russification of the Kazakh elite. Although the new regime took
immediate steps to revive a sense of Kazakh nationalism, it was initially propelled mainly by a desire among Kazakhs to displace Russians in the state bureaucracy and take their better jobs and apartments. The more difficult process of throwing out the Russian language and culture was a much bigger challenge, one that would involve mobilizing the quiescent rural Kazakh population, where
Russification was thinner. And that expansion of Kazakh awareness
would bring new political and economic struggles over the realloca-
tion of property and privileges among Kazakhs themselves.

Third, the Kazakh political elites were not just Russified; they
were also Sovietized. The end of the Soviet Union brought no significant circulation of elites, that is, replacement of communists by
non-communists or lower-ranking and therefore only nominal communists. Nazarbayev and his ruling circle had been selected and promoted to positions of power by the Communist Party of the Soviet
Union. It taught them to rule, and it taught them how to view politics, economics, and international affairs.

With these three entanglements with Russia in mind, President
Nazarbayev's policies toward the CIS become far more comprehen-
sible.[84] First, he was furious over Yeltsin's scheme to end the Soviet
Union. He did not see how Kazakhstan could make it as an independent state with no close, formal ties to the Slavic version of the CIS,
i.e., Russia, Belarus, and Ukraine. Second, once admitted to the
CIS, he consistently sought the creation of central institutions that
could save most of the economic and military structures of the Soviet system. It is unclear whether he merely opposed a sudden rupture and wanted a long period of transition to full independence, but
he certainly understood the implications of a rapid breakup.

Notwithstanding two unhappy years of trying to persuade Yeltsin
and other CIS heads of state of the wisdom of CIS economic and
military institutions, Nazarbayev was still trying to advance these
ideas in the spring of 1994.[85] At the same time he had to defend the
idea of a truly independent Kazakhstan. While asserting unequivo-
cally that Kazakhstan's fate is inexorably tied to that of Russia, on

several occasions he also warned against the bloody consequences of any attempt to detach northern Kazakhstan and move it into the Russian Federation.[86] Russia's new military doctrine, promulgated officially in the fall of 1993, infuriated the Kazakhs. Speaking about its assertion of Russia's duty to protect Russians in the former Soviet republics, Nazarbayev drew the parallel to Hitler's assertion of the right to protect the Sudeten Germans in Czechoslovakia in the late 1930s.[87]

By opening ties with China and seeking East Asian investment, Nazarbayev sought to achieve some balance to his dependence on Russia, but economic assistance was a stronger motive.[88] At the same time, by agreeing to support Russia's involvement under the CIS banner in Tajikistan in the summer and fall of 1993, he set a precedent that might later haunt him. As for cooperation with the other Central Asian states to defend their common independence, such concerns had very little impact on Nazarbayev's calculations in 1992-94.[89] Bilateral relations were important to him, but prospects for a multilateral Central Asian alliance appeared dim.[90]

The domestic political atmosphere in Kazakhstan changed very little after the breakup of the Soviet Union. The old Soviet structures remained in place, the main change being the removal of virtually all non-Kazakhs from high posts. The policy of Kazakhization at lower levels proceeded with greater caution, so as not to catalyze a strong Russian separatist movement in reaction. Press censorship was relaxed marginally, but political opposition groups were not given freedom to compete effectively. The Alash party, for example, was accused of Islamic radicalism, hardly an accurate characterization of its leadership, which opposes establishment of an Islamic regime,[91] and was treated as a dangerous organization. How far Nazarbayev will be able to proceed without provoking a political backlash from the Russian minority is the key question. Some observers noted severe strains in the Kazakh Russian community in spring 1994 and warned that violent clashes between Russians and Kazakhs might soon occur.[92]

Economic development. In economic policy, the regime was reluctant to face up to the need for a serious program for transition to a market economy. Objective pressures for such a move grew, but by late 1994 no serious steps had been taken toward a genuine and feasible transition program. To the extent that the government had a vision of economic development, it was the East Asian model: a strong authoritarian regime sponsoring a market system. Yet government officials failed to see that Kazakhstan lacked several of the critical ingredients to make that model relevant,[93] most obvious among them a legal basis for private property and a system of civil courts that can reliably arbitrate contract disagreements and other civil disputes. Great inflows of foreign investment are another. Clearly the attractive thing about the East Asian model was that it seemed to justify the old communist political elites' hold on power, allowing them to continue dominating the state bureaucracy in the name of keeping order.

In 1993-94 two observable tendencies augured very badly for Kazakh political and economic development. First, privatization was being carried out only at the discretion of oblast (province) political chiefs. Therefore, only small commercial firms had any prospect of becoming private, and they could achieve private status only as opportunities for local political patronage and on uncertain legal grounds. None of this was at all conducive to a fundamental transition to a market system. Second, rather than finance the government largely by taxation, direct and indirect, the government sought to skim the profits from oil exports for the state coffers. The temptation was strong, in light of the Chevron oil company's commitment of $20 billion in hard currency for rights to Kazakh oil reserves.[94]

Several studies of political development and state-building have pointed out the connection between a regime's capacity to tax, especially through direct taxes (the most demanding to collect), and a state's overall strength. Regimes that depend on capital transfers, either through state enterprise exports (as in the oil producing states of the Middle East) or through direct foreign aid funds (as in several U.S. client states), become (or remain) weak states. They are spared the necessity of building intrusive state institutions that penetrate all social strata and political enclaves, institutions essential for effective taxation.[95] The Kazakh regime, counting on foreign investment and abundant future profits from oil exports, was headed down the road to becoming a weak state.

Given the Slavic minority problem in Kazakhstan and the social and economic bifurcation between the old communist elites and the politically excluded lower urban and rural social strata, oil revenues would deprive the regime of virtually all incentives to overcome the bifurcation, to create participatory political institutions, and to expand the political franchise. This set of trends in Kazakh domestic politics and economic policy suggests that the regime will become increasingly fragile, caught between social mobilization and frustration in the broader populace and pressures from Moscow to return to colonial status.

Suppose, however, that the pressure from Moscow does not materialize. What difference would that make? The regime would still stand as an obstacle to political and economic development. Elsewhere in the Third World, such regimes have typically fallen into what Huntington has called "praetorianism."[96] They resort to repression, and many become military dictatorships. The old communist institutions (with new labels) may temporarily succeed in maintaining order in Kazakhstan without further political development, but eventually the military will become more important, especially because the nation has lost the old ideology as a legitimizing principle. Of course, this assumes that there will indeed be a Kazakh military. Will there be one?

Military development. After some hesitation and ambiguity during the spring of 1992, Kazakhstan accepted the Non-Proliferation Treaty's terms and agreed to eliminate strategic nuclear weapons from its territory by 1997.[97] Unlike Ukraine, Kazakhstan had no personnel competent to operate such forces; moreover, Nazarbayev was reluctant (for reasons noted earlier) to defend Kazakh independence the way Kravchuk attempted in Ukraine. Haggling over the space launch facility at Baikonur and biological weapons facilities, however, marred the military relationship with Russia from January 1992 through most of 1993.[98] Nonetheless, Nazarbayev has not allowed these matters to prevent agreements on Russia's lease and maintenance of personnel at key nuclear and space facilities.

Unlike all other Central Asian states, Kazakhstan has been fairly open about its military plans. When it became clear that a unified CIS armed forces would not emerge, Nazarbayev launched a program for a Kazakh national military. In May 1992, probably as an adjunct to the CIS collective security treaty, Kazakhstan signed a bilateral treaty committing Russia and Kazakhstan to become a single strategic zone, providing for joint control of airspace and military

facilities in both countries.[99] Thereafter, Kazakhstan began the difficult task of establishing a national military while dividing up conventional weaponry and facilities with Russia.

The Kazakh defense ministry set a troop strength of 70,000, but
dependency on Russian officers was great, approximately 97 percent.[100] In a discussion with the chief of the general staff, a young
Kazakh major general, one of the authors learned that he was trying
to find ways to accelerate the creation of a largely Kazakh officer
corps, the sine qua non for a military loyal to the Kazakh leadership.
He was sending many young men to Russian officer training schools,
and he saw no real prospects for escaping dependency on Russian
weaponry and supply. Moreover, giving Russia leases on key military bases (such as the Baikonur space launch center) insured a long-
term Russian military presence.[101] Political developments are unlikely to wait for two decades while a reliable Kazakh military is
created.

In the meantime, the old Soviet 40th Army has become the
core of the Kazakh military force structure, and a number of
former Soviet tactical aviation units have been taken over. A few
military schools were also turned over to the Kazakh ministry of
defense. The few military industrial firms in Kazakhstan were
joined under common management, and in spring 1992 the government undertook efforts to keep them integrated with Russian
military industries.[102]

Summary. Given the tensions between the Kazakh regime and
the Russian minority, one is forced to conclude that only Russian
enthusiasm for Kazakh independence can secure it. Even if that is
forthcoming, an independent Kazakhstan will be a weak state, similar to many in the Third World. It will struggle with praetorianism
and social pressures from the politically excluded strata of the population (including members of the native nomenklatura who are being
pushed aside because they do not belong to the more powerful lin-
eages). Economic progress, to the degree it depends on foreign capital controlled by the Kazakh state and invested in oil production for
export, will merely weaken the state further and exacerbate domestic political problems. The outlook for Kazakhstan is not bright, either within a Russian-dominated CIS or a loose CIS that leaves
Kazakhstan as a truly sovereign state.

Uzbekistan

Political development. With the largest population in the region (more than 22 million) and the largest dominant indigenous ethnic group, the Uzbeks, Uzbekistan has the greatest potential for sustaining its independence. Never a nomadic people in modern times, highly conscious of the past glories of Tamerlane, possessing ancient cities—Bokhara, Samarkand, and Khiva—studded with remarkable buildings from those times, deeply aware of its cultural and religious past, Uzbekistan's social and political culture gives it a contemporary political weightiness not present in any other Central Asian state. In this regard, it differs sharply with Kazakhstan. Kazakhs convey the outward impression of connections to the Orient, to their migrant heritage, as a social residue of the Mongol invasions. Uzbeks convey a strong sense of kinship with the Middle East, more like Syrians or Iraqis than like the Kazakhs, Kyrgyz, and Tajiks.

Yet like Kazakhstan, the Uzbek leadership did not welcome the demise of the Soviet Union. During the last three decades of Soviet rule, the Uzbek communists had worked out a *modus vivendi* with Moscow, accepting titular non-Uzbek senior party officials in their apparatus while creating their own system of rule through family and clan patronage and vast corruption.

Islam Karimov, the Uzbek party chief at the time of the dissolution of the Soviet Union, had no trouble making himself president of the newly independent Uzbek state. Gorbachev's *perestroika* had not significantly circulated throughout the republican party cadres; therefore, Karimov, very much the local party boss, was able to keep his team of party comrades in place through the end of Soviet rule. Thus it was not surprising for Karimov to be highly supportive of establishing strong central institutions under the CIS. He did not have to contend with a large Russian ethnic community or potential territorial dispute, but he shared Nazarbayev's concerns about the economy. Karimov had no enthusiasm for a market economy and was keenly aware of Uzbekistan's ties to the Russian economy through cotton exports and the aviation industry. Therefore, rather than allow the CIS to disrupt the old Soviet economic system, he wanted all parties to agree to keep the old system under the CIS name.

More than any other state in the region (with the possible exception of Turkmenistan), Uzbekistan under Karimov retained the repressive political regime he inherited from the Soviet period. The main opposition movement, ERK, was founded by a mix of intellectuals and Muslim leaders, but it was hardly a bastion of Islamic radicalism as the regime consistently charged. ERK and other smaller political groups made no headway toward gaining the right to participate in the Uzbek political process; instead, they were persecuted, which gave Karimov a very bad name as a violator of human rights.[103] Although the official Uzbek line about opposition groups was that they were threatening to bring radical Islam to Uzbekistan, the real reasons for opposing them were clearly different. First, Karimov's clique did not want to share power, especially while the government was making the rules on control of property. Second, a large number of Tajiks live in Uzbekistan, especially in the Samarkand region.

This second factor explains Karimov's vigorous support for allowing the old communists to retain power in Tajikistan. He feared that clan and regional struggles over political power in Tajikistan might spill over into the Tajik-inhabited parts of Uzbekistan. In fact Karimov's attitude toward Tajikistan has been to try make it more or less a satrapy of Uzbekistan because a vigorous and independent Tajik nationalism could tear Uzbekistan apart.

The violence between Uzbeks and Kyrgyz in the Fergana Valley around Osh during 1991 also threatened Uzbekistan with broader civil disorder. Karimov and Akayev met and put an early end to it. Officials in both governments believed that the whole affair was inspired by Russian intelligence operatives.[104]

The Kazakh pattern of governing through regional strong men also characterized Karimov's regime. The main difference, albeit a small one, was the higher degree of central control in Uzbekistan. The regime distrusted local political chiefs and watched them more closely. In this regard, Karimov himself made the Uzbek political system distinctive. His paranoia was notorious; it prevented cooperation and coordination within the government and maintained an atmosphere of the deepest suspicion and mutual mistrust.[105] Structurally, the Uzbek political system differed little from the Kazakh system, but Karimov's personality gave it a distinctive character missing in Kazakhstan.

As economic hardships accumulate, the potential for political unrest grows. Because Karimov adamantly refuses to allow a secular political opposition to emerge within a legal system of political competition, religion and ethnicity will inexorably become the fallback unifying principles for illegal opposition. Islam and Tajik ethnicity are the obvious candidates. Given the importance of several Islamic holy places in Uzbekistan, and given the deeper roots of Islam there, Karimov's repressive policies could eventually inspire a political movement committed to Islamic principles for the state and the economy. That development, however, will require time.

Economic development. From the beginning of the CIS, Karimov struggled to keep Uzbek economic ties with Russia and other CIS states as close to those of the Soviet period as possible. Informal and bilateral relations became the main linkages, as the Soviet GOSPLAN and the union ministries lost control of economic planning and allocations. Meanwhile, Karimov backed most of Nazarbayev's attempts to create a "single economic space" in the CIS and establish institutions to manage the unified economy. When it became clear that no such unified economic system would be created, and especially with the breakup of the ruble currency zone, Uzbek economic plans had to accommodate the new and unhappy realities. By mid-1993, Karimov himself was admitting that Uzbekistan faced an economic "crisis" and that it would have to take a new approach.[106] In July he announced that Uzbekistan would make a transition to a market system but that the state would retain strong levers for "steering" the economy and retaining "social justice." He invited foreign capital and firms to invest. Some Western businessmen showed interest, but they remained fewer than in Kazakhstan and risked far less capital. Some western corporations expressed an interest in investing in gold mining and cigarette production.

Karimov reluctantly sought the kind of panacea Nazarbayev appeared to have in Chevron's promises to Kazakhstan. Yet he was unwilling to make the dramatic legal changes and other moves essential to attract serious foreign interest. Nor could he offer the kind of massive oil and gas reserves found in Kazakhstan and Turkmenistan. Moreover, his population was too large to support with profits from such commodity exports. In late 1994 the Uzbek economic crisis was deepening.

To Uzbek officials, privatization was simply the transfer of the most attractive properties to high-ranking government officials as favors from Karimov. The local political boss in Samarkand—previously the first secretary of the oblast's communist party and before that the party boss in Tashkent—proudly told one of the authors about four hotels in Samarkand that had been privatized and one that was being constructed privately by a Swiss contractor. They were all his private holdings! What other privatization was occurring? He pointed to many commercial shops along the main streets of the city center. He was building the shops and leasing them to merchants. This vignette probably gives a fair picture of privatization in Uzbek cities countrywide and insight into how senior Uzbek officials understand a market economy. If they follow this pattern to its logical conclusion, the Uzbek economy will eventually resemble those in Syria, Iraq, and other such Middle East countries: highly statist, with a limited commercial competitive market sector. The chief political leader will continue to treat the entire economy as his patrimony.

Military development. Like Kazakhstan, Uzbekistan signed a bilateral military treaty with Russia in addition to the CIS collective security treaty. Although much less is known about Uzbek programs for establishing a national military, it is safe to assume that the pattern is similar to the Kazakh model. The old Turkestan military district had its headquarters in Tashkent, and a number of ground and air force units were stationed there. Uzbekistan took over some of these forces and installations and shared others jointly. The Uzbek national forces were initially based on a motor rifle division and an airborne division. Planning envisioned a troop strength of 30,000, multiethnic composition, and not only ground forces but also air defense and air forces.[107] Russian officers remained the primary source of Uzbek officer cadres. As in all states in the region, Uzbek natives seldom achieved officer status in the Soviet military and almost never high rank. Thus the Uzbek military faces the same difficulties as that of Kazakhstan in building a truly national military establishment not Russian-dominated.

In the meantime, Uzbek-Russian military ties will probably remain cooperative but also palpably strained. The chief of the Uzbek general staff was a Russian major general in December 1993. The visible tension between Uzbek officials and this lonely Russian was painfully apparent at a meeting with the foreign minister where other foreign ministry aides and the chief of the general staff were also present. Questioned by one of the authors about Uzbek military plans, manpower policies, logistics, and relations with the Russian military, he was evasive and visibly nervous, turning most questions over to the foreign minister or his aides.

Russian military influence in Uzbekistan clearly remained strong in late 1994. General Grachev's successes in strengthening Russian military influence elsewhere in the CIS brought no objections from Uzbekistan. Moreover, Karimov was consistently a strong supporter of the CIS collective security treaty and an enthusiastic advocate of Russian military support for the regime in Tajikistan. Karimov would probably like to have an independent military loyal only to him, but that will take many years to create. Dependency on Russia goes beyond officer cadres to include weapons and logistics, as his Russian chief of staff has pointed out. As mentioned previously, however, the Uzbeks were not in as precarious a position as the Kazakhs, with their large Russian minority and potential territorial dispute. Moreover, the large Uzbek population undoubtedly makes even General Grachev pause when considering the challenge of a popular resistance movement to Russian military influence. Both sides, therefore, have good reasons to be patient and work cooperatively. Time, however, may well be on the side of the Uzbeks.

Summary. Uzbekistan has greater potential for maintaining its sovereignty than any other state in Central Asia. Its large Uzbek population and potentially cohesive culture and historical identity provide political gravity lacking elsewhere. At the same time, its political elites are the most repressive in the region, quite willing to cooperate with former communists and conservatives in Russia and without any serious ideas about economic and political alternatives to the Soviet system they grew up in. With even a modicum of economic success, a repressive regime could survive for a long time by co-opting new elites into its privileged circle, paying off potential opposition leaders, and killing off others. Nonetheless, political instability later in the 1990s should not be ruled out. And if such instability becomes serious, even Russia will find subduing it a daunting challenge.

Turkmenistan

Turkmenistan rivaled Tajikistan as the most backward Soviet republic. Located on the old Soviet periphery, sharing a long border with Iran and Afghanistan, and very large in territory, it is nonetheless very small in population, approximately four million. In 1992, the Turkmen portion comprised slightly more than 70 percent of the total, while Russians made up approximately 9 percent and Uzbeks numbered approximately 10 percent. The Russian minority is approximately the same proportion as in Uzbekistan, but because the real numbers (one-tenth of four million versus one-tenth of more than 22 million) are much smaller in Turkmenistan the problem is much more manageable. Turkmenistan's population is almost 60 percent rural, more than any other CIS state, and virtually all the Russians live in urban areas.[108] The working population was even more skewed toward agriculture and services, with only 10 percent working in industry. Yet Turkmenistan was the second largest producer of natural gas and cotton in the USSR, reflecting its considerable endowment of natural resources.

Political development. President Saparmurad Niyazov, the Turkmenistan communist party chief during the last years of the Soviet Union, proved extremely skilled in handling Turkmenistan's transition from a Soviet republic to an independent state. He managed two objectives before and during the USSR's dissolution. First, he slowly expanded local autonomy from Moscow. Second, he ran a highly repressive domestic regime, disallowing any political opposition and denying the Turkmen intelligentsia, local Russians, and outsiders a chance to shake his indigenous political foundation.

At the same time, he maintained the patina of a democratic process. For example, after the August 1991 crisis in Moscow, when other republics were declaring independence, Niyazov first launched public discussion, then a popular referendum in October, albeit a highly controlled one. It yielded a 94 percent majority for independence. Most other republics declared independence first and held referenda much later.[109] Niyazov, elected president in 1990, ran again under the new constitution in June 1992. He was unopposed and collected more than 99 percent of the vote. When a few intellectuals tried to become politically active, Niyazov dealt roughly with them;

he allowed no organized opposition.[110] His repression of Muslim clerics was equally effective as late as late 1994.

Although Niyazov's domestic policies won him no international awards for protecting human rights, they did deny Russia and Iran the opportunity to meddle effectively in Turkmenistan's internal affairs. Accordingly, Russian leaders had to deal with Niyazov on his own terms, and Iran had to deal with him on a proper diplomatic basis. Niyazov has executed what he calls his twin policies, "Open Doors" and "Positive Neutrality." The first calls for foreign investment and the second asserts Turkmenistan's independence.[111] He has talked about the Turkish development model—a secular state in a Muslim society—while developing his closest foreign ties with Iran.[112]

In dealing with Russia, Niyazov steadfastly defended Turkmen independence while rejecting the multilateralism of the CIS. He understood the need for a successor institution to the Soviet Union, but he scorned the vague and ambiguous character of the CIS collective security treaty signed May 1992. He refused to sign it. Proposals for a multilateral economic union in the CIS never drew his enthusiasm. He consistently espoused that bilateralism was better than multilateralism.[113]

Niyazov was able to get away with rejecting Moscow's pleas for CIS military and economic integration, for a number of reasons. First, he did not antagonize the local Russian population, particularly Russian officers and their families. Indeed, he offered them dual citizenship—Russian and Turkmen passports—which would allow ethnic Russians to enjoy the same rights as Turkmen while keeping one foot on the Russian side. Second, his rhetoric and policies made it clear that Turkmenistan intended to depend on Russia for military security—but that the relationship had to be based on bilateral agreements. Third, his highly dictatorial regime—which raised him to a virtual cult figure—prevented Russian intelligence operatives from stirring up internal problems for him. Given all the problems elsewhere in the CIS for the Russian military, Niyazov's bilateralism was enough to appease even hard-line Russian imperialists.

Where the course followed by Niyazov will lead later in the 1990s is not quite clear. Eventually, some Muslim clerics and the small circle of Turkmen intelligentsia may pose political problems. If

Niyazov passes from the scene, uncertainties will become great, and if his economic plans fail, the political situation will undoubtedly worsen.

Economic development. Because Turkmenistan sits on large natural gas deposits, Niyazov has attracted strong interest among foreign investors. His big challenge is constructing a pipeline for exporting gas to world markets. Very early in 1992, Niyazov sought Turkish assistance in providing capital and geographical outlets for a pipeline.[114] Iran would also have to cooperate in such a pipeline, because Turkmenistan has no border with Turkey. Accordingly, Niyazov pursued pragmatic and neighborly ties with Iran, and Rafsanjani's Tehran government reciprocated. In fact, throughout 1992 and 1993, both Iran and Turkey appeared to be competing for influence in Ashgabat. Neither country, however, could provide the level of investment needed. Therefore, Niyazov courted Western Europe, the United States, the IMF, and the World Bank.[115]

As regards internal economic reform, Niyazov talked about market reform. In practice, however, he allowed little change, even in agriculture, where privatization of the collective farm system would seem to be both politically feasible and economically productive. Citing Kuwait as his model for economic development, Niyazov was obviously convinced that he could use profits from gas exports to subsidize his dictatorial regime, buy off the opposition, and maintain internal stability and independence for Turkmenistan.

In 1994, although his optimism about the country's economic future remained high, Niyazov was far from overcoming all the obstacles he faced. He had yet to secure adequate capital investment and Iranian and Turkish cooperation for the pipeline to the West. In principle his strategy ought to work, but he did not hold all the cards in late 1994. Iran, Turkey, and foreign bankers still held the trump cards. Nonetheless, improvements in agriculture and modest local manufacturing had readied Turkmenistan to sustain a modest but acceptable level of income while waiting for the big profits from gas exports.

Military developments. Niyazov kept Turkmenistan involved in CIS military planning discussions from the beginning. Indeed, he had initially declared that Turkmenistan would not create its own army. By the Tashkent summit in May 1992, however (when he refused to sign the CIS collective security treaty), it was clear that he intended to resist creation of an integrated CIS military. He created a ministry of defense and began to develop bilateral agreements with the Russian military for its extensive participation. On 31 July 1992, Turkmenistan entered an agreement on "friendship and cooperation" with Russia, which contained several protocols for close military cooperation.[116]

Throughout the rest of 1992 and 1993, Turkmenistan tried to build a small national army of its own, based on the former Soviet 52nd Army (which had been stationed there) and depending heavily on Russian assistance. Russia and Turkmenistan signed a specifically military agreement on 2 September 1993, which required Turkmenistan to shoulder most of the costs of defense in the country for both Russian and Turkmen military units and entitled Russian citizens to serve in the small Turkmen military.[117] Of approximately 300 military units, totaling approximately 110,000 personnel, 200 were put under Turkmen command, 70 remained under Russian jurisdiction, and 30 were to be withdrawn or disbanded.[118] Despite its heavy dependence on the Russian military—including 2,000 Russian officers to help train Turkmen forces—Turkmenistan established military assistance ties with Ukraine and Turkey, although these were comparatively minuscule.[119]

Manning the country's long southern borders with Afghanistan and Iran, of course, was an equally sensitive issue, and here Niyazov made no effort to expel Russian Border Troops. On the contrary, he eventually accepted heavy dependence on them. Russia and Turkmenistan finally reached bilateral agreements in December 1993, regularizing joint operations and forces for controlling the frontiers.[120]

Summary. Perhaps remarkably, given the weakness and backwardness of Turkmenistan, Niyazov steered his country through the first two years of the CIS without yielding to most of Russia's attempts at restoring its former hegemony over the former Soviet republics. While refusing to sign the CIS collective security treaty and showing reluctance to agree to a new economic union, he was able to deflect Russian pressures by offering the Russian military bilateral agreements allowing retention of Moscow's control of the border and virtually all military affairs in Turkmenistan. The Russian military presence would seem to make Turkmenistan effectively a Russian colony, but these appearances were deceptive as late as the end of 1994. Niyazov's firm control of the domestic political system was thwarting a Russian "divide and rule" strategy, as in the Transcaucasus and Tajikistan. It was also holding Iranian influence at bay.

To make his political strategy viable in the longer run, however, Niyazov needs to find ways to export gas to Western markets. To export through Russian-controlled pipelines would make Turkmenistan as vulnerable as Kazakhstan and Azerbaijan to Moscow's pressures. Yet to find non-Russian alternative outlets, Niyazov must obtain capital and political support for pipelines through Iran and Turkey. Given the shortage of capital in Iran and Turkey for such ventures, the money will have to come from Western investors. Such investors, however, will have to comply with U.S. policy toward Iran, a policy that strongly discourages investments there.

Turkmenistan's political future, therefore, is to a large degree hostage to U.S. policy toward Iran. Changing that policy will not be easy. Iran's behavior makes it difficult, of course, and Niyazov's record on human rights makes him unlikely to receive support in U.S. political circles. In time, if he fails to deliver on his economic plans, Niyazov could encounter intransigent domestic resistance to his repressive style of rule. And that would encourage both Russia and Iran to attempt to meddle in Turkmen affairs.

Kyrgyzstan

Political development. Kyrgyzstan is one of the region's smaller countries. Its population is approximately 4.7 million and is 52 percent Kyrgyz, 21 percent Russian, 13 percent Uzbek, and 14 percent others. Like all the other state boundaries Stalin drew in Central Asia, Kyrgyzstan's borders create problems of ethnic overlap, precisely as Stalin intended. Most of the country is mountainous, including some of the most spectacular parts of the Tian Shan mountain range. Like the Kazakhs, the Kyrgyz were settled forcibly by the Russians, beginning in the 19th century and ending only during the Soviet era. Sometimes the Kyrgyz and the Kazakhs have been considered the same people, but temperament and the effects of topography distinguish them. The Kyrgyz are much less numerous than the Kazakhs, are less placid and even-tempered, and possess a culture developed on high grazing plains and rugged mountain terrain.

Gorbachev's *perestroika* had a significant impact on Kyrgyzstan's capital, formerly Frunze and now known by the old Kyrgyz name, Bishkek. The city lies at the foot of the northern slopes of the country's mountains and is smaller than Almaty in Kazakhstan and Tashkent in Uzbekistan. During the last year of Soviet rule, the liberal-minded intelligentsia in Frunze were able to oust the old party elites, and they elected Akayev to lead the country. This fortunate happenstance gave Kyrgyz political development a reforming cast not only lacking in but strongly opposed by all its neighboring states. Akayev understood what transforming the old political and economic system entailed, and he set out to achieve it. The problem, as he admitted in the authors' presence in December 1993, was the thinness of elite support, especially in the parliament and in local government, for such a dramatic transition.

Therefore, the outward commitment to reform in Kyrgyzstan, so strong in 1993 and 1994, may prove short-lived. Akayev gave reform an additional boost by submitting his programs to a popular referendum in January 1994. His reform approach won out against antireform sentiment in the parliament, but the fact that he had to take the risk of a vote demonstrated the fragility of the political forces for reform.

Dependence on Europeans (such as Slavs and Germans) in high-skill economic posts and in science, engineering, and other intellectual sectors leaves Kyrgyzstan no choice but to get on well with Moscow and try to persuade these non-Kyrgyz cadres not to emigrate, as a large number were doing in 1993.[121] Even so, ethnic Kyrgyz occupied virtually all the top government posts under Akayev; Vice President German Kuznetsov, a Russian, was an exception. Having long suffered second-rate status during the Slav-dominated Soviet period, Kyrgyz elites understandably moved into the key positions previously denied them (along with the housing). Carrying that policy too far, however, would provoke serious problems with both Moscow and local Russians, on whom the industrial sector of the local economy depended heavily. That limit was being approached in 1993. Kuznetsov, for example, resigned from the government and emigrated to Russia in July 1993 because he was excluded from all important decisions.[122] The Kyrgyz leadership responded by retreating from the policy. Akayev neither wanted to nor could expect to get away with excluding all the local Russians from senior posts. Nonetheless, some Kyrgyz nationalists criticized his tolerance toward non-Kyrgyz.[123]

Economic development. As is clear from the earlier discussion of CIS economic issues, Kyrgyzstan was the only new Central Asian republic with a leader committed to a transition to a market economy and also able to comprehend what that involved. Thus Kyrgyzstan set the pace for economic reform. It signed foreign economic agreements in East Asia before most other Central Asian CIS members and gained IMF support ahead of all others. President Akayev, as mentioned earlier, took the lead in breaking out of the Russian ruble zone by introducing his own currency in the summer of 1993.

The influx of foreign capital, however, was trivial for several reasons. First, Kyrgyzstan has no vast oil or gas reserves that can attract foreign companies as in Kazakhstan, Turkmenistan, and even Uzbekistan. Second, attracting investment other than in extraction of mineral commodities for export requires an infrastructure of private property laws, reliable civil courts, and a modern banking structure. Although Akayev's reform programs promised to develop some of these features, they were still absent in 1992-94. Third, Kyrgyzstan's mountainous terrain lacks a modern ground transportation infrastructure, which deterred some Western firms from trying to expand gold production there.[124] Even Bishkek is off the beaten path and hard to reach. And whereas Kazakhstan and Uzbekistan gave Lufthansa rights to regular flights to their capitals, the Kyrgyz could not persuade the German company that stopping in Bishkek would cover its costs. Also, the remainder of Soviet Aeroflot was becoming increasingly unreliable in 1993-94, making Western air transport access even more important in attracting foreign investment.

Kyrgyzstan's economic development outlook in late 1994 was not bright. True enough, Akayev and a few of his aides were the most reform-minded leaders in the region and were staking their careers on successfully achieving the economic transition. Yet Kyrgyzstan lacked both the economic institutional infrastructure and a sufficiently broad base of support for political reform.

Military development. In the first two years of the CIS,

Kyrgyzstan's military aspirations were extremely modest. In December 1991 Akayev decreed the formation of a "national guard" comprising a small number of personnel from the Ministry of Interior and other security personnel, but it failed to take shape until August 1992, when it comprised approximately 800 personnel.[125] It was a security force, not a proper army. In January 1992 the Kyrgyz government had affirmed the right to a national military but denied any intention of creating it in the near future, attributing the delay to costs.[126] Only at the end of May 1992 did Kyrgyzstan follow the pattern of most other CIS states and formally assert authority over all Soviet forces on its territory. This step accelerated the disintegration of most of them.[127] More than 200,000 Soviet military personnel were stationed in Kyrgyzstan.[128] They were primarily ground forces but also included the large aviation training center near Bishkek, where many foreign students and Soviet officers received pilot training. By mid-1993, this center ceased to function.[129]

The Kyrgyz military leadership, initially a committee of national security under Akayev, was upgraded to a general staff in August 1993.[130] It had to remove most of the large complement of non-Kyrgyz military personnel before it could attempt to create significant forces of its own. It seems that the Kyrgyz government simply let these units deteriorate; their officers sold off their weapons and equipment and ceased to keep them effective as military organizations. As in all other Central Asian countries, building a cadre of native officers was the most time-consuming challenge; Kyrgyzstan began sending young Kyrgyz to officer training schools not only in Russia but also in Uzbekistan and even Turkey.[131] In 1993-94, the core of its defense program involved plans for a 5,000 to 7,000 man force based on the old Soviet 8th Motor Rifle Division.[132] Although modest in size, even this small structure would depend on Russian supplies of weapons and logistics. Whether Bishkek could find the cash to pay Russia for such support remained an open question in 1994.

Kyrgyz leaders expressed intense interest in the Swiss "defense model" for a wholly defense-oriented strategy based on a mountainous terrain. They held discussions with Swiss officials in 1993, and more were anticipated.[133] Apparently, the government also planned to have each region of the country house local paramilitary structures for conducting insurgency operations against any future invader.[134] Given Bishkek's fiscal plight, this scheme made better sense than attempting to build ground, air, and air-defense forces that would inevitably be in Russian officers' hands even if Kyrgyzstan paid for them.

Akayev consistently cooperated with Russia on most CIS military issues in 1992-94. He signed the collective security treaty at the May 1992 CIS summit meeting, and at Moscow's request he sent a Kyrgyz battalion to reinforce Russian Border Troops on the boundary with Afghanistan.[135] The incompetence of the battalion soon led to its withdrawal, but Kyrgyzstan could not be accused of failing to cooperate in CIS joint military operations.

Summary. Akayev's commitment to liberal reforms put Kyrgyzstan out of step with all other Central Asian states from the beginning of the CIS. That was apparent from his decision to introduce an independent Kyrgyz currency and leave the ruble zone. This move upset his neighbors thoroughly. A short time later, however, Russia changed its monetary policy, which angered Nazarbayev and Karimov even more and displaced their irritation with Akayev. On most foreign policy issues, Akayev was sufficiently deferential and cooperative with his big neighbors to avoid making Kyrgyzstan the focus of serious regional disputes. At the same time, the liberal reforms Kyrgyzstan carried through caused it to diverge from its neighbors in ways that eventually caused difficulties.

In military policy, Akayev managed to hold down Kyrgyzstan's defense expenditures, although that involved the political risk of letting the residual Soviet forces there rapidly decay and their officers express strong discontent. Kyrgyz military reform plans remained extremely modest, and the notion of borrowing concepts from the Swiss defense model made good sense because conducting defense was easier than offense. Like all other countries in Central Asia, Kyrgyzstan had very few officers in the Soviet military. Therefore, as in Kazakhstan, Uzbekistan, and elsewhere, building a Kyrgyz national military establishment required building native officer cadres.

While pursuing a long-range policy of pursuing greater military independence, Akayev made Kyrgyzstan a dependable ally for Moscow in CIS military affairs: he cooperated with Russia's intervention in Tajikistan, signed the collective security treaty, and avoided oppo-

sition stands except when Kyrgyzstan's minimum limits for sovereignty were at stake.

Kyrgyzstan made too little progress in political and economic liberalization to cause serious unease in neighboring dictatorships or in Moscow. Moreover, outside capital and business interests showed little interest, although Akayev was able to secure some foreign economic aid and credits. Kyrgyzstan's future, therefore, looked uncertain in late 1994. Its admirable, reforming leader was facing passive resistance from his own parliament and society on the one hand and very modest assistance from abroad on the other.

Tajikistan

Political development. When the Soviet Union collapsed, Tajikistan, with almost 6 million people, was less prepared than any other republic for dealing with the new realities. No significant democratic nationalist front grew up there during *perestroika*, as occurred in Kyrgyzstan, nor did it develop a consolidated communist elite that could hold power, as occurred in Kazakhstan, Uzbekistan, and Turkmenistan. The absence of a powerful democratic nationalist movement is not surprising. Tajikistan was the most backward and poorest of the Soviet republics and had lost its two great cultural centers, Samarkand and Bokhara, to Uzbekistan under Soviet nationality policy. Tajikis had a particularly weak level of national awareness. Thus only a weak Tajik intelligentsia emerged to carry the banner of democracy as Soviet power collapsed. A Muslim awakening, however, did occur during the last couple of years of *perestroika*. This movement was manifest in the Islamic Renaissance Party, not a radical political movement but one with fairly broad appeal in the rural parts of the country where awareness of the country's Islamic heritage had never died. The movement's leadership, however, favored a secular state and, as part of the political opposition, cooperated with the Democratic Party, a much smaller and weaker group composed mainly of the small Tajik secular intelligentsia.

The communists were also caught in disarray. The Tajik communist party never penetrated and replaced the country's regional clan political structure. It merely became an overlay, and depended on the social structure of the clans for its underpinnings.[136] Thus

reformist communists did not take over the communist party in Dushanbe as they did in Russia, the Baltic republics, and elsewhere. Instead a struggle for dominance ensued among regional-based clans. The northern-Leninabad-based Khodjent clan was able to respond to demonstrations in February 1990 by replacing first party secretary Rakhmon Nabiyev, one of its clan members, with Kakhor Makhkamov, another of its members.[137] The opposition was based on Shodmon Yusup's small Democratic Party and Davlat Usmon's much larger Islamic Renaissance Party and had widespread roots at the village level. The Democratic Party proved too small to be of significance because it was not clan-based, but the much stronger Islamic party enjoyed both the support of several clans and the trans-clan cultural appeal of Islam.

Although Nabiyev faced what appeared to be sure political defeat after strong opposition demonstrations in October 1991, he won the presidential election in November by a healthy majority.[138] Things settled down until the spring of 1992, when the opposition began a two-month period of anticommunist demonstrations. Nabiyev was forced to create a coalition government which included Islamists, Democrats, and others. Rather than stability, this prompted the beginning of fighting (in late May 1992) which lasted into the fall. The northern Leninabad Oblast clan, the Khodjenti led by Nabiyev, had lost its primacy and alienated its regime partner, the southern Kulyabi clan, ostensibly over concessions to the Islamists. The Kulyabi clan's leader, Sangak Safarov, who spent many years in prison on several criminal charges, created a popular front with a military organization and fought the Islamic Renaissance-Democratic forces all summer, gaining an edge over them by early fall.

Fragmentation and corruption in the ranks of the regime also made it increasingly vulnerable, and although it tried to strengthen its base by making the Pamiri clan leader acting president in September 1992, it behaved as if it were about to create an Islamic state. That brought aid to the Kulyabi from Uzbekistan (Saudi Arabia, Iran, and Pakistan were said to be aiding the Islamic Renaissance Party) which allowed them to drive out the increasingly Islamicist-dominated regime in October. The charge that it was intent on establishing a theocratic Islamic regime was probably exaggerated, but it helped rally domestic and external anti-regime forces. The office of the presi-

dency was abolished, and Imomali Rakhmonov, a Kulyabi, was made head of the parliament and head of state.

Thus the struggle from fall 1991 through fall 1992—though ostensibly between communist and Islamic Renaissance-Democratic forces—had a more important underlying dimension, namely clans competing for power. Within the regime, the northern Khodjenti from Leninabad had lost out to the Kulyabi from the south. They had shared power, the Khodjenti being on top and the Kulyabi being second-rank partners, under the communist banner. The civil war of 1992 allowed the Kulyabi to reverse the hierarchy and displace the Khodjenti.[139]

All other clans in the east, mainly the Pamiri and Garmi, fought against the regime (i.e., Safarov's Kulyabi forces) in 1992, and other clans of the remote southeastern region, Gorno-Badakshan, would soon become deeply involved in efforts against the regime. The Islamic Renaissance Party, the Rastokhez (the Tajik nationalist movement), the Lali Badakshan (the Badakshan nationalist movement), and the Western-oriented but very weak Democratic Party were the formal groups in the opposition. For the most part, they also rested on clans, but the Democratic Party was an exception, and the Islamic Renaissance Party had, as noted, a trans-clan rural appeal.[140] Like the communists holding the government, the opposition evinced inter-clan fissures and feuds.

The regime and other Central Asian governments, particularly Uzbekistan, used the Islamic character of the opposition as a means to stir up fear and justify support for the old communist Khodjenti-Kulyabi. Yet the key opposition leader insisted consistently that he favored a secular state.[141] Ali Akhbar Turadzhonzoda became the undisputed leader of the Islamic Renaissance-Democratic bloc in 1991-93; he came from a family with a long religious tradition and grew up following the path of "official Islam" in the Soviet Union. In 1990 he was appointed as supreme religious authority of official Islam in Tajikistan and elected to Tajikistan's supreme soviet. There he pushed for legal reforms which would have ended the outlawing of Islamic practices in the country. Kulyabi mullahs, however, refused to support him, and he became the object of attacks from outside Tajikistan. Both these factors suggest that Islam was not really the basic issue that led to fighting in Tajikistan.

The 1992-93 civil war produced large numbers of casualties; estimates ranged from 20,000 to more than 50,000.[142] A large number of refugees, between 40,000 and 70,000, fled to Afghanistan, especially during the first half of 1993.[143] That, of course, brought Afghan mujahidin into the conflict. Gulbeddin Hekmatyar, the leader of the Afghan Islam Party, apparently provided training camps for Tajik guerrillas cadres.[144] Masud, one of the most distinguished Afghan military leaders in the fight against Soviet occupation, was an ethnic Tajik, which provided a point of appeal and pride for some Tajik refugees. The Tajik Islamic religious leader, Turadzhonzoda, also fled to Afghanistan. Given Hekmatyar's reputation as a radical Islamicist and the inability of the Rabbani regime in Kabul to control Hekmatyar's activities in the north, there was circumstantial evidence for the charge by Russian, Uzbek, Kazakh, and other outside parties that radical Islam posed a genuine threat to Tajikistan. More likely, however, because the Tajik Democratic Party never disowned its Islamic party allies, the charge was without solid grounds.

The underlying political reality was a struggle among Tajik clans. The Kulyabi were ensconced in Dushanbe, effectively protected by the Russian 201st Motor Rifle Division, and most of the southern clans were retreating to Afghanistan's mountainous terrain, as they had during the Basmachi resistance against Soviet power in the 1920s.

Ironically, some Russian leaders misunderstood the true structure of the political struggle in Tajikistan in 1991-92. After the August 1991 coup attempt, Yevgenii Ambartsumov, a key member of the foreign affairs committee in the Supreme Soviet, called on the Russian government to support the Tajik anticommunist forces in Dushanbe.[145] He and other Russian democrats presumed the Tajik democrats to be the primary opposition, knowing nothing of their trivial numbers or the strength of the Islamic cultural awareness and clan structure that provided the basis for genuine political alignments and loyalties. Russian Border Troops remained in charge of the Afghan border, and the 201st Motor Rifle Division remained in Dushanbe, leaving Russia implicitly involved in Tajik political affairs. The Russian defense ministry and Marshal Shaposhnikov (as head of the CIS military organizing effort) sought to tie Tajikistan into a "single strategic space" and did not treat the country as genuinely sovereign. Meanwhile, Kozyrev and his foreign ministry em-

phasized the fundamental change in relations among former Soviet republics. Yeltsin stood apart and avoided expressing a clear position. All of this changed sharply in the summer of 1993.

On 13 July 1993, more than 20 Russian border guards were killed by fighters from Afghanistan. This action catalyzed a turning point in Russian relations with Tajikistan. General Grachev flew in to assess the situation, followed by Barannikov, minister of security and head of the Russian Border Troops. President Yeltsin also became engaged; he put foreign minister Kozyrev in charge of coordinating the overall Russian policy, and he called the attack a direct threat to Russia's national security.[146] The "domino" effect of Islamic radicalism was cited not only in Moscow but also by the regime in Dushanbe and by other Central Asian leaders as threatening the entire regime. A Russian-Tajik treaty was drawn up, signed, and ratified by both sides with remarkable speed, in two days time, committing Russia to defend the border and the incumbent Tajik region.[147] Some Russian parliamentary opposition drew analogies between this commitment to Tajikistan and the Soviet involvement in Afghanistan, but the criticisms were brushed aside.

This dramatic policy change, of course, was rooted in domestic Russian political considerations, particularly Yeltsin's fear that his critics would accuse him of failing to defend Russia's traditional territorial interests in Central Asia and of letting Russian soldiers be killed with impunity. The reasons hardly rested on an objective assessment of Russia's interests in Tajikistan, but the consequence was to put Russia and other CIS states, especially Uzbekistan, Kazakhstan, and Kyrgyzstan, firmly on the side of Russian hegemony in Tajikistan and to shore up the Kulyabi clan's rule of the entire country. Not only were the Garmi and Pamiri excluded, but the Khodjenti of the northern, economically better off, regions were also shut out. Moreover, the Khodjenti are geographically closer to Uzbekistan and potentially detachable from Tajikistan by Uzbekistan. More than any other Central Asian republic, Uzbekistan fears a strong and independent Tajikistan because of the large Tajik population in Uzbekistan, and therefore prefers to keep Tajikistan weak and in effect an Uzbek satrapy.

Drug trafficking complicated the political situation further. Little is known for certain about this factor in Tajik politics, but narcotics trade may have been the actual cause of the 13 July clash between Russian Border Troops and Tajik border crossers. Rumors were rife in 1994 that the Russian military itself was involved in the drug trade. It can be argued that drug trafficking was the most important factor in determining sides, the course of the civil war, and other political developments in Tajikistan.[148] Moreover, when Nabiyev brought opposition leaders from the Democratic Party and the Islamic Renaissance Party into the regime in May 1992, they used their positions less to help construct a competitive political system than to pillage the country for their personal economic advantage.[149] Therefore, any attempt to characterize the various parties and factions in Tajik politics as communist, Muslim, democratic, or other tends to mislead more than inform us about political goals, alignments, fissures, etc.

In 1994 Tajikistan's stability depended on Russia, particularly on its Border Troops on the Afghan frontier, the Russian motor rifle division in Dushanbe, and economic assistance from Moscow. Internally, there was no balance of political power among the country's clans, and the prospects of getting the dominant Kulyabi to share power looked poor, although the Russian foreign minister had begun to urge the regime to engage the opposition in dialogue rather than civil war. Moreover, Russia's diplomatic efforts in Saudi Arabia, Iran, Pakistan, and Afghanistan to isolate the Tajik opposition forces were hardly a success. The key problem was in Afghanistan where the Kabul regime had little control over Afghan territory in the north. And local leaders there were sympathetic to Tajik resistance groups instead of Russia's plight.

Economic development. The breakup of the Soviet command economic system left the Tajik economy as much adrift and unprepared to adjust as any other in Central Asia. The civil war, however, virtually displaced serious planning by the regime for economic reform and transformation. The gross domestic product declined rapidly in 1992 and 1993, and by 1994 this fragmented and war-torn society was in far worse economic shape than any other in the region. To the extent that it was an "economy" at all, it was an appendage of the Russian economy: it was dependent on Moscow for aid, a currency system, banking, and most other macroeconomic policies.

Military development. The civil war created a unique environment for Tajik military institutional developments. The regimes, first of Nabiyev and later of Rakhmonov, made no attempt to "nationalize" the Russian Border Troops or the 201st Motor Rifle Division (MRD). They were preoccupied with internal struggles. Moreover, the 201st MRD was commanded by Major General Mukhriddin Ashurov, a native Tajik. By the summer of 1992, Ashurov's forces were the last source of political stability in the country, officially proclaimed to be neutral but occasionally involved in the conflict in and around Dushanbe. At the same time, Ashurov was tilting the activities of the Russian forces in favor of the Kulyabi opposition forces in the south at the expense of the non-communists in Nabiyev's coalition government.[150]

The coalition government attempted to create a Tajik national guard and to articulate a Tajik "military doctrine."[151] These efforts, however, could not possibly meet the demands of the civil war. Therefore, the government accepted the idea of deploying CIS military forces in areas where the situation was tense.[152] This decision evoked confusion and anger from opposition groups and led to no effective CIS action. Only late in the fall, after Nabiyev had been deposed and the Kulyabi clan returned to power, did significant action for building military institutions occur. The Tajik presidium of the supreme soviet issued a decree creating the Armed Forces of Tajikistan and establishing a ministry of defense.[153]

The Russian hand in these developments was clear in January 1993, when a Russian, Colonel Aleksandr Shishlyannikov, was appointed as minister of defense of Tajikistan and promoted to major general. Although he was an ethnic Russian, he was born in Tashkent and served at length in Central Asia. He was chief of staff of a corps in Uzbekistan when appointed to the Tajik post.[154] The Uzbek government also undoubtedly cooperated in this move. Shishlyannikov made clear that the 201st MRD would not be "privatized" like Russian forces elsewhere, and General Grachev in Moscow declared that it would remain in Tajikistan until at least 1999.[155] Teams of CIS officers began to assist Shishlyannikov, and unlike the previous summer, they were allowed to begin work.[156] In February the CIS made efforts to send Uzbek, Kyrgyz, and Kazakh forces under the CIS banner to assist the government in closing the border with Afghanistan.[157] A Kyrgyz battalion and a few small Uzbek units were eventually sent, but Kazakhstan continued to hesitate.

These Central Asian contributions were of no significant help, largely because of poor training, and even the Russian forces proved unable to close the border, as the 13 July affair would demonstrate a few months later. Meanwhile, the Tajik Armed Forces made little progress, leaving both internal and external security effectively in Russian hands. The magnitude of this task was reflected in Yeltsin's decree "On Measures to Settle the Conflict on the Tajik-Afghan Border and to Normalize the Situation on the Russian Federation's Borders," issued on 27 July. It assigned tasks to the Russian ministries of security, internal affairs, defense, finance, health, and several other agencies.[158] Because the Tajiks were embroiled in their own inter-clan struggles and could not create an effective military and police system, let alone a system of social services, Russia had stepped in to act as surrogate for the Tajik state.

Summary. Tajikistan fragmented along clan lines because the old communist leaders apparently did not foresee that the Soviet Union might collapse, as Nazarbayev, Karimov, and Niyazov did. They cracked down early, keeping a firm hand on power and disallowing opposition groups under any banner to have a serious chance for open political participation. Nor did Tajikistan have a sufficiently organized secular democratic movement to achieve the kind of transition Akayev accomplished in Kyrgyzstan. Actually, during the last years of *perestroika,* Tajikistan had perhaps the most pluralist political development, but it served as a mere patina over the clan and cultural fissures in the country. When forced to accept that they ran a "sovereign" state, the old communist elites themselves were engaged in clan struggles, which created an opportunity for Islamic political forces and much weaker democratic forces to bring down the government. In the summer of 1993, to impose a degree of order in Tajikistan, Russia decided to provide essentially a colonial government.

Russian arms, troops, and modest economic assistance, however, would not soon alter the unstable structure of power in Tajikistan. Uzbekistan was no less involved, because of its own Tajik minority and the closeness of the Khodjent clan in Leninabad Oblast, not to mention probable Uzbek involvement in drug trafficking through Tajikistan. The large refugee population in northern Afghanistan added another external entanglement of large importance. Finally, as the struggle continued and the opposition used the Islamic banner to create inter-clan alliances, the government had to consider the potential for a radical Islamic movement. In other words, the policies of Russian and Central Asian leaders to prevent Islamic radicalism may prove to be the very things that create it.

Armenia

Political development. Two factors have dominated Armenian political life over several centuries. First, as a small Christian ethnic group surrounded by Muslim Turks and under Ottoman rule since the fall of Constantinople in 1453, Armenians have struggled for both survival and independence. Second, Armenia has long sought outside sponsorship for its independence, dating back at least to the late 17th century, when the head of the Armenian church appealed to the courts of Europe and the Holy Roman Emperor, and eventually to Peter the Great of Russia.[159] None of these parties came to Armenia's defense until Russia did so during Catherine the Great's rule. Karabakh, with a large Armenian population, came under Russian rule in 1813. Russia's imperial ambitions, Christian religion, and antagonism toward Turkey coincided well with Armenia's desire to escape Turkish dominance.

During *perestroika* and after the collapse of the USSR, these two factors again dominated Armenian political development. When Gorbachev relaxed political controls, Armenians took the opportunity to raise the issue of Nagorno-Karabakh's status: predominantly populated by Armenians but located in the Azeri Soviet Socialist Republic. Nagorno-Karabakh had been incorporated into Azerbaijan by the Soviet government after the Revolution. As one of the few areas of Transcaucasia with a historical Armenian majority, it had great emotional value to Armenians. When the Soviet Union started to disintegrate, Armenians in Nagorno-Karabakh pushed for separation from Azerbaijan and incorporation into Armenia, which led to the current warfare. The "Karabakh Committee," formed in 1987, organized protests in Yerevan in February 1988. The soviet of the Nagorno-Karabakh Autonomous Oblast formally requested in Moscow and Baku that the oblast be united with Armenia. Moscow ruled against the Armenian demand later that year, and the Azeris started to react forcefully to developments in the disputed oblast. By the end of the year, the war over Nagorno-Karabakh had begun.

Moscow proved unable to resolve the conflict by negotiating a settlement or imposing one by force. This stimulated increasing discontent in Yerevan and during 1990 prompted talk of Armenian sovereignty and independence from the Soviet Union, especially after the pogroms in Sumgait against Armenians and the failure of Soviet forces to intervene promptly to stop them. The "Karabakh Committee" became the Armenian Pan-National Movement in November 1989, and as anger at Moscow grew during 1990, the Movement's chairman, Levon Ter-Petrossian, defeated the secretary of the Armenian Communist Party in the presidential election. Ter-Petrossian, however, did not pursue an anti-Moscow policy but took a conciliatory approach, behind which he hoped to establish an Armenian military capable of winning the war with Azerbaijan.[160]

This task would define Armenian domestic politics. The Armenian diaspora returned Armenians from abroad, including Armenian-Americans, and they joined the struggle. Ter-Petrossian retained power while the country pursued the war with Azerbaijan, worked in international diplomatic circles for assistance, and attempted to manage relations with Moscow. The politics of survival, greatly reinforced by memories of the Turkish massacres of Armenians in 1915, gave Armenia a social and political cohesion unmatched elsewhere in the Transcaucasus. Social subgroups in Armenia did not have the fragmenting effect characteristic of Georgian and Azeri politics. Moreover, when Azerbaijan declared its independence in August 1991 and later refused to join the CIS, Ter-Petrossian was able to secure Russian military assistance and use it to gain a military advantage in 1992-93. Once again, as in the past two centuries, Armenia used the Russian connection to provide a strategic balance against its Muslim enemies.

In spite of Armenia's internal political coherence, a split of sorts did develop, especially after the breakup of the Soviet Union. Dashnaks—Armenian activists from the diaspora—moved into both the Yerevan government and the Nagorno-Karabakh political leadership. They strongly opposed Ter-Petrossian's pragmatic policy toward Turkey (in which he sought Turkish support as an alternative to dependency on Russia) and his greater willingness to reach a settlement with Azerbaijan. The Dashnak elements favored war over a settlement and resisted all dealings with Turkey. Although no conclusive evidence appears to be available in open sources, one should not be surprised to find that Russian intelligence operatives had influence among the Dashnaks. Some Russian officials may have used the Dashnak connection within Ter-Petrossian's regime to undermine his willingness to compromise with both Turkey and Azerbaijan. If so, Armenia proved vulnerable to the Russian "divide and rule" tactics that were so transparent in Georgia and Azerbaijan.

Economic development. "Development" is hardly an appropriate term for describing economic affairs in Armenia between 1988 and 1994. Devastated by a terrible earthquake and periodically denied energy—electricity, gas, and oil—from the outside sources on which it wholly depended, economic life in the country became primarily a matter of survival. Western aid, private and governmental, afforded modest relief, but in late 1994 Armenian economic affairs could only be described as desperate.

Military development. The Soviet 7th Army was deployed in Armenia when the USSR was dissolved, and its weaponry and supply stocks became the primary source for building an Armenian military. Armenia created a ministry of defense in January 1992, and it set to work drawing up the necessary regulations and institutions for a national army. The first plans involved only a ground force, eschewing air forces and air-defense capabilities.[161] Already involved in a war, the Armenian military had first to solve its manpower problem. During 1992 they rounded up deserters, and the government set a legal basis for conscription and created the administrative bodies to implement it.[162] These developments created tensions with the Russian 7th Army, as defense ministry officials began to take control of parts of the former Soviet military establishment in the country.[163]

Unlike all other countries in Central Asia and the Transcaucasus, Armenia could staff its new army with a fairly large number of Soviet officers who were ethnic Armenians. At the very beginning of the CIS, in January 1992, nearly sixty generals and senior field grade officers were available for the ministry of defense,[164] and another 5,000 were serving in Russia, Ukraine, and Belarus. Later that year the Armenian defense ministry began to appeal to them to return home and join the new Armenian military.[165]

This fairly large source of officers gave Armenia a distinct advantage in building the foundations for genuine independence. No less important, of course, was the country's sense of national identity and ethnic cohesion, because it permitted effective conscription of regular soldiers. Yet in spite of these huge advantages, Armenia remained dependent on Russian military supplies, especially weapons and munitions. Ter-Petrossian, unlike some of his more nationalist-extremist ministers (especially the foreign minister, American-born Raffi Hovanissian), was sufficiently pragmatic to attempt to improve relations with Turkey in 1992. Georgia's independence cut off ground communications with Russia, and Armenia's need for outside sources of military supplies dictated alternative sources if Armenia was to remain independent. Ter-Petrossian did not succeed in this strategy, however, and in late 1993, as Russia reasserted control in Azerbaijan and Georgia, it also was able to exercise its leverage over Armenia. As mentioned earlier, the role of the Dashnak radicals in the Armenian government may provide part of the explanation for Ter-Petrossian's failure to come to terms with Turkey.

Another military development complicated Armenia's situation. Nagorno-Karabakh created its own militia, which gave it a degree of autonomy vis-a-vis the Yerevan government. Apparently, Russian military advisors helped train and supply this force throughout 1992 and early 1993.[166] The autonomy of Nagorno-Karabakh leaders proved a stumbling block against several international efforts to negotiate a settlement of the war over Nagorno-Karabakh. It was not the only such obstacle but nonetheless troublesome.[167]

Summary. The struggle to unite Nagorno-Karabakh with Armenia stimulated an early and sustained Armenian independence movement and a high degree of domestic political cohesion. It also destroyed Armenia's economy, intensified hostile relations with Azerbaijan, harmed traditionally good relations with Iran, pushed Turkey to side with Azerbaijan, and left Armenia once again dependent on Moscow for its survival. Although relations between Yerevan and Moscow waxed hot and cold between 1989 and 1994, Yerevan never risked complete alienation from Russia, although it came close in the fall of 1993 when Russia tilted to the Azeri side of the dispute.

Not surprisingly, therefore, Armenia consistently supported Russian military policies in the CIS during the first two years of the CIS' existence.

Azerbaijan

Political development. The Azeri Popular Front arose as a political movement under the liberal climate of *perestroika* in May 1989, appealing to a national-minded intelligentsia and the country's lower socioeconomic stratum. Popular Front leaders exploited the war in Nagorno-Karabakh by appealing to anti-Armenian sentiment, and in late 1989 they gathered sufficient strength to take power in the border towns of Lenkoran and Dzhalilabad, and they used those positions to force open the entire Soviet border with Iran.[168] In effect, the Popular Front was using the conflict with Armenia to compete for power with the ruling communist party. Because of the bloody events in Baku during January 1990, pogroms against Armenians, and demonstrations by the Popular Front, Gorbachev sent in Soviet military forces to restore order. They came belatedly, after considerable disorder, not only to restore order but also to destroy the Popular Front and revitalize the Azeri communist party leadership.

Ayez Mutabilov was appointed as the new party first secretary. To broaden his political base, he sided with the nationalists during the spring of 1990. He won the presidency of the republic in the May election and retained the leadership in Baku for two years. Soon after the dissolution of the Soviet Union, however, in March 1992 while the war was going poorly for Azerbaijan, Popular Front forces caused Mutabilov to resign the presidency. Yagub Mamedov, as head of the parliament, became acting president. This power-sharing attempt between the communists and the Popular Front did not reverse the military situation. By mid-May Armenian forces were on the verge of taking Stepankert, the capital of Nagorno-Karabakh. Mutabilov returned to power, pushing out Mamedov and prompting Popular Front protestations. The resulting political crisis led the parliament to dissolve in favor of a national council dominated by the Popular Front. The Front's leader, Abulfez Elchibey, was quickly elected president on 7 June, as he promised to reverse the deteriorating military situation.

Although Elchibey's government failed to achieve significant military success, it did launch a new set of policies. It scorned Moscow, tried to build an independent Azeri army, established close ties with Turkey, and struck oil production deals with several Western companies. Described by some observers as idealistic but feckless, Elchibey marked the end of rule by the old communist *nomenklatura*. His colleagues proved venal, however, and exploited the government just as the *nomenklatura* had done, causing greater hardships for the lower socioeconomic stratum which provided their support.[169] In addition to alienating its domestic political base, the new regime also inflamed its relations with Russia. Elchibey's openly pro-Turkish policy and his flirtation with foreign oil companies did not go down well in Moscow. And his refusal to hold parliamentary elections displeased the moderate intelligentsia who could have augmented his political support.[170]

Still, he held power for a year before being ousted by a military rebellion. The military commander, Surat Huseinov, had become a national hero by making territorial gains against the Armenians in the fall of 1992. In the spring of 1993, however, under pressure from Armenian attacks, he withdrew troops to Gyandzha and thereby allowed Armenian forces to recoup lost gains. The Popular Front government accused Huseinov of trying to destabilize the regime and summarily dismissed him, notwithstanding the defense minister's testimony that he had withdrawn on orders from the supreme commander of the Azeri military.[171] This puzzling episode may be explained by Elchibey's conviction that a Russian-inspired coup was about to unfold with Huseinov as its leader. In any case, Huseinov refused to accept his dismissal and remained near Gyandzha with troops loyal to him.

During the next three months, the military situation worsened. (Russian aid to Armenia was having its effect, as was Azerbaijan's inability to mobilize as effectively as Armenia.) The last Russian forces were expelled from Azerbaijan, leaving their weapons and equipment at Gyandzha. It appears that Azerbaijan government forces started the series of events leading to Huseinov's military march on Baku by attacking his brigade encamped near Gyandzha to prevent him from acquiring the Russian weapons and equipment. Huseinov soon took the garrison at Gyandzha, acquired the Russian arms, and moved to the outskirts of Baku.

Meanwhile, Elchibey began trying to strike deals with the old communists Mamedov and Gaidar Aliyev (former Azeri Communist Party chief and alternate member of the Politburo until Gorbachev expelled him in 1987). Both declined to settle for the government posts Elchibey offered. While Huseinov threatened Baku, Aliyev persuaded Elchibey's supporters that he was a better alternative than Huseinov.

After Elchibey's departure, Aliyev rapidly took charge of the situation, dealing with the various factions competing for power. Huseinov entered Baku on 27 June, and after hard bargaining with Aliyev he agreed to settle for less than the presidency, accepting the post of prime minister. (Aliyev had hoped to save this position for Mamedov, who had served as acting president for a few months in 1992.) Aliyev became chairman of the national assembly and acting president, thus preserving the appearance of legality and continuity in the new institutions.[172]

As mentioned earlier in the section on CIS military developments, there is much evidence to support the charge of Russian complicity in Huseinov's military revolt and Aliyev's maneuvering, but it seems doubtful that everything was fully staged. More likely, local Russian military and intelligence officers took advantage of opportunities as they arose. They did not arise all that favorably in February 1993, when Huseinov was first suspected of being party to a Russian-backed coup, but they did work out favorably in June.

Aliyev, of course, went to Moscow in September to agree to make Azerbaijan a member of the CIS. And he reversed Elchibey's pro-Turkish policy. He only temporarily relinquished deals with Western oil companies, however, when Moscow turned up the pressure on him in July, later reopening talks with British firms about investing in Azerbaijan's oil industry.[173] Russia consolidated its grip on Azerbaijan in the fall and winter of 1993-94. By January 1994 Russia achieved regularization of its troop presence and an agreement for Russian Border Troops to control Azerbaijan's border with Iran.[174]

Economic development. As in Armenia, the war caused a dramatic decline in living standards in Azerbaijan. The old command economic system fell apart. No serious reform programs were implemented. And the regime was absorbed with mobilizing and supplying its military forces. Indeed, things would have been better if the regime had confined its attention to the economic demands of the military: senior officials in the Elchibey regime were busy exploiting all opportunities for corruption.

In this respect, the situation in Azerbaijan differed somewhat from that in Armenia. Azerbaijan's oil reserves evoked another significant economic difference. The regime was attempting to save itself economically not by internal market reforms but by exports of mineral commodities, as in Turkmenistan and Kazakhstan. It also sought Turkish economic aid, but Turkey had to little to provide, and Russia was not about to tolerate a dependence on Turkey. Unlike economically barren Armenia, Azerbaijan could earn significant foreign currency through oil exports. The Turkish connection and the deals with Western oil firms—including plans for an oil pipeline to the Black Sea which would not transit Russian territory—probably inspired Russian nervousness and willingness to act decisively in Azerbaijan in the summer of 1993.

Military developments. In creating a national army Azerbaijan got off to a slower start than Armenia did. President Mutabilov issued a decree setting up a ministry of defense in early September 1991, and the ministry immediately faced huge problems in financing, manpower, and weapons and supplies.[175] The Russian 4th Army (i.e., the former Soviet 4th Army) was deployed in Azerbaijan as were significant air defense facilities, air forces, and a major military headquarters in Baku. In December 1991, Mutabilov decreed that all of these assets belonged to Azerbaijan, but he could not could ensure that the Russian commanders would cooperate. They did in fact resist, most of them continuing to follow orders from the Russian command lines.[176] The process of taking over military assets was messy, not well organized, and more often than not a matter of Russian troops and officers simply selling their supplies and equipment to the highest bidder. Nonetheless, during the CIS heads of state meeting in the Tashkent in May 1992, Russia agreed on a schedule for withdrawal of its forces from Azerbaijan.[177]

The regime's key problem was to find ethnic Azeri officers. Few existed, and most of them served outside Azerbaijan. Thus, training a new officer corps became first-order business.[178] The only short-run solution was to accept non-Azeri officers from the old Soviet military, which the defense ministry offered to do in the spring of 1992.[179] The government made the terms sufficiently attractive that more than 300 Russian officers transferred by midsummer.[180] The ministry of defense sought to attract entire units of the old Soviet forces to become part of the Azeri military. Despite these promising beginnings, progress was slow and generally resisted by significant parts of the government and society.[181]

The army depended increasingly on mercenaries, reportedly paid $250 a month, for the 8,000-man force committed to the war in Karabakh. By mid-1993, the total manpower level was 18,000, most of which comprised volunteer self-defense detachments. Some of the old Soviet air-defense system was retained, but plans for an Azeri air force envisioned its full existence only by the year 2000. The Soviet Caspian Sea Flotilla became the basis for the Azeri navy, comprising approximately 15 vessels. The larger emphasis, dictated by the war with Armenia, was on ground forces.[182]

Central control over the Azeri military apparently remained a serious problem after Surat Huseinov's coup against the government. Addressing the Supreme Soviet on television on 24 August 1993, Aliyev explained (at great length) how units in some areas prevented support of the war effort, confessing the following: "Unfortunately in recent years Azerbaijan's defense is not in the Army's hands, but in the hands of the armed formations that belong to disparate armed units and mafioso groups, and instead of defending the homeland they follow their private interests."[183] Although efforts to gain control showed some progress during the winter of 1992-93, casualties continued to plague the forces engaged in war and the local units, especially in Nakhichevan, where they were still defending former President Elchibey in his home town.[184] The army's overall effectiveness remained woefully poor in the spring of 1994. Aliyev continued to appeal for public support, reporting that 20 percent of the country was under Armenian occupation and that his calls for peace to Armenian President Ter-Petrossian were getting no effective response.[185]

Summary. The contrast between developments in Azerbaijan and Armenia is striking. Political fragmentation made the creation of an Azeri military extremely difficult and opened the door for Russian "divide and rule" tactics. Although Azerbaijan was located on the periphery of the USSR and blessed for a time with good relations and support from Turkey and Western oil companies, the Azeri leadership failed to take advantage of the opportunity to consolidate the country's independence. The Armenians, had they enjoyed the same position, probably would have escaped Russian control, but this goal proved to be beyond Azeri means and political skill. The lack of a significant pool of ethnic Azeri officers played a key role because it made the national army dependent on Russian officers, and in this case also Russian mercenary soldiers. By the fall of 1993, therefore, Azerbaijan became a member of the CIS, after nearly two years of resistance.

Georgia

Political development. Georgian politics became radicalized during Gorbachev's rule, after the bloody events in Tbilisi in April 1989, captured on television, in which Soviet troops battered young Georgian women to death with shovels. The event caused a crisis within the Soviet Politburo, deeply angered Shevardnadze (who had spent a decade and a half as Georgia's communist party chief), and inspired denials of responsibility from Gorbachev and other Politburo members.

Zviad Gamsakhurdia, jailed for a time as a dissident during Soviet rule, was elected chairman of the Georgian Supreme Soviet in October 1990. Nationalist fever was running high, and Gamsakhurdia provided the rhetoric to raise it higher; non-Georgian ethnic minorities, especially the South Ossetians, took fright at the political dynamics in Tbilisi. They demanded union with North Ossetia, which is part of the Russian Federation. By the end of the year, war broke out in South Ossetia in reaction to Georgia's nationalistic policies. The following spring, in March 1991, Georgia held a referendum, in which a majority voted to secede from the Soviet Union. Georgia declared independence in April. When the Soviet Union was dissolved, Georgia persisted in its stubborn refusal to cooperate with Russia: it declined to join the CIS and demanded early withdrawal of Russian forces from its territory.[186]

From the very beginning, Georgia's blustering and stubborn policy of breaking away from Moscow's control carried the seeds of its own failure. Its first major error was to frighten its own minority regions with the chauvinistic rhetoric of Georgian nationalism. The resulting separatist movements in Ossetia and Abkhazia opened the door for Russian meddling. The second problem was Georgia's failure to effect a political consolidation among the Georgians themselves. Gamsakhurdia's dictatorial policies soon led to civil strife among Georgian political elites and their clan- and regional-based supporters. In September 1991, fighting broke out in Tbilisi, which led to Gamsakhurdia's ouster and his retreat with his followers into the countryside. The following spring, Eduard Shevardnadze, having resigned as Soviet foreign minister the previous November, agreed to return to Georgia to be elected chairman of the state council.

By this time, the political fragmentation in Georgia was beyond short-term repair. No Georgian military was created; instead, several militias, loyal to various individuals, had formed, none of them capable of effective military action. Russia reacted by cutting off energy and other economic supplies to Georgia and by sending peacekeeping forces to South Ossetia initially and into Abkhazia later. By the fall of 1992, war had broken out in Abkhazia, where Abkhazians were less than 20 percent of the total population but were able to win the struggle with covert Russian military support.

Most of 1993 was marked by the struggle over Abkhazia. General Grachev ignored Georgian sovereignty when he came and departed Georgian territory in March. This embarrassed Shevardnadze by showing his helplessness to prevent such unauthorized transiting of the Georgian border. Grachev and other Russian officials repeatedly denied any Russian involvement in the Abkhaz war, although Georgian officials and foreign observers saw unambiguous evidence to the contrary.

Russian military leaders in particular were delighted at the opportunity to humiliate the man they blamed for giving away Eastern Europe and Germany and helping Gorbachev destroy the Soviet Union. They carried this delight to the point of a devastating defeat of Georgian forces in Abkhazia during July 1993, when Shevardnadze went in person to conduct the defense of Sukhumi, the capital of Abkhazia. After imposing humiliating terms on Shevardnadze in Abkhazia (which he initially rejected), Russia opened another attack on Shevardnadze's regime by allowing, and perhaps even inspiring, Gamsakhurdia's forces to launch new operations in western Georgia.

Until then, Shevardnadze had tried to resist Russia's demands that Georgia join the CIS and accede to the establishment of permanent Russian military bases in Georgia. He knew that his opponents in the national council would accuse him of betrayal for surrendering Abkhazia and then yielding to additional Russian demands. By risking his life in the defense of Sukhumi he had reduced the plausibility of such charges, but he realized that only by taking Georgia into the CIS and accepting Russian bases could he prevent Russian intelligence and military operatives within Georgia from tearing the country apart in a civil war. The various warring Georgian factions, such as Gamsakhurdia's, made it easy for Russia to create that threat. Thus 1994 saw Georgia brought to heel by Russia; Georgia joined the CIS and signed a treaty that not only authorized Russian military bases but also gave Russian Border Troops control of the Georgian border with Turkey.[187]

Even more than Azerbaijan, Georgia was torn apart by internal political factionalism and violence. Unlike the Armenians, who possess a much stronger sense of national cohesion, Georgians proved able only to proclaim loudly their nationalism. They could not act as a nation. Rather than compromise and join together to resist Russia, regional and factional leaders were always ready to sell out to Russian operatives for a chance to settle scores with their Georgian opponents. After nearly two centuries of Russian hegemony, Georgia seemed to have lost its capacity for independent self-defense.

Economic development. Civil war and Russian actions cutting off economic ties to Georgia threw its economy into a much sharper depression than would have otherwise been the case. The government tried a coupon currency for a time because the money economy had dried up. Barter and corruption replaced practically all other economic exchange activity. Outside communications—such as civil airlines and telephones—dropped to trivial levels, leaving the country isolated. Emigration, primarily to Russia in search of better living conditions, reached nearly 100,000 during 1991-92.[188] In these circumstances, it became impossible for Georgia to attract foreign business investment and economic aid. By 1994, the country was in desperate economic circumstances.

Military development. In the spring of 1991, President Gamsakhurdia established a Georgian National Guard which reached a manning level of between 7,000 and 12,000 by early 1992. It was eventually to reach 60,000 and be based on 14 helicopter assault battalions deployed at key points throughout the country where they could react quickly to internal security problems.[189] During the winter of 1992-93, this National Guard slipped from Shevardnadze's control and threatened to become a serious political problem. He temporarily dissolved it, but then revived it in October 1993 under the command of Major General Dzhemal Chumburidze in the city of Kutaisi, changing it to the First Army Corps.

A paramilitary organization, the Mkhedrioni (horsemen, in Georgian), had a small corps of 300 in a concentrated unit and another 2,000 members distributed throughout the ministries of defense and internal affairs.[190] These troops were loyal to Jaba Ioselani, a Georgia "strong man" reportedly possessing a record as a violent criminal, who chose to cooperate on his own terms with Shevardnadze.

Longer-term plans for a Georgian army included two army corps of mechanized brigades, one to be stationed in Tbilisi and the other in Sukhumi. A small air force of three separate aviation detachments and some air defense units plus a small naval squadron located at the port of Poti on the Black Sea were to make up the rest of the armed forces.

Manning the Georgian military, of course, ran up against the lack of ethnic Georgian officers in the old Soviet military. Unlike Armenians, very few Georgians had chosen military careers in the Soviet period. Thus building an officer corps became a major hurdle. A mixed system of contract soldiers and conscripts was authorized by law, but the yield from call-ups of conscripts proved extremely poor in 1992-93. As in Azerbaijan and the Central Asian states, military manpower—especially the shortage of officers—was a major constraint on the establishment of an effective Georgian national military.

Four Soviet divisions were stationed in Georgia when the Soviet Union was dissolved. These became the object of a struggle between the Russian military command structure and Georgian military officials. Attacks, raids, and thefts of weapons and equipment were com-

mon throughout 1992-93.[191] Also, so-called privatization of many
of the companies and battalions in these forces proceeded on the
initiative of local commanders. Thus most of the materiel transfer
from the old Soviet military to the Georgian forces was informal,
chaotic, and without central direction.

The two nations continued to dispute the legal status of Russian
forces in Georgia until Georgia was forced to join the CIS. Initially
agreeing to withdraw the forces by 1995, Grachev began pressing
for long-term stationing agreements in 1993.[192] In October 1993,
after Shevardnadze's humiliation in Abkhazia, the Russian and Georgian general staffs met in Tbilisi and initialed agreements on the maintenance of Russian forces and bases in Georgia.[193] The hasty agreements of the fall of 1993 were finally tied up in a Russian-Georgian
treaty signed by Yeltsin and Shevardnadze in early February 1994.
Provisions included long-term military base rights and Russian control of the border with Turkey.[194]

Bringing Georgia under Russian military hegemony also brought
potential new difficulties. A number of ethnic regions in the North
Caucasus are hostile to Russian as well as Georgian rule. North Ossetia
is in the Russian Federation. Moreover, Chechnya has asserted its
independence of Russia since the creation of the CIS. Several other
potential separatist groups in the North Caucasus threaten the region
with spreading anti-Russian violence. As members of the Russian
parliament pointed out to Yeltsin before he signed the treaty with
Georgia in February 1994, ethnic hostility could provoke civil wars
in Ossetia, Abkhazia, and other parts of the northern areas of Georgia, and that violence could spill over into Russian Federation territories. Russia had been sponsoring the separatists in Ossetia and
Abkhazia, and several of the ethnic groups of the North Caucasus
were assisting them. Under the treaty, however, Russia was recognizing Georgia's territorial integrity, apparently at the expense of these
minorities, and was proposing to assist in training and equipping the
Georgian military—the very military Russia had helped them oppose. The speaker of the Russia Duma, Ivan Rybkin, and Yegor
Gaidar, leader of the Russia's Choice party, both warned that the
treaty might cause violent reactions in several of the ethnic regions
on the Georgian-Russian border. Moreover, they expressed doubt
that the Duma would ratify the treaty.[195]

Summary. Somewhat like the situation in Tajikistan, Georgian internal politics and factional struggles left the country ill-prepared for independence. Unlike Tajikistan's old-line rulers, who wanted Russian sponsorship, Georgia was determined to throw it off. Yet regionalism, clan and family linkages, systems of local "strong men," and the virtual absence of loyalty to the Georgian state made all Georgian resistance to Russian "divide and rule" tactics feckless. No one understood this better than Shevardnadze. When he accepted the leadership in the spring of 1992, he said that the situation was beyond repair but that he felt a sense of duty to try to fix it.

Virtually the only Georgian leader pursuing the country's larger interests over his personal aims, Shevardnadze achieved at least as much as could have been expected. Although he managed to remain in office, occasionally threatening to resign, he had not created a coherent Georgian state by late 1994. He did, however, save it from complete dismemberment by a Russian-stimulated series of separatist movements and civil wars after the defeat in Abkhazia. Joining the CIS put him at great risk, providing his enemies—especially Gamsakhurdia—a basis for charging him with treason.

The apparent peace and calm achieved through the Russian-Georgian treaty of February 1994, however, could prove short-lived. As the Russian leaders Rybkin and Gaidar noted, the treaty could provoke violence in South Ossetia and Abkhazia and in Chechnya and Ingushetia on the Russian side of the border. Shevardnadze had long been aware of this danger, and in 1993 he told Yeltsin and other Russian leaders that their actions in destabilizing Georgia internally would spread back into Russia through separatist movements in the North Caucasus. The same danger confronted Russia, he insisted, in their strategy of destabilizing Ukraine.[196]

Conclusion

We have followed three threads—military institutions, economic developments, and the domestic dynamics within the states of Central Asia and Transcaucasus—to uncover the messy and complex picture of CIS development. In many ways the founding of the CIS was a chaotic, ill-conceived, and poorly planned affair. For Moscow, however, the plan had at least two rationales—military and economic—which sometimes conflicted and sometimes reinforced each other. Through much of 1992 and 1993 a mere casual look at CIS affairs gave the impression that the organization was stillborn, doomed to wither away or at most remain a formality. By late 1994, however, that judgment was disputable. Although its initial conceptualization seems to have failed to materialize, the CIS has taken on a form and content that belie stillbirth and may forestall an early death.

This was most apparent in the military sphere. The initial attempts to replace quickly the old Soviet institutions with CIS structures adequate to create a stable confederation if not a true federation (something the military leaders could call a "single strategic space") failed miserably. Not surprisingly, military issues dominated the agenda during the first 4 to 6 months of CIS organizational meetings, but by the early spring Yeltsin and most senior Russian leaders realized that a unified CIS armed forces could not be created, certainly not in the short run. Establishing a Russian defense ministry in the late spring and summer of 1992 not only signaled Russian recognition of that failure but also prompted an intra-Russian military competition between the leadership of the CIS military and the Russian military, one that the Russian military was bound to win. By the summer of 1993, when Marshal Shaposhnikov gave up on his task and resigned his post as commander of the CIS military—such as it was—the CIS appeared to be a dead letter.

A closer look at the bilateral relations between Russia and the Central Asian and Transcaucasian states, however, reveals that Moscow was not about to let these countries go their own way militarily. The May 1992 collective security treaty marked a basic change in institutional strategy by providing a CIS structure on which to hang a series of individual Russian successes in forcing or wooing individual states into binding military relationships. In other words, building a CIS military from the top down gave way to building it from the bottom up, one country at a time if necessary, allowing countries to vary considerably in their connections to the CIS. By late 1994, all the Central Asian and Transcaucasus states had been gathered into the CIS military system in one form or another. Only Ukraine, and perhaps Moldova, still maintained genuine independence within the CIS *military* system.

Although this progress in CIS military affairs is impressive considering the circumstances, it should not conceal the dramatic degradation in military capabilities compared to the old Soviet Armed Forces. The coherence of force structure and force deployments in all five branches of service has suffered enormously. Aspects of the air defense system, the space and warning system, the strategic rocket forces, and the navy were permanently destroyed. Moreover, the ground forces—more than 200 divisions of ready and reserve forces—suffered major reductions. Many were simply destroyed by "privatization" or transfer to non-Russian republics. Others faded because new conscripts could not be found to fill them. The most any CIS military scheme could achieve was to limit damage, not prevent it.

A brief review of CIS economic relations reveals the confusion and contradictory nature of Russia's economic policies. The implication of the policies of Russian market reformers was the destruction of the ruble zone and most of the old planned industrial connections among the CIS states. At the same time, however, antireformers and industrial bureaucrats continued to sustain parts of those old connections. When Gaidar and his reformers lost out politically in late 1993, the prospects for reestablishing much of the old command industrial linkage among most of the CIS states began to look promising. Belarus was to join the Russian ruble zone with the right to create money. Nazarbayev was still proposing centralized economic structures for the CIS. Yet the problems of currency stabilization and the expulsion of Kazakhstan and Uzbekistan from the ruble zone in 1993 damaged the old economic relations so thoroughly that restoring them became more difficult. Even Nazarbayev and Karimov spoke of the impossibility of returning all the way to the old system.

CIS economic policies also demonstrate that Russia could not frame and implement a coherent strategy for building a CIS economic system. Economic policies were internally inconsistent at times, and they occasionally worked against concurrent military policies of the Russian defense ministry and Marshal Shaposhnikov in the CIS military organization. It is true, however, that several key Russian senior officials sought to reestablish some substitute for the Soviet Union and fully reassert Russian hegemony over Soviet territories.

Whether Russian hegemony is called a new Russian imperialism or by some other name, clearly a significant set of Russian military and political leaders want to regain control over as much of the former Soviet Union as possible, as apparently do the managers of the oil industry and pipeline sector. The military links within the CIS—multilateral where possible, bilateral where necessary—are their tools for that goal. Russian leadership on military affairs within the CIS cannot be explained as a series of random happenings, initiatives by local commanders, and bureaucratic inertia. During more than two years, Russia has shown a strong sense of direction and perseverance even when facing great resistance from other CIS states.

This reality is far more obvious in light of the third thread of our analysis, the dynamics of each individual state in Central Asia and the Transcaucasus. It is quite true that some of the non-Russian CIS countries wanted to retain the Russian security umbrella, and that they were sad to see the Soviet Union dissolved. But it is also true that elites in those states who genuinely sought liberal economic and political reform understood that the Soviet system had to dissolve to make such reform possible and that the CIS, if allowed to become a vehicle of Russian imperialism, would make such reform impossible. Local elites that opposed economic and political reform but wanted to achieve autonomy from Moscow also faced complex dilemmas in their relations with Russia.

Could one argue that such reform was merely a theoretical alternative of no practical consequence, and that political order was far more pressing, making Russian hegemony the only solution to that problem? The case of Tajikistan and much of the Transcaucasus might suggest a positive answer. One could argue that these countries were already deep in civil war. Neither the United Nations nor any other outside agent was coming to help them escape chaos and fratricidal war. Therefore, Russia was playing a positive role in taking on this task. A closer look at the facts, however, seriously undercuts this argument and suggests precisely the opposite conclusion: Russian involvement seems to have caused much of the violence and civil war.

Although Russian involvement may not be entirely responsible for the Tajik civil war, it increased its intensity and scale. Perhaps Moscow wholly misunderstood the domestic political alignments in Tajikistan, but the 201st Motor Rifle Division stood by at times when it might have intervened to prevent the inter-clan strife, and it took sides at times and in ways that increased the violence. For all the Russian rhetoric about defending the border with Afghanistan, that border remained highly porous, allowing paramilitary groups to cross both ways. It also remained porous for drug trafficking. Although the evidence is ambiguous, significant Russian military involvement in drug trade—including transporting large shipments into Russia as well as selling passage through the border—is a factor in the Russian involvement that deserves serious scrutiny. The several mysterious assassinations of Russian officers in May and June 1994 in Dushanbe[197] could as easily be explained as related to drug trade as to political opposition groups. The possible involvement of members of the Russian military in the lucrative drug trade—in conjunction with local criminals—may considerably increase instability and violence in Tajikistan in the future.

In Azerbaijan, Russian military and economic policies contributed to the violence. When Soviet forces entered Baku in January 1990, they tried to destroy the Popular Front political organization. After the collapse of the Soviet Union, Russian forces continued to oppose Popular Front leadership, both internally and externally. By aiding Armenian military forces, Russia provoked crises in Azerbaijan's ruling circles, and by supporting the disaffected military leader Surat Huseinov, Russian operatives contributed to the forcible overthrow of the Elchibey regime. Moreover, after Gaidar Aliyev became head of state and brought Azerbaijan into the CIS, Russian officials worked to ensure that international peace initiatives for an Armenian-Azeri settlement would not succeed.[198]

In economic policy, Russia consistently opposed Azerbaijan's efforts to export oil through pipelines not transiting Russian territory. By the summer of 1994, Russia's attempts to conceal the true motives for this resistance had become too transparent to take seriously; for example, Russia argued that ecological considerations made it unwise to move oil on any path not through Russian territory.[199]

Russian policy in Armenia also contributed to the increase of violence and war. Throughout 1992 and 1993, Russian military advisors assisted Armenian forces in Nagorno-Karabakh and Armenia. They were sufficiently effective to allow Armenia to carry the war into Azeri territory and occupy as much as 20 percent of it (by Azeri accounts). Russia also used intelligence linkages with certain Armenian factions to exploit splits within the Armenian government on policy toward Turkey.

Russian policy in Georgia unambiguously aimed at raising the level of violence and ethnic conflict to tear Georgia apart, even though, as Shevardnadze pointed out, they risked the spread of that violence into the Russian Federation in the North Caucasus. This perverse role of Russian policy broke into the open when members of the Duma, including the speaker, complained that a peace treaty with Georgia after Shevardnadze's capitulation could provoke violence through the North Caucasus.

Undoubtedly, violence would have been widespread in the Transcaucasus without Russian involvement, but Russian policy did not try to reduce it. On the contrary, Russian military and intelligence operatives worked actively to increase and spread it, risking on occasions a complete loss of control, as in Armenia in late 1993. And Russian policy toward the role of United Nations officials corroborates the duplicitous character of official Russian rhetoric about trying to prevent violence and contain civil wars in the region. Also belying the official rhetoric were Russia's role in controlling information and access in Abkhazia, undercutting an international settlement between Azerbaijan and Armenia in the summer of 1993, and demanding UN financial support in Tajikistan while telling UN officials they could not bring their "spies" into the CIS command there.

The absence of violence and civil war in some areas along the southern tier of the CIS can be explained mainly by the presence of highly dictatorial local leaders who asserted strong local authority not only after the collapse of the Soviet Union but also in the last couple of years before its collapse. Niyazov, for example, simply allowed Russia no cracks to exploit in Turkmen domestic politics. Karimov did the same in Uzbekistan, and Nazarbayev followed the same policy. The most vulnerable, Nazarbayev's regime in Kazakhstan, could easily have come completely unhinged if Russian military and intelligence operatives had successfully incited the Russian minority to open resistance. The size of the potential conflagration, however, probably deterred even the most reactionary Russian officials and should continue to do so at least until the rest of Central Asia is vanquished.

Akayev's democracy in Kyrgyzstan has also escaped civil war thus far, appearing as an exception to the proposition that in the CIS only dictatorships can resist Russian dominance. Stirring up a civil war there has been within Russian capabilities, and the riots in Osh in 1991 suggest that Russia has done some meddling. Karimov, however, acted quickly to repress them, in cooperation with Akayev. Akayev alone probably could not have contained the violence.

The only country in both regions with genuine domestic political coherence is Armenia, and Armenia's ability to recruit young men for the military units in Nagorno-Karabakh and in Armenia reflects this social integration. This factor should allow Armenia to defend its sovereignty from Russian meddling, but other factors cancel it out. Dependency on Russia for economic ties, military logistics, and officer training provide opportunities for Moscow to keep its grip on Armenia. Ter-Petrossian's pragmatic attempt to come to terms with Turkey posed a serious threat to the dependency levers, but his own ministers were able to scuttle Ter-Petrossian's wise diplomacy.

A strong domestic dictatorship alone, however, may not be sufficient for long-term maintenance of sovereignty. An indigenous military capability could also prove critical. Niyazov, Karimov, and Nazarbayev all found themselves unable to establish effective national militaries during the first two years of the CIS. Nor could the democrat Akayev. These regimes will not overcome their dependency on Russian weaponry and logistical support in the foreseeable future. They can neither create domestic military industrial bases nor easily find alternative foreign suppliers, not least because of lack of money.

This dependency, however, is not nearly as important as their lack of competent officer corps. In principle they could fairly quickly shift their logistical dependencies to China, India, Pakistan, or some other outside source, perhaps within a couple of years—if money were not a problem. But they cannot overcome their officer shortages in a couple of years, and probably not even in five or ten. Moreover, as long as they use Russian military schools to train officers, they will remain vulnerable to the affinities those officers gain for Russia. Genuine independence of their future officer corps, therefore, will depend on domestic officer training and alternative foreign schooling in Turkey, Pakistan, Western Europe, and the United States.

In light of this analysis, do any or most of the Central Asian and Transcaucasus states have real prospects of maintaining their independence?

The answer has to be constrained by the structural conditions this analysis has identified. Summarizing them again briefly, therefore, is instructive:

• Of first importance, the absence of native officer cadres left all these states except Armenia beholden to Russian officer cadres. Allowing Russian military units to remain on their territories, depending on Russian sources of military supply, and depending on Russian officer training schools offered too many avenues of political penetration for Russian elites, all of whom developed their political skills in the old Soviet political culture.

• Of second greatest importance, the absence of a significant number of able political elites who understood and desired reforms placed severe limits on what reforms could be carried out. The top leadership in Georgia (Shevardnadze) and Kyrgyzstan (Akayev) promised a lot, but in neither country was there a significant second and third level of such people. Another dimension of this problem is the lack of a national consciousness of the European or East Asian sort. Armenia stands as the lone exception among the states of the Transcaucasus and Central Asia. None of the others possesses a population knitted together socially by that kind of national identity.

• Third in degree of importance, the economic predicament bequeathed these states by the old Soviet command planning system left them with unprecedented structural changes to accomplish before economic recovery could even begin. Turkmenistan's oil and gas makes it an exception to some degree, but economic well-being based wholly on oil exports does not always create a stable and productive society. Several of the Middle East oil-producing states, for example, have retained traditional and highly repressive societies while remaining stable although fragile. Following their model—which Turkmenistan and perhaps Kazakhstan and Azerbaijan wanted to do to some degree—would provide only a temporary reprieve for these CIS states. Sooner or later they will have to implement fundamental domestic economic reform. Only Turkmenistan, if its natural gas reserves rapidly enable it to achieve large export revenues, has prospects for avoiding such a traumatic transition.

These structural realities, of course, are all domestic. The prospects for any of the regimes coping with them successfully against Russian resistance are trivial. That raises the question of Russian policy in the CIS as a determinant of their future sovereignty or subordination to Moscow's hegemony. Is there any reason to believe that Russia's policy will not change?

Two sets of developments will provide the answer. First, if Ukraine maintains its own domestic stability and does not collapse back into Moscow's hands, that development will force the CIS, if it is to continue to include Ukraine, to permit a much wider degree of autonomy among members. Some could remain mere satraps of Moscow, but others might use cooperation with Ukraine, combined with growing internal stability, to keep Moscow at arm's length.

Second, Russian domestic political development will prove critical. In the summer of 1994 the fight over the state budget indicated a decline in the defense ministry's influence.[200] The State Duma was offering only half the funds General Grachev had demanded. To the degree that the Russian budget process is conducted under public scrutiny in the competitive arena of the parliament, the costs of the Russian policy of using the CIS to restore much of the former Soviet empire will be visible and other claimants will seek to take the funds that policy requires. Thus domestic politics in Russia could conceivably turn around Russia's CIS policy, however slowly. Still, President Yeltsin could use his decree authority to increase the military budget, undercutting this political process.

Another aspect of Russian domestic affairs could constrain that policy. Corruption, poor discipline, drug trafficking, and similar developments within the Russian military greatly weakened it during the first two years of the CIS. Commitments in Tajikistan, Armenia, Azerbaijan, and Georgia could continue those developments despite the Russian defense ministry's strongest efforts to restore order and discipline. Critics in the Russian parliament had a point in July 1993 when they warned that Yeltsin's commitments to Tajikistan would embroil Russia in "another Afghanistan."

Another factor in Russia's domestic politics is the influence of old antidemocratic, former communist leaders in the other CIS countries. Nazarbayev, Karimov, Niyazov, various officials in Tajikistan, and several officials in Belarus have encouraged the hard-liners in

Moscow to resist reforms, especially in the economic area, and they have allowed their local intelligence and police operatives (former KGB and MVD officials) to retain close liaison with their Russian counterparts. The relationships have not always been friendly or cooperative, but they certainly have not fostered pro-reform sentiment in Russia. These non-Russians could become sources of support and finance for antireform forces in Moscow.

In sum, the CIS was a hastily devised institution that initially appeared doomed to a short existence. By 1993, however, the Russian military was using it with increasing effectiveness as a cover for interfering in the domestic affairs of all the states of the Transcaucasus and most of the states in Central Asia. As Yeltsin and his foreign minister, Andrei Kozyrev, took a much harder line toward Russia's "near abroad," Moscow seemed to have reached a de facto consensus on restoring as much of the old Soviet empire as possible under the banner of the CIS. Kozyrev's frequent assertions to the United Nations and other foreign audiences that Russia was playing a "peace-keeping" role within the CIS were flatly at odds with the truth. Russian policy in Central Asia and the Transcaucasus was actually increasing violence and conflict in several places. Moreover, it was stymieing efforts by the UN and other outside forces to achieve settlements in the Transcaucasus.

Has this policy restored the "empire"? In many respects the answer is yes. At the same time, a number of developments—inside Russia, in Russian economic policy toward the CIS, and within some of the CIS countries—were hampering and constraining the new imperialism. On balance, the trend toward a new empire was considerably stronger than the counter-trends in the first two and half years of the CIS' existence.

Notes

[1]That is, the Russian Socialist Federated Soviet Republic (RSFSR). It became the Russian Federation in January 1992.

[2]Georgia and Azerbaijan did not join initially, although they occasionally sent representatives to CIS meetings.

[3]FBIS-SOV-239, 12 December 1991, 25-26. Both Gorbachev and Yeltsin appeared before an assembly of Soviet military leaders in Moscow on 10-11 December, each trying to persuade them to support his position.

Yeltsin prevailed, and they agreed to the abolition of the Soviet Union, some because it evoked the idea of a purely Slavic state, others because they believed it would merely mean putting up a new sign on the old Soviet Ministry of Defense building. This critical meeting has received little attention in Western analysis; yet it was perhaps the most important for Yeltsin's move to create the CIS. Had the military leadership backed Gorbachev, Yeltsin could hardly have proceeded with his plan.

[4]Of the 15 Soviet republics, the three Baltic countries (Lithuania, Latvia, Estonia) refused to join the CIS and remained wholly outside it, not joining later as did Azerbaijan and Georgia.

[5]FBIS-SOV-91-246, "Text of Alma Ata Declaration," 23 December 1991, 29-30. This provides TASS reporting on the meeting.

[6]FBIS-SOV-91-250, "Provisional Agreement on Official Bodies Signed," 30 December 1991, 11.

[7]FBIS-SOV-91-251, "Further Reportage on Minsk Commonwealth Summit," 30 December 1991, 15-20.

[8]FBIS-SOV-92-001, "Minsk News Conference Held on 30 December," 2 January 1992, 23-25.

[9]See JPRS-UMA-92-002, 16 January 1992, 45. This is a translation of a piece from *Nezavisimaya gazeta,* 31 December 1991, which reported a dispute between General Konstantin Kobets and Marshal Yevgenii Shaposhnikov over the shape of a CIS military structure.

[10]The Strategic Arms Reduction Talks (START) treaty between the U.S. and the former USSR provided for reductions in both sides' strategic nuclear forces. Because four of the successor states to the USSR (Russia, Belarus, Ukraine, and Kazakhstan) hosted strategic nuclear forces, the issue of implementing the treaty required the cooperation of Belarus, Ukraine, and Kazakhstan with Moscow and Washington. It became a severe cause of tension between Ukraine and Russia. The Conventional Forces in Europe (CFE) reduction agreements signed by NATO and Warsaw Pact countries regulated conventional arms reductions in Europe. It put limits to the types and numbers of arms the Soviet Union could locate in its various military districts. Upon the collapse of the USSR, some of these districts became regions of newly independent countries. Russia asked for CFE agreements to be revisited in light of its loss of its western and Transcaucasian regions.

[11]For the complexities of this arms control issue see Sergei Rogov, "Russian Defense Policy: Challenges and Developments," January 1993, prepared for the Center for Naval Analyses, especially pages 10-20.

[12]Because START implementation is a much-reported affair and not central to the more complex issues of the CIS military, it will not be treated in more detail here.

[13]FBIS-SOV-92-012, 17 January 1992, "Conference of Heads of Member States Begins," 8-11.

[14]See FBIS-SOV-92-032, 18 February 1992, 18-27 for all items.

[15]JPRS-UMA-92-008, 4 March 1992, "Agreement on a Single Budget," 15-16.

[16]FBIS-SOV-92-054, 19 March 1992, "Preliminary Agenda for Kiev Summit Detailed," 15-17; FBIS-SOV-92-055, 20 March 1992, "Agenda Debate Viewed," 15, and "Agreements Signed," "Armed Forces Heads Appointed," and "Peacekeeping Forces Set Up," 17-18.

[17]FBIS-SOV-92-055, 20 March 1992, "Agreements Signed," 17-18.

[18]Russian and Soviet flag officer ranks are as follows: one star, major general; two stars, lieutenant general; three stars, colonel general; four stars, general of the army. Marshal of the Soviet Union was a Soviet rank which does not yet exist in the Russian military.

[19]Ibid.

[20]Ibid., 48.

[21]Russian officials have generally used "mirotvoricheskye voiska" when referring to "peacekeeping forces," although the Russian term literally means "peace-creating," or what in English would be called "peacemaking." This ambiguity is important to keep in mind in dealing with all Russian policies on "peacekeeping" activities.

[22]"Military and Security Notes," *RFE/RL Research Report*, Vol 1., No. 14, 3 April 1992, 49.

[23]FBIS-SOV-92-055, 20 March 1992, "Agreements Signed," 17-18.

[24]See "Military and Security Notes," *RFE/RL Research Report*, Vol. 1, No. 14, 3 April 1992, 48-50.

[25]One of the authors learned this in April 1994 during a conversation with General Anatolii Gribkov, former chief of staff and later commander of the Warsaw Pact Forces. He did not explain why they disliked Shaposhnikov, but he made it clear that they did.

[26]FBIS-SOV-92-094, 14 May 1992, "Shaposhnikov Cited on Priorities," 11.

[27]Ibid., 12.

[28]"Military and Security Notes," *RFE/RL Research Report*, Vol. 1, No. 22, 29 May 1992, 55-56, summarizes the results of the Tashkent CIS summit meeting.

[29]FBIS-SOV-92-198, 13 October 1994, "Leaders Reach Agreements at Bishkek Summit," 2-9; see also following items in that issue.

[30]FBIS-SOV-93-184, 24 September 1993, "INTERFAX Outlines Main Points of Economic Union Treaty," 5.

[31]*Security Through Cooperation—93* (Moscow: Center for Information and Analytical Support of the Commonwealth of Independent

States, 1993),   32.

[32]Ibid., 56-57.

[33]FBIS-SOV-93-113, 15 June 1993, 3, "Post of Commander in Chief Abolished."

[34]FBIS-SOV-93-245, 23 December 1993, 16-17, "CIS Armed Forces Command Abolished."

[35]See Kozyrev's Stockholm speech, as reported by Reuters, "Speeches to European Conference," 14 December 1992. He gave a short, very hard-line speech, accusing NATO and the WEU of military ambitions in the Baltic states as well as interference in Bosnia. He set distinct limits on Russia's rapprochement with Europe and threatened that Russia, as a great power, would defend itself and its friends against damage to their interests. After letting the shock of this turnabout in Russian policy sink in for a few minutes, he took the floor again, disavowing the substance of those remarks and explaining them as a "rhetorical device" to show to the West the kind of Russian foreign policy the opposition forces in Moscow were demanding. Ten months later, speaking to the UN General Assembly, he made a speech that contained most of the points of his "rhetorical device," only this time it was official Russian foreign policy.

[36]RFE/RL Daily Report No. 138, 22 July 1993.

[37]RFE/RL Daily Report No. 143, 29 July 1993.

[38]RFE/RL Daily Report No. 43, 3 March 1993.

[39]RFE/RL Daily Report No. 150, 9 August 1993.

[40]RFE/RL Daily Report No. 147, 4 August 1993.

[41]Ibid.

[42]See Fiona Hill and Pamela Jewett, "Back in the USSR," Strengthening Democratic Institutions Project, JFK School of Government, Harvard University, January 1994, 10.

[43]The authors learned this from discussions with high level Georgian officials on two different occasion in 1993. Apparently the use of these bases to aid Armenia was kept quiet, and for obvious reasons. Publicity would have complicated Russia's relations not only with Azerbaijan but also with the political oppositions in Georgia. Shevardnadze's government, not at all sympathetic with such assistance, was powerless to stop it.

[44]Hill and Jewett, op. cit., 11.

[45]Ibid. See also Thomas Goltz, "Letter from Eurasia: The Russian Hidden Hand," *Foreign Policy* 92 (Fall 1993), 92-116, for more details and further analysis of the Russian role.

[46]Hill and Jewett, op. cit., 12.

[47]Ibid., 16.

[48]FBIS-SOV-93-046, 11 March 1993, "Grachev Interviewed on Current Situation," 56-58.

[49]Hill and Jewett, op. cit., 57-59.

[50]RFE/RL Daily Report No. 196, 12 October 1993.

[51]RFE/RL Daily Report No. 23, 3 February 1994. Apparently, the details of the treaty for bases were not completed. Georgian officials told one of the authors (in June 1994) that hard bargaining was still in progress. Russia was trying to get Georgia to pay all the costs of the Russian military occupation forces!

[52]RFE/RL Daily Report No. 53, 17 March 1994.

[53]See RFE/RL Daily Report Nos. 34, 45, 49, and 51, February and March 1994, for a few examples. All such demands were heard in 1993, especially in the fall, beginning with Kozyrev's September address to the UN General Assembly; the frequency picked up considerably during the winter of 1994.

[54]RFE/RL Daily Report No. 65, 6 April 1994.

[55]Ibid.

[56]That is, the Russian Socialist Federated Soviet Republic.

[57]INTERFAX, 2 April 1992.

[58]RFE/RL Daily Report No. 102, 29 May 1992.

[59]RFE/RL Daily Report No. 197, 13 October 1994.

[60]Hill and Jewett, op. cit. 56-57.

[61]Ibid., 23-27.

[62]John Lloyd, *The Financial Times*, January 7, 1994, reported this agreement to the surprise not only of the West but also to many people in Russia and Belarus.

[63]Helen Bell et al., *Kazakhstan: The Gold Road to Oil and Gas in Central Asia* (New York: Petroleum Intelligence Weekly, 1993), 9.

[64]Hill and Jewett, op. cit., 30.

[65]Gregory Gleason, "The Political Economy of Dependency," *Studies in Comparative Communism* 24:4 (December 1991), 342-44.

[66]International Monetary Fund, *Economic Review: Azerbaijan* 1993, 9.

[67]See, for example, Paul Henze, *Whither Turkestan?* (Santa Monica, CA: Rand Corporation, 1992), 9; International Monetary Fund, *IMF Economic Review of Uzbekistan* (Washington, D.C.: International Monetary Fund, 1994), 16; Maxim Shashenkov, *Security Issues of the Ex-Soviet Central Asian Republics* (London: Brassey's, 1992), 10; *Hearings, Subcommittee on Europe and the Middle East, Committee on Foreign Affairs,* U.S. House of Representatives, Washington, D.C., 28 April 1992, 66; Patrick Cockburn, "Dateline USSR: Ethnic Tremors," *Foreign Policy* 74 (Spring, 1989), 172-73; and John Lloyd and Steve

LeVine, "IMF Warns of Rouble Zone Unrest," *Financial Times,* November 12, 1993, 16.

[68]Boris Z. Rumer, *Soviet Central Asia: A "Tragic Experiment"* (Boston: Unwin Hyman, 1989). This study delves deeply into the logic, economic and military, of the development of Central Asia under Soviet rule, and it concludes that the region had suffered enormously in the relationship.

[69]RFE/RL Daily Report No. 62, 30 March 1994. In the spring of 1994, Nazarbayev advanced a plan for a Eurasian economic union to coordinate all economic, military, and political relations. This was essentially a revival of the scheme he had pushed in the spring of 1993, and a goal that he had consistently favored since the breakup of the Soviet Union.

[70]Helen Bell, op. cit., 13.

[71]RFE/RL Daily Report No. 226, 26 November 1993.

[72]Hill and Jewett, op. cit., 13.

[73]See American-Uzbek Chamber of Commerce Session, Washington, D.C., 14 January 1994; *The Economist,* February 19, 1994, 124; and Peter Rutland and Timur Isataev, *Kazakhstan: First Steps Towards Economic Independence* (Stockholm: Institute for East European Economics, 1993), 27.

[74]Hill and Jewett, op. cit., 13. See also Steve LeVine, "Kazakhs accuse Moscow of stopping oil exports," *Financial Times,* 31 May 1994, 18.

[75]See "Azerbaijan," *The Economist,* December 11, 1993, 36; and Steve LeVine and Robert Corzine, "Russian Muscle," *Financial Times,* January 21, 1994; and John Lloyd and Steve LeVine, "Russia demands veto over Caspian oil deals," *Financial Times,* 31 May 1994, 2.

[76]See Alan Richards, "Political Economy Review of Kazakhstan," an unpublished paper for Chemonics, a firm performing contract work in Central Asia for the U.S. Government. The paper provides a good summary of the problems facing Kazakh leaders and these leaders' tentative thinking about how to deal with them.

[77]Ahmed Rashid, "Out of Steppe," *Far Eastern Economic Review,* June 17, 1993, 30.

[78]RFE/RL Daily Report No. 114, 18 June 1993.

[79]RFE/RL Daily Report No. 150, 9 August 1993.

[80]A permanent one for Kazakhstan (the tenge) and a temporary "som coupon" for Uzbekistan, which was replaced by a permanent som in the spring of 1994.

[81]John Lloyd and Steve LeVine, "IMF warns," *Financial Times,* November 12, 1993; and David Buchan, "Western banks," *Financial Times,* October 29, 1993.

[82]RFE/RL Daily Report No. 67, 8 April 1994.

[83]The circle of Western students dealing with Central Asian societies has been small. Alexandre Bennigsen and Edward Allworth helped keep alive the study of this region in the early decades of the Cold War period. Richard Pierce, *Russia in Central Asia 1867-1917* (Berkeley: University of California Press, 1960), also provided a solid study. Helene Carrere d'Encausse and Martha Brill Olcott have done prolific work in the past two decades. The Transcaucasus has been equally neglected, but Ronald Grigor Suny, *The Making of the Georgian Nation* (Stanford, CA: Hoover Institution Press, 1988), and Audrey L. Alstadt, *The Azerbaijani Turks* (Stanford, CA: Hoover Institution Press, 1992) are excellent recent exceptions. The barrier of local languages still limits Western study of contemporary politics in both regions, and most of the reporting comes through the Russian press, hardly a high-fidelity channel although vastly improved over Soviet press reporting and often quite insightful.

[84]For full explication, not only of Nazarbayev's views on the CIS and Kazakhstan's need for close relations with Russia but also an insider's story on the breakup of the Soviet Union and the agreements that founded the CIS, see his interview in the Russian press, FBIS-SOV-92-093, 13 May 1992, "President Nazarbayev Interviewed," 61-66.

[85]RFE/RL Daily Report No. 62, 30 March 1994.

[86]FBIS-SOV-92-093, 13 May 1992, 64, "President Nazarbayev Interviewed."

[87]FBIS-SOV-93-226, 26 November 1993, 58, "Nazarbayev Interviewed on Ties with Russia."

[88]This became clear when one of the authors, as part of a small private delegation, met with Nazarbayev in December 1993. When asked about the counterbalancing role of China, Nazarbayev admitted it but put the emphasis on economic assistance. He also waxed eloquent in accusing Russia of being unable to abandon its imperial tendencies, complaining bitterly about the new Russian military doctrine.

[89]At the same meeting, in December 1993, one of the authors raised this matter with Kazakh foreign ministry deputies. They were evasive when reminded of the implications of their policy in Tajikistan. They appeared worried about it but unwilling to talk openly about its negative aspects.

[90]Again, this impression was gained from the meeting with Nazarbayev and several talks with his aides.

[91]U.S. Congress, Commission on Security and Cooperation in Europe, *Implementation of the Helsinki Accords* (Washington, D.C.: Government Printing Office, January 1993), 191-99.

[92]Ian Bremmer, "Is There A Future for Kazakhstan?" *Association for*

the Study of Nationalities—Analysis of Current Events 5, No. 15 (April 22, 1994), 3, offers this judgment with fewer qualifications than most observers. Also, Bess Brown, RFE/RL Daily Report, no. 54, 18 March 1994, 3, reports on the low proportion of ethnic Russians compared to ethnic Kazakhs in the new Kazakhstani parliament.

[93]Allan Richards, op. cit.

[94]Ian Bremmer, op. cit.

[95]See William E. Odom, *On Internal War* (Durham, NC: Duke University Press, 1991), 191-92; Lewis W. Snider, "The Political Performance of Third World Governments and the Debt Crisis," *American Political Science Review* 84 (December 1990), 1263-80; and Joel S. Migdal, *Strong Societies and Weak States* (Princeton, NJ: Princeton University Press, 1988), 279-86.

[96]Samuel P. Huntington, *Political Order in Changing Societies* (New Haven: Yale University Press, 1967), 78ff.

[97]Roy Allison, "Military Forces in the Soviet Successor States," Adelphi Paper No. 280 (October, 1993), 57.

[98]See Jeffrey Lenovitz, "Control of Kazakh Launch Disputed," *Aviation Week and Space Technology,* July 26, 1993, 26; and FBIS-SOV-92-010, 15 January 1992, "Nazarbayev, Shaposhnikov Discuss Defense Issues," 69.

[99]Allison, op. cit.

[100]Ibid., 58.

[101]One of the authors spoke with him at length on these issues in December 1993.

[102]JPRS-UMA-92-012, 8 April 1992, "KEMPO Unites Kazakh Defense Industries," 69-70.

[103]The authors and a few other Americans met with one Uzbek dissident at the American Embassy in Tashkent in December 1993, where they learned something of the opposition's goals. Islam as a cultural affair is very much on the agenda of some opposition groups, but political liberty, not an Islamic dictatorship, is the stated aim of most oppositionists. Admittedly, it is difficult to judge the real situation on such impressionistic evidence.

[104]One of the authors heard this account from Kyrgyz officials in December 1993, but a few days later in Tashkent he received confirmation from Uzbek officials only of their belief that Russian operatives were to blame for the outbreak of violence.

[105]During the authors' brief visit to Uzbekistan in December 1993, the depth of mistrust was palpable. One small episode demonstrates this vividly. Karimov promised that the visiting group would be permitted to see any dissidents they wished to. On the way from the meeting, the

American Embassy informed us that the six persons who planned to see us that evening had been arrested or were afraid to come. Confronted with this information, the foreign minister and other officials simply denied that the detentions had occurred. After only one dissident showed up, having been released under the impression he would not come, these officials were at a loss for an explanation the next day. Some insisted that police officials were sabotaging Karimov. Others speculated that situation was caused by confused instructions. Because these officials were strongly interested in impressing us favorably, their consternation was believable. Their reactions suggested that paranoia and mutual mistrust were indeed extremely high. In Kazakhstan and Kyrgyzstan, where we also visited, scheduling mistakes were corrected by calls and clarifications. Not so in Uzbekistan!

[106]RFE/RL Daily Report No. 137, 21 July 1993.

[107]Allison, op. cit., 61.

[108]See David Nissman, "Turkmenistan (Un)transformed," *Current History,* Vol. 93, No. 582 (April, 1994), 185.

[109]Bess Brown, "Turkmenistan Asserts Itself," *RFE/RL Research Report,* Vol. 1, No. 43 (30 October 1992), 27.

[110]Christopher J. Panico, "Turkmenistan Unaffected by Winds of Democratic Change," *RFE/RL Research Report,* Vol. 2, No. 4, (22 January 1993), 6-10, offers a good analysis of both Niyazov's technique of rule, human rights abuses, and nascent opposition groups.

[111]Ibid., 9.

[112]See Bess Brown, op. cit., 30. See also FBIS-NES-94-016, 25 January 1994, 53-54, for an Iranian commentary on Niyazov's successful visit to Tehran in early 1994.

[113]For a sense of his views on proper relations within the CIS, see FBIS-SOV-93-172, 8 September 1993, 84-86, "President Niyazov Outlines Attitude Toward CIS," and FBIS-SOV-93-244, 22 December 1993, 57-58, "President Niyazov on Ties with Russia, CIS."

[114]FBIS-SOV-92-047, 10 March 1992, 47-48, "Cooperation Agreements Reached With Turkey."

[115]Bess Brown, op. cit., 30-31.

[116]Panico, op. cit., 10.

[117]FBIS-SOV-93-169, 2 September 1993, 54, "Military Agreements Signed." Also, FBIS-SOV-92117, 17 June 1992, 53-54, "Official Interviewed on Armed Forces, Defense." Turkmenistan agreed in 1992 to carry a large part of the cost of military installations and social support costs for Russian troops, putting the Russian defense ministry in its debt.

[118]JPRS-UMA-93-031, 25 August 1993, 3, "Turkmenistan: Allied with Turkey and Ukraine."

[119]Ibid.

[120]FBIS-SOV-93-246, 27 December 1993, 78-79, "Bilateral Agreements Signed with Russia."

[121]RFE/RL Daily Report No. 199, 15 October 1993. During the first six months of 1993, 57,000 people emigrated from Kyrgyzstan, including nearly 30,000 Russians. The president's staff submitted to the government a number of measures aimed making it more attractive to remain in Kyrgyzstan.

[122]RFE/RL Daily Report No 136, 20 July 1993.

[123]RFE/RL Daily Report No. 6, 11 January 1994. The Asaba nationalist party disapproved of Akayev's desire to grant dual citizenship to Russians and other foreigners who were important to the Kyrgyz economy.

[124]FBIS-SOV-92-150, 6 August 1993, "Akayev Describes Gold Deal With Canadian Firm," 37. Canada's CAMECO promised to invest $45 million of its own money and to borrow $250 million more to exploit Kyrgyz gold deposits, some as high as 4,000 meters elevation.

[125]FBIS-SOV-93-155, 13 August 1993, "The Guards Have an Anniversary and Discipline Problems," 55.

[126]FBIS-SOV-92-014, 22 January 1992, "Presidential Adviser on Organization of the Military," 84.

[127]FBIS-SOV-92-105, 1 June 1992, "President Takes Control of Troops on Territory," 53. This source also recounts the story of the 282 Guards Regiment of the Panfilov Division, formerly part of the Soviet 40th Army of Afghanistan infamy. Its officers, almost entirely Russian, were upset at being put under Kyrgyz subordination; they threatened to sell their equipment outside the CIS to earn money for their families, and wondered whether they could transfer to Russia for service in another unit or whether they would be discharged and left to their own resources. This was a typical pattern throughout the Soviet ground forces within the CIS.

[128]FBIS-SOV-93-165, 27 August 1993, "Army Facing Shortage of Officers," 34.

[129]JPRS-UMA-93-028, 11 August 1993, "Future of Aviation Training Regiment in Kyrgyzstan Discussed," 56-57.

[130]FBIS-SOV-93-160, 20 August 1993, "General Staff of Armed Forces Created," 48-49.

[131]RFE/RL Daily Report No. 156, 17 August 1993.

[132]Allison, op. cit., 62.

[133]A senior Kyrgyz officer reported this to one of the authors during his visit there in December 1993.

[134]Ibid.

[135]JPRS-UMA-93-031, 25 August 1993, "Kyrgyz Volunteer Battalion To Be Sent to Afghan Border," 35.

[136]Svetlana Lolaeva, "Tajikistan in Ruins," *Democratization* Vol. 1, No. 4 (1993), 32-43.

[137]Ibid., 34-36. "Clans" in Tajikistan are based primarily on territory, not bloodlines.

[138]Ibid., 37.

[139]Ibid., 37-43. See also Bess Brown, "Tajikistan: The Conservatives Triumph," *RFE/RL Research Report,* Vol. 2, No. 7, 12 February 1993, 9-12.

[140]Keith Martin, "Tajikistan: Civil War without End?" *RFE/RL Research Report,* Vol. 2, No. 33, 20 August 1993, 18-29.

[141]Ibid., 21.

[142]Ibid., 23.

[143]Ibid., 25.

[144]Lolaeva, op. cit., 41.

[145]Ibid., 40.

[146]Keith Martin, op. cit., 27.

[147]Ibid.

[148]The authors heard this explanation from two Americans who spent time in Tajikistan and observed political and military affairs quite closely. Russian Deputy Foreign Minister Anatolii Adamshin lent credence to this judgment by asserting in August 1993 that drug trafficking was the basis of almost all events in Tajikistan. See FBIS-SOV-93-152, 10 August 1993, "Adamshin Says Drug Trafficking Behind Problem," 5.

[149]Lolaeva, op. cit., 39.

[150]JPRS-UMA-92-033, 2 September 1992, "Dushanbe Commander on Army Involvement in Factional Conflict," 21-22. Colonel Dzhurabek Asimov, deputy chairman of the republic's national security committee (precursor to the ministry of defense's formation), accused General Ashurov of favoring Kulyab forces in a fight on 27 June 1992 in Kurgan-Tyube Oblast. He added, "I would prefer that some general named Ivanov and General Ashurov be the garrison chief and commander of the 201st Division, someone who would think about the army and not about supporting President Nabiyev." At this time, Nabiyev, although still president, had admitted Democrats and Islamicists to a coalition government at the expense of the Kulyab clan.

[151]FBIS-SOV-92-119, 19 June 1992, "Presidential Decree Forms National Guard," 67-68; and FBIS-SOV-92-136, 15 July 1992, "Staff Member Details Future Military Doctrine," 61.

[152]FBIS-SOV-92-169, 31 August 1992, "CIS Forces Dead; Shaposhnikov Arrives for Talks," 39.

[153]FBIS-SOV-92-245, 21 December 1992, "Presidium Issues Decree on Armed Forces," 73.

[154]FBIS-SOV-93- 017, 28 January 1993, "Newly Appointed Defense Minister Interviewed," 45-46.

[155]FBIS-SOV-93-029, 16 February 1993, "Russian 201st Army Division To Remain Until 1999," 57.

[156]FBIS-SOV-93-021, 3 February 1993, "CIS Military Visit to Tajikistan 'Fruitful'," 44-45.

[157]FBIS-SOV-93-046, 11 March 1993, "First Contingent of CIS Troops Arrives in Tajikistan," 3.

[158]FBIS-SOV-93-145, 30 July 1993, "Yeltsin Edict on Tajik-Afghan Border Published," 3-4.

[159]Fiona Hill, "Report on Ethnic Conflict in the Russian Federation and Transcaucasia," *Strengthening Democratic Institutions Project,* JFK School of Government, Harvard University, July 1993, 66-67.

[160]Ibid., 74.

[161]FBIS-SOV-92-030, 13 February 1992, "Defense Minister Interviewed on Service, Army," 91-92.

[162]FBIS-SOV-92-221, 30 October 1992, "Leaders Speak at Meeting on Defense, National Army Creation," 61-62.

[163]FBIS-SOV-92-026, 7 February 1992, "Defense Ministry Takes Control of Troops," 95.

[164]FBIS-SOV-92-030, 13 February 1992, "Defense Minister Interviewed," 91.

[165]FBIS-SOV-92-249, 28 December 1992, "Defense Minister Urges CIS Officers to Join National Army," 42.

[166]One of the authors was told by Georgian officials that Russian military training camps for Armenians from Karabakh were maintained in Georgia covertly not far from the Armenian border.

[167]Hill, op. cit., 80.

[168]Ibid., 72-73.

[169]Elizabeth Fuller, "Azerbaijan's June Revolution," *RFE/RL Research Report,* Vol. 2, No. 32 (13 August 1993), 24.

[170]Ibid., 25.

[171]Ibid.

[172]Ibid., 27-29.

[173]Hill and Jewett, op. cit., 13.

[174]Ibid., 13-15.

[175]FBIS-SOV-91-174, 9 September 1991, "Supreme Soviet on Forming Army," 100.

[176]FBIS-SOV-92-028, 11 February 1992, "Baku To Insist on National Army," 92-93.

[177]FBIS-SOV-92-103, 28 May 1992, "Army Commander on Russian Troop Withdrawal," 76-77.

[178]FBIS-SOV-92-028, 11 February 1992, "Baku To Insist on National Army," 92-93.

[179]FBIS-SOV-92-109, 5 June 1992, "Azerbaijani Minister, Commander Interviewed," 13-14.

[180]FBIS-SOV-92-122, 24 June 1992, "Over 300 Officers Transfer to Azerbaijani Army," 14.

[181]FBIS-SOV-92-184, 22 September 1992, "Minister Urges Leaders To Develop Armed Forces," 60.

[182]JPRS-UMA-93-031, 25 January 1993, "Survey of CIS Armed Forces, Readiness," 1-2.

[183]FBIS-SOV-93-163, 25 August 1993, "Aliyev Addresses Supreme Soviet on Gumbatov," 49-52.

[184]JPRS-UMA-94-004, 26 January 1994, "Azerbaijan's Progress in Establishing 'Regular Army' Viewed," 39-41.

[185]FBIS-SOV-94-072, 14 April 1994, "Aliyev Address National Assembly on Progress of War," 55-59.

[186]See Hill and Jewett, op. cit., 45ff, for a succinct account of these events.

[187]Ibid. The authors take most of this account and the judgments about Shevardnadze's actions from discussions with Shevardnadze and other Georgian senior officials in Tbilisi in December 1993.

[188]Unpublished research paper, "Respublika Gruziya," no author, provided to one of the authors by an institute in Tbilisi in 1993.

[189]Ibid.

[190]Ibid.

[191]FBIS-SOV-93-024, 8 February 1993, "Defense Ministry: No Plans to Re-station Troops in Georgia," 10.

[192]RFE/RL Daily Report No. 68, 8 April 1993, and RFE/RL Daily Report No. 23, 3 February 1993..

[193]RFE/RL Daily Report No. 196, 12 October 1993.

[194]See RFE/RL Daily Report No. 23, 3 February 1994 and Daily Report No. 52, 16 March 1994.

[195]Yevgenii Krutikov elaborated these considerations, opinions, and issues in *Megapolis-Ekspress,* No. 6, February 9, 1994, 15.

[196]During discussions with Shevardnadze in December 1993 in Tbilisi, the authors heard him recount these warnings to Yeltsin and others.

[197]See RFE/RL Daily Report No. 105, 6 June 1994, for a report on these killings.

[198]Hill and Jewett, op. cit., 16, conclude that by sending Russian

troops to support Azerbaijan, Moscow threw ". . . its commitment to the cessation of hostilities into question."

[199]RFE/RL Daily Report No.106, 8 June 1994.

[200]RFE/RL Daily Report No. 108, 9 June 1994, reported that the State Duma increased the defense budget from the recommended 37 trillion rubles to 40 trillion. Defense Minister Grachev and several other officials were demanding 80 to 87 trillion rubles, and a counter offer of 55 trillion was suggested. Failure to reach the 80 trillion figure, and not even the 55 trillion level, suggests that the defense ministry will have far fewer resources with which to pursue its policies of hegemony in the CIS.

T W O

The New Russian Military

As the previous chapter's analysis of developments in the Commonwealth of Independent States (CIS) makes clear, military issues were first placed on the agenda when the CIS was formed, remained the central issue after the program for a joint armed forces collapsed, and by late 1994 were still the most substantive aspect of CIS relations, particularly in Central Asia and the Transcaucasus. Whether the military connection will continue to be the tie that binds these two regions to Moscow depends in large part on what happens in the Russian military establishment.

With the passing of the Soviet regime and its Communist Party discipline, power to make foreign and military policy became fragmented. Although President Yeltsin retained strong legal authority for the office of the presidency in the new Russian constitution, real power to determine military doctrine and foreign policy was left in large degree to individual ministries, with erratic involvement by the parliament and an important new role for the media and opinion makers. Russian military leaders, military institutions, and military industrial programs inherited an unprecedented autonomy, especially for making policy toward the CIS countries. If Russian military leaders have plans that are hindered by deep entanglements in Central Asia and the Transcaucasus, Russian political leaders will find it difficult to keep them engaged there. If, however, the military's plans and doctrinal views give these regions great importance, Russian political leaders may find it difficult to disengage from them.

Thus the new Russian military establishment's plans, structure, resources, and activities should provide a number of clues as to Russian intentions toward the CIS and to Moscow's capabilities for imposing its hegemony over Central Asia and the Transcaucasus. To understand these aspects of the Russian military, it is necessary to set aside temporarily concern with CIS regional affairs and to undertake an exploratory analysis of the new Russian military establishment and its doctrine, strategy, and internal policies.

The New Russian Military

> About the army: you know that for a long time Russia made no decision about setting up its own army, trying to preserve the single Commonwealth Army. Well, that did not work. A state commission has now been set up . . . under Colonel General Volkogonov to carry out the primary work on establishing a Russian Army and Navy.[1]

With these brief words to the Sixth Congress of People's Deputies in April 1992, President Yeltsin announced the creation of a purely Russian military establishment separate from the Armed Forces of the Commonwealth of Independent States. In May, he appointed General Pavel Grachev as minister of defense with the task of organizing the new Russian forces as rapidly as possible. No other Russian institutional development would prove as critical for Russia's role in Central Asia and the Transcaucasus. The defense ministry would not only provide the means for Russia's deep involvement in the domestic politics of these regions; it would also aggressively seek that involvement.

By 1994, notwithstanding enormous difficulties, the Russian military establishment was taking inchoate shape. In the process, it became a major influence on the future course of Russian domestic and foreign policies. In particular, it weighed heavily on Russia's aims in and influence on Central Asia and the Transcaucasus. To understand the development of such a complex institution and its role in Russian foreign and domestic policies is not easy. We can begin to do so, however, by examining the following six issues, which offer a kind of cross section of the military and its functions:

1) Russian foreign policy;
2) military doctrine;
3) military manpower policy;

4) military industrial policy;

5) command, control, and force structure; and

6) military strategy.

Russian Foreign Policy

A state's foreign policy defines in the broadest sense the major tasks for its military. Thus the kind of foreign policy Russia chooses bears centrally on the kind of military establishment it must have. Russian foreign policy was hardly consistent in 1992-94, evolving as it was under the constraints of many factors, internal and external, but it showed distinct shifts and trends.

Initially, the Yeltsin government had to develop two foreign policies, one for the "near abroad," i.e., the former USSR, the other for the "far abroad," i.e., the remainder of the world. Because policy for the "near abroad" is treated in the first chapter of this study, it can be temporarily set aside.

Policy toward the "far abroad" can be broken into three axes— West, i.e., Europe and North America; East, i.e., East Asia; and South, i.e., the subcontinent and the Middle East.

Throughout 1992 and 1993, Yeltsin's foreign policy on the West axis not only maintained but even expanded the cooperative approach of the last three years of the Gorbachev period. Moscow treated Europe and North America as a whole, seeking economic and technical aid, cooperating in arms control and security matters, and expanding a wide range of cultural and social connections. On the potentially divisive issue of the former Yugoslavia, Yeltsin avoided breaking solidarity with the West, although differences surfaced. Most important, he showed no inclination to play Europe against the United States or vice versa, at least into early 1994.

On the East axis, Yeltsin tried to follow up on the breakthroughs of Gorbachev's policy, beginning with a rapprochement with China, expanded ties with South Korea, and improved relations with Japan. On the southern Kurile Islands issue he had to yield to domestic resistance, particularly within the Russian military,[2] and give up on early return of these so-called Northern Territories to Japan, which might have normalized fully relations with Tokyo. After postponements and a cancellation, Yeltsin finally visited Tokyo in October

1993, and although both sides tried to put a good face on the event, their relations only marginally improved. At the same time, Russian policy in this region has not been anti-American or played to pressures for U.S. military withdrawal. On the contrary, the Russian deputy foreign minister who is responsible for this region, G. F. Kunadze, has long insisted that the U.S. military presence is essential for regional stability in East Asia.[3]

On the South axis, Russia was neither uncooperative with the United States nor very active. Backing radical Arabs was no longer Moscow's policy, and ties with Israel were normalized. At the same time, concern about Islamic radicalism finding fertile ground in Russia's "near abroad," particularly in Central Asia, sharpened. Afghan involvement in the civil war in Tajikistan heightened Russian fears of this threat, though these fears in fact appeared to be more a pretense for interference in Tajikistan than a result of Islamic realities. Azerbaijan and the Northern Caucasus, in the view of some Russian leaders, hold similar potential for Middle Eastern states to meddle on Russia's southern "near abroad."

A major result of these new lines of Russian foreign policy was a dramatic change in Russia's perception of military threats. Only a few years ago, the West and East axes posed huge military threats in Soviet eyes. In 1992-94, they posed virtually none while the passive southern axis presented a larger but more diffuse and less definitive military challenge. During the last years of the Soviet Union, the radical reformers in Moscow argued that the Western powers posed no genuine military threat. The defense ministry spokesmen strongly disagreed. In 1992-93, however, most of the senior military implicitly came to accept the earlier assessment by their radical critics and to agree that Russia faced no serious prospects of external attack, although they did not see this as a permanent condition.[4]

Such a dramatic reversal of Russia's perception of external threats derived almost wholly from an equally dramatic reversal of foreign policy goals. Marxism-Leninism, the basis for Soviet foreign policy, defined all of the nonsocialist world as an irreconcilably hostile camp to be eventually destroyed, by Soviet offensive military operations in extremis, or, preferably, by internal revolutions bringing socialist forces to power. Committed to Western principles of interstate relations, Russian foreign policy by contrast seemed directed at making

Russia more like Western societies.

In other words, Moscow had shifted in the space of three or four years from a stubbornly expansionist foreign policy to acceptance of the dramatic political and military realignment involving the collapse of the Warsaw Pact and the Soviet Union. For the Russian military, defense requirements went from overwhelming to virtually nonexistent, although the military remained concerned with internal stability and, in the longer term, with the "near abroad." This change in requirements was reflected in rapidly declining military capabilities, brought on partially by policy intent and partially by the forces of decay and disorder unleashed during the last two years of the Soviet Union's existence.

How settled was Russia's commitment to this foreign policy? As long as the foreign ministry under Andrei Kozyrev had the upper hand in dictating it, Russian foreign policy looked settled, but deep resistance existed in the so-called power ministries, i.e., the ministries of defense, security, and internal affairs, as well as within the parliament and among reactionary political circles. During the summer and fall of 1993, Yeltsin began to lend his support to a number of actions favored by the power ministries, backing in particular General Grachev and the defense ministry. Kozyrev followed Yeltsin's lead in greater involvement in Central Asia and the Transcaucasus, trying at the same time to assure the West that the involvement was benign and meant to maintain regional stability. At the United Nations General Assembly in September 1993, Kozyrev demanded that the UN treat Russian military actions in these regions as official UN peacekeeping endeavors.[5]

By the fall of 1993, Russian foreign policy appeared to have shifted from its initial status quo orientation, aimed at doing nothing to reverse the loss of Moscow's control over the former Soviet republics, to a careful but assertive policy on the southern axis, aimed at reestablishing Moscow's hegemony based both on formal arrangements within the Commonwealth of Independent States and on the physical presence of Russian military forces in as many of the CIS members as possible. Contemporary Western opinion on the nature of Russian foreign policy in late 1993 and early 1994 was divided on whether such a shift in Russian foreign policy had actually occurred. Those who argued that it had not often described Russian actions in the other CIS republics as reflecting no central direction or conscious policy in Moscow. They also attributed, rightly in several cases, Russian military involvement to encouragement and complicity by local leaders. There was, in this view, simply no evidence of a "new Russian imperialism" because there was no evidence that Russian leaders subscribed to such a policy or were implementing it.[6]

But do the statements of leaders and opinion makers in 1992-93 support the view that there was no planning or scheming to regain the old Soviet territories? Although "imperialism" was not to be found in their vocabulary, they did express widely differing views on the merits of accepting the loss of control over the non-Russian republics, on the nature of military threats to Russia, and on the kinds of policies required either to change or maintain the new legal status quo. Those reluctant to accept the new status quo and to deemphasize the military aspects of Russian foreign policy were most numerous and vocal in the new Russian defense ministry, although the defense ministry hardly monopolized this viewpoint. Both old communists and new Russian nationalist-patriotic spokesmen shared their opinions and offered demagogic rhetoric if not clear policy concepts in support of them. Within the government, Vice-President Alexander Rutskoi was the highest-level spokesman for this position. Hardly a sophisticated strategic thinker, he nonetheless served as a mouthpiece for the more imperial-minded officers in the general staff academy and the defense ministry, providing a comprehensive statement of this line of thought early in 1993 in the form of an article in the leading military journal.[7]

Rutskoi conceded in this article that no serious military threats to Russia existed, but he insisted that military affairs are dynamic, that a few states are acquiring greater military potential, including nuclear weapons, and that the present peaceful state of affairs could, therefore, be short-lived. For Russia specifically, he argued, the large "possible threat" would be the movement of military forces into states on the CIS borders. Other and more immediate threats were civil wars within the CIS, including within Russia.

The potential adversaries Rutskoi seemed to have in mind were the United States, Western Europe, and China, since only they could possibly move large forces into Eastern Europe or along the CIS borders in the east. He also foresaw possible rearmament by Japan following a decline in U.S. power. Notwithstanding the potential for adversarial relations with these states, he prescribed expanded relations and policies of cooperation with them all. In the Middle East and South Asia, he declared, Russia has historically been influential and must remain so in the future. For him, the urgent military problems were closer at hand. When he voiced concern about states' acquiring greater military potential, including nuclear weapons, that could pose a threat to Russian territory, he might well have had in mind other CIS states, including Ukraine, Belarus, and Kazakhstan, as well as North Korea, Iran, and Iraq.

The primary focus of his policy aims, therefore, was the former Soviet republics. Rutskoi insisted unambiguously that the CIS and the Baltic states must be a single strategic space, tied firmly in a collective security system through treaties and possessing a common strategic nuclear force as well as common technical and support systems for all of its military forces. He outlined a military development program through the year 2000, whose similarity to variants emerging from the defense ministry was too great to be coincidental.

In a word, Rutskoi proposed for Russian foreign policy a thinly veiled formula for reclaiming the old Soviet borders as well as Russian "great power" status on all three axes. He encouraged cautious cooperation with the West and Japan. Rutskoi's position on practical matters like relations with former Warsaw Pact states and the Baltic republics was to consider their inclusion in NATO wholly unacceptable, a direct threat to Russia. Cooperation with the United States in the Middle East and Southwest Asia was for him secondary to maintaining Russia's influence in these two regions.

This is not a status quo foreign policy. It is a formula for regaining lost power and prestige, obviously requiring considerable Russian military power. Finally, it seems to put foreign policy above domestic reform as a priority. Implicitly it requires domestic policies devised to support foreign policy. Rutskoi does not exclude liberal democracy and market economics, but they certainly do not take first place for him. Rutskoi, of course, was arrested after the violence inspired by him and others in the parliament on 3-4 October 1993, and for that reason, his arguments might be dismissed, but that would be a mistake, and not only because he and others charged with causing the violence in October were granted amnesty and allowed to reenter the political scene in Moscow. The more important reason for not dismissing such foreign policy aims is that his article was effectively a summary of the strategic thinking within the defense ministry in 1992, thinking that persisted there and among conservative political circles in 1993 and 1994, and that may have been the basis for policies implemented in 1993-94.

On the opposite side of the debate, Sergei Blagovolin, formerly a professor at the Institute for International Economics and International Relations (IMEMO) and an aide to former Politburo member Alexander Yakovlev, offered two months earlier what was probably the maximalist liberal alternative.[8] He focused first on what Rutskoi ignored—the many political and economic processes at work in the rest of the world, particularly the world economy, the European Community, NATO, technological change, and the transnational social and cultural forces giving the West a distinctive and attractive character. In order to counter the opinion still dominant in military and reactionary political circles, he took pains to explain why liberal democracies, owing to their internal constraints, could not pose serious offensive military threats to Russia. In assessing the prospects for world order or world chaos, Blagovolin saw the role of the United States as key but worried that it might shrink from its leadership role in supporting order in Europe and East Asia. U.S. reluctance to act would, in his judgment, be a tragedy for Russia.

Within this larger international context, he reviewed the three axes for Russian foreign policy. The West axis took priority, and his goal there was to see Russia become part of the Western economic, political, and cultural community. Only by succeeding with its domestic transformation to a liberal political and economic system could Russia hope to join that community. Thus Blagovolin, setting aside concern for great power status, inverted Rutskoi's priorities. Great power status would naturally arise through a cooperative relationship with the United States. Both the U.S. and Russia are deeply involved in Europe and East Asia, he said, and if the United States takes an appropriate leading role in these regions it will need Russia as a key partner. No other state can join the United States in balancing the two key areas of the world, he argued; thus Russia's status is not threatened but rather ensured by aligning with the West.

Blagovolin warned Russians against the temptation to try to split

Europe from the United States. Such a move would destroy the very community Russia must join in order to become a modern and prosperous liberal society. In fact, he treated the disintegration of the West as Russia's greatest external threat, an eventuality that would leave Russia alone, outside a stable international system.

Concerning Russia's "near abroad" and Eastern Europe, he judged the maintenance of stability, especially in Eastern Europe, as beyond Russia's means, and he welcomed the entry of Eastern European states into NATO. He argued that CIS states, including Russia, should not join NATO because they did not yet have the domestic political conditions or professional militaries to participate effectively in the Atlantic Alliance, but he believed that all should strive for expanded security relations with NATO and dependency on the Western security system, with NATO as the system's foundation, not the Conference on Security and Cooperation in Europe (CSCE). Within the CIS, he noted, no state other than Russia had adequate military power to play a stabilizing role, but the CIS should not try to become another NATO; CIS members simply do not share enough in common to make such an alliance work. For him, the "far abroad" was more important to Russia's security than the "near abroad." The road to Russian security led through Washington and Bonn, not through Dushanbe, Tashkent, and Tbilisi.

Thus the military requirements for Blagovolin's foreign policy are fairly small, depending on a minimal strategic nuclear force coupled with a continued rapid reduction in all other forces. For the next ten years, he insisted, Russia should focus on modernization of small conventional forces since this was the trend in NATO and elsewhere, and it made sense for Russia to seek close collaboration with the United States in its own modernization process. According to Blagovolin, the closed "enclave" nature of the old Soviet military-industrial complex has to be almost entirely abandoned in recognition that advanced military technology requires modernization of the entire economy, not just the military sector.

These two quite different variants of foreign policy reflect the reemergence of the traditional struggle within Russia between Westernizers and Slavophiles.[9] Blagovolin explained the reasons for Westernizing Russia and gave the process his full blessing. Rutskoi could neither grasp the process nor accept it. Within the Russian foreign ministry, Blagovolin's views seemed to enjoy considerable (although not universal) support during 1992 and early 1993. Within the Russian defense ministry, Rutskoi's article clearly reflected the dominant sentiment, and it may even have been ghostwritten by someone in that ministry.[10] By the summer of 1993, the foreign policy line within the foreign ministry began to yield priority to the line in the defense ministry (also partially supported by anti-Yeltsin forces in the parliament). The former required more rapid reduction of the present forces and more emphasis on modernization through a market industrial base and cooperation with the West. The latter demanded a slower reduction of forces, more active involvement in CIS peacemaking, and modernization of the old military-industrial base, apparently with greater administrative, i.e., non-market, control and less help from the West. The former variant took Russia's great power status as inevitable but less important than membership in the Western community of liberal democracies. In this view, the West would be Russia's salvation, not its adversary. The latter variant viewed the West not as hostile but still as a potential adversary seeking to encroach on Russia's traditional areas of influence.

The common ground between the two variants lay in the perceived need for technical modernization by the military. Both variants called for it, and both recognized that force reductions were essential to achieve it. Otherwise, they were not only incompatible but in fact thoroughly antithetical to one another.

To what degree was the foreign policy advocated by Blagovolin truly a reflection of the foreign ministry's actual policy line? Blagovolin's views were not as consistent with the foreign ministry's as Rutskoi's were with those of the defense ministry, but they did overlap to a considerable extent. A so-called working document in the foreign ministry, which set forth the outlines of policy in some detail, makes this overlap clear. Elaborated in large part in the Russian press in late 1992,[11] it dealt first with "short-term tasks" to be performed in the former Soviet territories. Concerning military security, the task was "to stop armed clashes and settle conflicts around Russia, prevent their spread to Russian territory, and ensure a strict observance of rights of minorities, such as the rights of ethnic Russians, in adjoining countries." The CIS was to be turned into "an effective formation of sovereign states" based on "common interests and voluntary participation," and to become an "international regional organization" with legal foundations. This change required a "flexible and patient approach to the establishment of the CIS. . . that would allow for. . . deep interaction with interested countries only." On human rights, Russia would compromise but not make unilateral concessions, and it might take unspecified retaliatory measures where Russians' rights were abused in other former Soviet republics. Another task to be carried out was "to concentrate full control over the nuclear forces of the former USSR in Russia's hands by withdrawing such forces onto its own territories and their subsequent scrapping." And concerning economic affairs, the aim was to develop a "unified space" over the entire former Soviet territories, apparently including the Baltic republics within some sort of trade zone.

Concerning Eastern Europe, this document says, the strategic aim was to keep this region from becoming a buffer walling Russia off from the West. Fulfilling this aim required building new relations with East European states, a task made more difficult by the appearance of an additional belt of states, including the Baltic republics, Belarus, and Ukraine, between Russia and Eastern Europe.

The document noted tensions between the United States and Europe and pointed to the dangers of U.S. isolationism. It put great stress on the US-Russian relationship, in particular on the need for cooperation and on the U.S. as a source of economic assistance to Russia, but it warned that as the "only superpower," the United States might resort to occasional imperialist actions that Russia must resist. Russia must take the initiative in designing the relationship and secure U.S. assistance in gaining G-7 membership for Russia. The document invited greater U.S. participation in settling conflicts and protecting human rights within the CIS but remained wary of efforts by the United States to replace Moscow's influence in some regions.

In the Asia-Pacific region no less than in Europe, the United States was seen as the critical partner in maintaining stability, but that did not eliminate the need for an independent Russian role in the "polycentric system" of relations in this region. Achieving economic integration with the market economies of Asia was a major aim. In the case of Japan, this would require settling the Northern Territories dispute. Observing that Russia no longer shares an official ideology with China, the document nonetheless cited good neighborly relations between the countries as the only policy alternative. It called Korean reunification the best way to abolish tensions on the peninsula and remove the threat of North Korean nuclear proliferation.

In treating the south, the document identified Iran as a problem and Turkey as a partner; it also saw cooperation with the United States as essential for preventing nuclear proliferation and maintaining regional stability. Tajikistan and Afghanistan were cited as sources of instability affecting neighboring states. In the subcontinent, the goal was good trading relations with India and neutrality in the Indo-Pakistani dispute.

This foreign ministry version of Russian foreign policy, then, shared much with Blagovolin's, but it in some respects also tilted toward the Rutskoi variant. On the CIS in particular, it was more threatening than Blagovolin on protecting the Russian diaspora, but it did not imply as clearly as Rutskoi did military retaliation in the event Russians in the "near abroad" were mistreated. Nor did it require the unified military system that Rutskoi demanded for the CIS. It instead treated CIS members as truly sovereign states voluntarily entering an international regional organization.

The foreign ministry document's approach to Eastern Europe, though different from Rutskoi's, slightly overlapped with it. Where Rutskoi treated the expansion of NATO into that region as a military challenge to Russia, the foreign ministry document opposed it on different grounds: it feared that Eastern Europe would then act for the West as a buffer against Russia, isolating Russia from the West. In principle, NATO could expand eastward, as long as doing so was compatible with making the West more open to Russia, especially in economic affairs, such as G-7 membership. The foreign ministry's differences with the Rutskoi version were also evident in policy toward East Asia. The foreign ministry would concede the Northern Territories because economic ties to Japan would be worth the concession.

The big difference between the two versions, of course, was the foreign ministry's emphasis, like Blagovolin's, on joining the Western community of advanced industrial states. The foreign ministry's version made a gesture in Rutskoi's direction by warning against the reassertion of U.S. imperialism, but it mainly focused on the need to draw the United States into closer and highly cooperative ties and to collaborate with it on security in Europe, East Asia, and the Middle East.

The foreign ministry's version requires not a large Russian military but one able to deal with conflicts within the CIS. This requirement is again much closer to Blagovolin's than to Rutskoi's version, although the foreign ministry is it not as specific as Blagovolin on military modernization.

Russian foreign policy in 1992 and early 1993 was remarkably close to the foreign ministry variant. After Yeltsin had to retreat in his March 1993 attempt to close the old parliament, he showed more interest in the defense ministry variant. Throughout the spring and summer, General Grachev carried on an open quarrel with Georgia's leader, Eduard Shevardnadze, surreptitiously supporting Abkhaz separatists and quietly dealing with other anti-Shevardnadze military groups in Georgia. Grachev brought Shevardnadze to his knees by late summer, forcing him to make Georgia a member of the CIS. At the same time, a military revolt in Azerbaijan, almost certainly sponsored by Russian operatives, ended with the installation of Gaidar Aliyev, a former KGB official, former party chief in Soviet Azerbaijan, and former alternate member of the Politburo of the Soviet Communist Party, as head of state.[12] Aliyev soon reversed Azerbaijan's decision to remain outside the CIS. With a solid footing in Georgia, Armenia, and Azerbaijan, the Russian military was also taking charge of Tajikistan. Thus by mid-1993, Yeltsin and Kozyrev appeared to be adopting much of the "near abroad" foreign policy advocated by Rutskoi and the military leadership throughout the previous year.

Following Yeltsin's closing of the parliament in September, the violence in Moscow on 3-4 October, and the elections in December, it seemed that Russian foreign policy might once again have the chance to swing back toward the line of 1992. Once Yeltsin had arrested Rutskoi and the parliamentary leaders who shared his military and foreign policy views, he appeared to have new room to maneuver. To be sure, because he had had to depend on the ministries of defense, interior, and security to control events on 3-4 October, these ministries had gained new political prominence. A significant retreat in the foreign policy toward the "near abroad," therefore, was unlikely at once, but with the anticipation of liberal forces' winning most of the seats in the new parliament, i.e., the State Duma, the Westernizing foreign policy was not yet a dead letter. True enough, during a summer visit to Prague and Warsaw, Yeltsin had agreed that the Czech Republic and Poland could enter NATO, but he had reversed that position in a formal letter shortly after returning to Moscow. Kozyrev's foreign ministry team apparently was still struggling to retain its foreign policy toward the "far abroad" by supporting the defense ministry's policy toward the "near abroad," but as the incident in Prague and Warsaw revealed, it was rapidly losing the battle.

The December election results, the departure of virtually all liberal reformers from Chernomyrdin's government, the dynamics within the new State Duma, and the February 1994 amnesty of those accused of insurrectionary activities in August 1991 and October 1993— these developments revealed the declining political influence of Westernizing politicians on Russian foreign policy. Even those who had warned that Russia's return to deep involvement in the "near abroad" would prevent both modernization of the Russian military industry and liberal political development were emphasizing in February 1994 the overwhelming importance of Russia's concern for the Russian diaspora in the former USSR.[13] Further evidence of the primacy of the "near abroad," including the Baltic republics and possibly Eastern Europe, in Russian foreign policy was offered in remarks by a Russian diplomat to one of the authors in February 1994. While this official did not favor the policy, he said flatly that Russia would soon reacquire control of all the territories of the old Soviet Union and would also renew its influence in Eastern Europe. He was certain of this because Western passiveness had alerted Moscow that it would meet no resistance in such a course.

Whether Russia could achieve these goals remained debatable in late 1994, but there was already strong evidence that it was trying to do so.

Military Doctrine

The term "military doctrine" is fairly loosely used in Western writings, but in the Soviet Union it had a rigid definition. Consisting of two components, social-political and military-technical, it was said to encompass the state's official views on war, military forces, and preparations for war. In Western parlance, it might better be translated as the state's "military security policy" in its widest sense.

Implicit in this understanding of military doctrine are the philosophical assumptions of the state's leaders about the nature of war. Is it an instrument of policy, as Clausewitz insisted it could be? Or is it like stormy weather, which, when it comes, one must try to mitigate in order to survive? Or is it an eschatological phenomenon, part of the inexorable march of history toward some preordained goal? The Marxist-Leninist philosophy of war was a mix of the Clausewitzian and the eschatological views. Class struggle was the cause of war and the source of progress toward socialism. At the same time, as Marx insisted, revolution is an act of volition inspired by class consciousness. This voluntarist aspect of Marx's view of revolution and war permitted Lenin to introduce the Clausewitzian perspective into the Soviet view.

Because Marxism-Leninism split the world into two camps, socialist and capitalist-imperialist, it effectively defined the threat against which Soviet forces had to prepare to fight—essentially the entire nonsocialist world. Soviet military doctrine, therefore, was designed for dealing with the inevitable showdown between socialism and capitalism. Being materialists, Soviet military theorists also had to take account of the changing nature of technology and its impact on warfare. Thus industrialization and a modern economy were imperative. Because the quality of a society's manpower base was also considered a major determinant of military power, military planners concerned themselves with virtually all aspects of state policies for education, social matters, and physical fitness. Military doctrine, conceived in such broad terms, embraced a large part of the entire business of governing within the Soviet state.

Military doctrine in this system was never written down in any formal document. Its authority derived from the ideology informing it and from its approval by the communist party's highest organ, the Politburo. With that blessing, the defense ministry had party backing to take what it needed from all state resources. Justification of its actions to a parliamentary body or to the public was out of the question.

This elementary review of what military doctrine has long meant to the present generation of Russian military leaders is essential to an understanding of their obsession with developing and legitimizing a new, Russian version of the doctrine. They instinctively wanted it to perform all the functions of the old one—defining the threat, justifying force structure, and dictating adequate resources. Not surprisingly, reaching agreement on a new military doctrine was not easy. The social-political component was in the past defined by the political leaders, and the military-technical component was largely left to the military and their cadres of scientists, engineers, and industrialists.

The abandonment of the official ideology and the passing of the Communist Party created a terrible void for the military. It cannot be filled without a fundamental rethinking of Russia's purpose, its role in the world, and its relations with the CIS. That process has only begun, as the foregoing discussion of foreign policy makes clear. Even by 1994, after the long struggle over foreign policy appeared to be resolved, there was hardly a consensus on the political aspect of doctrine, not to speak of military-technical and resource issues. Yet with the defense ministry in the midst of a major restructuring, the new shape the ministry was to take became an urgent issue for its members. Were they to wait until a political consensus was hammered out in public and in the Russian parliament? They answered that question by moving ahead more or less independently, designing their own version of what they believed the doctrine should be and then struggling to gain approval in the parliament and the rest of the government. In this new political context, they saw a written, formal, and legal document for articulating military doctrine as imperative. If the basis of the new Russian state was to be law instead of an official ideology, military doctrine also would have to be in the form of a law.

The defense ministry managed to get two laws passed by the parliament, the "Law on Defense" (September 1992) and the "Law on Military Obligation and Military Service" (February 1993). The first of these statutes created a legal basis for institutional arrangements and authorities in the defense ministry, the government, and the presidency. The second provided a basis for recruiting manpower. Neither, however, answered the questions about the military's purpose, size, structure, or budget, or about what the military was to defend against.

In May 1992, the defense ministry published a draft document entitled "The Fundamentals of Russian Military Doctrine."[14] It identified two major threats to Russia. The first was the introduction of foreign military forces into states adjacent to the former USSR's borders and the buildup of ground, air, and naval forces near Russian borders. The second threat was violation of the rights of ethnic Russians living in all the other former Soviet republics. Identifying three types of wars, the document called global wars unlikely, local and civil wars far more probable. The second and third types, although smaller, could still involve large-scale conventional ground combat. Presumably, either of the two primary threats could provoke local and civil wars. And, presumably, Russian military power would be used to deal with such threats.

Two implications of this doctrine are important. First, the only foreign military powers that could conceivably move forces into states neighboring the CIS are China on the Sino-Russian border and NATO states abutting Eastern Europe. Thus this doctrine created a basis for a military reaction by Russia were any of the Eastern European states to join NATO. Second, the doctrine was an explicit warning to CIS countries that violated the rights of ethnic Russians living on their territories. In light of the more than 25 million Russians in the CIS living outside Russia—virtually none of them Russian citizens in the sense of having Russian passports and many formally citizens of the states of their residence—this warning dealt with more than hypothetical matters.

To respond to these threats, the defense ministry document specified three types of armed forces: 1) limited numbers of forces, primarily strategic nuclear forces, permanently ready for combat as a deterrent; 2) mobile forces as a reserve to shift quickly to reinforce against an attack from any direction; and 3) additional reserve forces to be mobilized in anticipation of the threat of war. The mission of these forces included the collective defense of the entire CIS under central direction. Gone was all mention of "purely defensive" forces, the policy under Gorbachev. Russia would develop all kinds of weapons and forces for both defensive and offensive operations.

While the doctrine considered the main tasks of Russian forces the defense of Russia and the CIS, it also allowed Russian forces to join with forces from other states for keeping the peace under the authority of the United Nations. Strategic nuclear weapons were seen to retain a critical role as a deterrent, yet Russia showed signs of backing away from a no-first-use policy. The new doctrine allowed for nuclear retaliation against conventional strikes at Russian nuclear forces, introducing considerable ambiguity to the no-first-use promise. With its emphasis on new technology for modern weaponry, the doctrine dictated an industrial requirement to keep Russian weapons on a technical level second to none in the world.

Overall, this draft doctrine called for a more capable military than did Gorbachev's "defensive sufficiency" doctrine, one able to defeat as well as repel an aggressor, respond to all possible variants of future war, and provide for a wide range of nuclear weapons employment, not just simple retaliation. It also reflected great sensitivity to the modern weaponry used in the Persian Gulf War.

Within military circles, some officers, especially General Igor Rodionov, head of the general staff academy, have called for an even more aggressive doctrine, including renunciation of the no-first-use pledge and assertion of military hegemony over the Baltic republics and most of the Black Sea littoral (including both former Soviet republics and ex-Warsaw Pact members).[15]

Following the issuance of the defense ministry document, military leaders complained periodically during the remainder of 1992 and most of 1993 that neither the Russian Security Council nor the parliament would officially promulgate this doctrine. Only after the closing of the parliament by force of arms in October did Yeltsin allow the Security Council to act. The final and official version of the doctrine, made law on 2 November 1993, was considerably toned down in its language, leaving many points either implicit or slightly ambiguous. Nonetheless, it identified the same threats, held open the possibility of first use of nuclear weapons, and essentially authorized the modernization of Russian military weaponry. While it might not include the specificity desired by the general staff, it provided a basis for most of the military policies long sought by the senior Russian military.[16]

Not surprisingly, the promulgation of the doctrine caused deep concern in the Central Asian and Transcaucasus republics. Presidents Nazarbayev of Kazakhstan, Karimov of Uzbekistan, and Shevardnadze of Georgia were particularly worried by it, and some

anxiety was probably felt in all other republics.[17] Nazarbayev, for
instance, pointed out the unnerving analogy between Russia's claim
to protect Russians in other CIS states and Hitler's assertion of authority over Sudeten Germans in 1938.

Military Manpower Policy

No single issue captures the turmoil, difficulties, and chaos within
the Russian military as does manpower policy. Conscription and recruitment tie the military to every stratum of society, and poor morale arising from horrible conditions in military units in turn stimulate
public demands for changes.[18] Dividing up the military among the
CIS states has placed hardships on military family members and confused individual soldiers and officers about where to place their loyalties. Large troop withdrawals from Europe and the Baltic states
vastly exceeded the personnel system's capacity to manage them,
and the failure to create the CIS joint forces merely added to withdrawal difficulties. The enormity of the manpower problems defies
a complete characterization. All that can be offered here is a snap-
shot of the key issues and how they were being addressed.

The Russian military was confronted at once by too many active
duty personnel and too few. Always top heavy in officers, the defense ministry began reducing their number, including flag officers.
At the same time, filling all vacancies in the enlisted ranks has proven
impossible, since a conscription cohort is released for active duty
every six months. In other words, about one fourth of the enlisted
personnel must be replaced twice each year. Sergei Stepashin, chairman of the parliamentary Committee on Defense and State Security
in the old, now defunct parliament, warned in July 1993 that after
the fall draft the army could have 630,000 officers but only 540,000
conscripts, a startling prognostication.[19]

In 1992, with the breakup of the Soviet Union, the Russian armed
forces were consistently reported at a strength of 2.8 million. Defense ministry plans envisioned reductions to 1.5 million, or about 1
percent of the population, a level to be maintained more or less permanently. By 1994 the number was to be near 2 million; the target of
1.5 million was to be reached by 1995. The armed forces were reportedly cut by 200,000 in 1992, leaving about a half million further

reduction for 1993.[20] But realities quickly outran these neatly planned reductions.

A complex new law "On Military Obligation and Military Service" was belatedly passed and signed on 11 February 1993.[21] Cutting the term for conscripts to 18 months and allowing for massive deferments (amounting to 80 percent of the total of each year's eligible youth), it confronted the defense ministry with the release of two conscription cohorts in the late fall of 1993 instead of the normal one cohort.[22] The defense ministry estimated that, as a result of this situation, only 27 percent of the required number of new conscripts would be available in the fall 1993 call-up.[23] This figure was probably an optimistic estimate unless it accounted for potential draft dodging and desertions. Moreover, the poor yield from call-ups in 1992 left the enlisted ranks woefully short, with staffing at only 55 percent by one report.[24]

Reluctance to serve in the military and the large number of exemptions permitted by the new military service law reflect both the dramatic change in public attitudes toward the military since the early years of Gorbachev's rule and a much weaker state incapable of enforcing the law. Brutal hazing of first year-soldiers, large numbers of noncombat deaths among soldiers, terrible housing, inadequate food (leading to some deaths by malnutrition[25]), and general disregard for soldiers' well-being by commanders became major headline stories beginning in late 1988.[26] Mothers' groups and organizations for servicemen's welfare sprang up to lobby the parliament and the military leadership to change this wretched state of affairs. Proposals for an all-volunteer military were advanced, and pressure for deferments for students mounted. Draft dodging in this public climate lost much of its stigma, and it reached staggering proportions in the non-Slavic republics. Even in Russia it has been practiced on a massive scale in the 1990s.[27]

To deal with the crisis, the Russian defense ministry took a number of steps. First, it introduced voluntary contract service. Under the authority of the military service law, the number of contract soldiers and sailors for 1993 was set at 100,000 by the parliament, which promptly failed to fund adequate salaries for them.[28] For a time, the salaries of contract volunteers fell so far behind inflation that their influx declined, and only 70,000 of the authorized number were recruited. General Grachev pressed the parliament for an additional authorization of 10,000 volunteers and a salary increase to 40,000 rubles per month, which, during the summer of 1993, began to restore the flow of volunteers. Later he requested additional authorizations of contract servicemen, putting the total at 150,000 and then close to 200,000. Contract service, however, could not meet the levels needed to maintain either the present or future force structure. In the winter and spring of 1994, Grachev was seeking a minimum manning level of 2.1 million, a figure considerably above the 1.5 million level prescribed in the Law on Defense.[29] Furthermore, the higher cost of contract servicemen contributed to general inflation and to an increase in the defense budget.

The defense ministry's second step was to ask for relief from the 18-month terms of service stipulated by the new military service law. Anticipating 580,000 discharges in the fall of 1993 and a yield of only 299,000—of which half would go to the ministry of interior (MVD) and another large portion to the Border Troops and security ministry (formerly the KGB), leaving 79,000 for the armed forces— he asked the parliament to postpone until 1995 the date of effectiveness for the new service law. Even if these estimates were less than fully accurate, the potential shortfall was certain to be significant. Moreover, at least one foreign intelligence service estimated that the actual strength of the Russian military was no more than 1.2 million in the spring of 1994.[30]

Senior military leaders claimed periodically, especially in 1993, that discipline and morale were improving and that hazing and accidental deaths were much less frequent than in the past, but there are strong reasons to doubt that more than marginal improvement occurred. The shortage of enlisted personnel meant that officers were forced to perform the tasks of rank-and-file soldiers and that it was practically impossible to carry out readiness training and exercises. Except for a few organizations, such as strategic rocket units, airborne divisions, and some special divisions and brigades being readied for action as the new mobile forces, the Russian military was probably not capable of serious military operations. That inability was an inescapable consequence of the manpower crisis among the enlisted ranks.[31]

The officer corps faced two major pains. First, the withdrawal of forces from Eastern Europe and the Baltics brought scores of thousands of officers and families back to Russia, where housing was virtually unavailable. The German government's generous financing of the construction of apartments in Russia to alleviate this shortage made only a minor difference. Strong political support was periodically expressed for making adequate funds for housing available, especially by Yeltsin's critics. Yeltsin promised additional financing early in 1992, but it failed to materialize on the planned scale.[32] While Gaidar headed the government in the fall of 1992, he also promised large sums for military housing, including for retirees,[33] but he and his reformers, especially Finance Minister Boris Fedorov, consistently resisted increases in military spending, which they rightly saw as inflationary.

In truth, the construction industry simply could not produce enough housing in the right places fast enough. About 400,000 apartments were needed, and construction programs built only a few score of thousands each year. Moreover, because other social groups also needed housing, local government authorities frequently ignored defense ministry demands. The scale of the housing and social support requirements for officers and their families defied a near-term solution, and it exacerbated the withdrawal problems from Germany and the Baltic republics, where officers occasionally refused orders to move because no housing was available at their new postings.

Reductions in officer ranks increased after the collapse of the Soviet Union. In 1992, 35,000 officers were reportedly removed from active duty.[34] In early 1993, about 30,000 more in the 25- to 30-year age range were dismissed, and 200,000 had to be discharged soon afterward to meet reduction goals. Yet another 33,000 left the Russian military for service in other CIS armies.[35] Added to this turmoil was the requirement to continue to post officers in units involved in "peacekeeping" in the Caucasus and Central Asia. In early 1993, about 2,500 such repostings were facing difficulty because all other CIS countries had dropped out of the personnel system for moving officers over the whole of the former Soviet territories.[36]

Flag officer ranks also experienced large reductions, dropping in total number by more than 50 percent between 1987 and 1993. Generals and admirals became objects of criticism when public fury was unleashed on the military in 1988 and 1989. Marshal Yazov, minister of defense at that time, refused to make public the total number of flag officers; the press was left to guess the number and derided the generals in the process. Only after the breakup of the Soviet Union was the total number admitted by Grachev, who in February 1993, while explaining his staff reductions in the defense ministry, put it at 2,218. That figure, he added, was one flag officer per 1,262 enlisted personnel and 312 officers. In 1978, the ratios had been one flag officer per 530 enlisted personnel and 169 officers.[37] By the summer of 1993, however, Yeltsin was promoting new flag officers at a surprising rate, 80 in the month of June.[38]

Another complication for manpower policy was the reappearance of the Cossack tradition in Russia. Several of the old Cossack "hosts" resurfaced and appointed leaders, or atamans, who demanded formal recognition of Cossack military organizations and the land and special privileges traditionally granted to them. Yeltsin was generally supportive of their demands and actually authorized their military units for integration into the Russia military and security forces.[39] But not all military leaders were happy to have Cossack units because they presented yet another personnel and force-structure management problem in a period of great organizational turmoil.[40]

Another officer problem was caused by the old Soviet system of political officers in the Main Political Administration (MPA), a communist party structure for control and indoctrination of the military. As late as the fall of 1992, 50,000 of these officers, including 329 generals, were still at work in their old positions in the Russian military.[41] The struggle of the residual MPA apparatus to find a new mission and remain alive is a separate story, but that it did not die easily is important to note in understanding the turmoil confronting the Russian officer personnel system.

Civil-military relations, of course, have become a new problem for Russia with the passing of the old Soviet system of rigid party discipline, counterintelligence nets, and the MPA party structure. All the predictions, both in the West and in Russia, that the military would seize power have not been born out. Such warnings surged before meetings by the Congress of People's Deputies in late 1992 and in the spring of 1993, when this body appeared determined to unseat Yeltsin. General Grachev was initially hesitant to use the army to repress the uprising on 3-4 October in Moscow, prompting Yeltsin to complain about his ambiguous response and to speculate that Grachev feared that some officers might not follow his orders.[42]

How was Yeltsin able to manage the military so successfully through at least early 1994? First, both Marshal Shaposhnikov and General Grachev sided with him during the crisis of 19-23 August 1991, and for their support were rewarded with top postings. Grachev, moreover, was able to pick some of his own team in the new Russian defense ministry, and he gathered several of his old Afghan war comrades in spite of public criticism.[43] A significant number of those tainted by collaboration with the "Emergency Committee" were eased out, although no full-fledged purge occurred, in spite of sufficient evidence to support one. Thus the senior military officers remaining in most of the key command and staff posts owed loyalty to Grachev if for no other reason than his reluctance to purge them for their behavior during the coup attempt.

A second factor in Yeltsin's successful management of the military was the generals' public embarrassment following actions against the civilian population during Gorbachev's rule, especially the massacre in Tbilisi in April 1989 and the abortive intervention in Lithuania in January 1991. The generals remained aware that the majority of the public was suspicious of them, and they also knew that the poor morale of their troops made them unreliable against crowds of Russian civilians.

Third, Yeltsin raised military pay several times and promised much other support. Although he could not always keep his promises, he was on record as supportive of most military welfare demands. Perhaps the most telling act in his courting of the senior military was the promotion of 80 officers to general and admiral rank in June 1993.

Fourth, the senior officers became sharply divided after the August 1991 crisis. Many retired officers, especially those who had been expelled for involvement with the "Emergency Committee," began independent political activities of two sorts. First, they became leaders in the unofficial Officers' Assemblies, an institution recently created on an earlier model in the Tsarist army and particularly active during and after the breakup of the Soviet Union. Until the crisis with the parliament in October 1993, these retired activists frequently convened in Moscow as well as in regional cities to voice their complaints and to push political leaders for preferred policies. Second, they gained influence in the old pre-1993 Russian parliament. A group of deputies, called Army Reform, was organized under the leadership of a forcibly retired colonel, Vitalii Urazhtsev, and began to launch vicious criticism at the incumbent defense leadership.[44] General Achalov, who served as commander of the airborne forces before Grachev and who had been retired for association with the "Emergency Committee," inspired similar attacks from the Officers' Assemblies. Thus the military elites were split among themselves, the "in's" backing Yeltsin and guarding against direct political activity by the military, and the "out's" struggling to find sympathy in parliament and in political organizations. A number of the "out's" discredited themselves by participating in the 3-4 October 1993 attempt to overthrow the Yeltsin regime, but because they were later granted amnesty, they may again become a challenge to the "in's."

Fifth, during the summer and fall of 1993, Yeltsin began to give the military its way in dealing with the "near abroad," particularly in Tajikistan, Georgia, Armenia, Azerbaijan, Moldova, and Belarus. This policy tended to undermine the demands of General Achalov and other retired officers who were angry about the loss of the empire.

A unified and corporate military position vis-a-vis the Yeltsin government was never very probable. The officer corps over the past couple of decades had allowed such poor standards of officer-troop relations and such abuse of the ordinary soldier that public hostility for their privilege-conscious behavior left them without either a base of social and political support or reliable troops in numbers adequate to rule the country. They had become identified as part of the corrupt communist party bureaucracy hiding behind the elaborate propaganda machine that cranked out "patriotic education" about World War II and military glory.

That Grachev and his colleagues gained any respect for successfully keeping the military out of politics in 1992 and 1993 is doubtful. Their detractors accused them of massive corruption, and in early February 1993 the presidium of the parliament directed a committee to investigate such charges.[45] Many of the documents from this effort became weapons in the struggle for the vote in the April referendum; Vice-President Rutskoi created a mild stir when he publicly announced their existence. Both Marshal Shaposhnikov and

General Grachev were targets of the smear campaign.[46] Shaposhnikov struck back publicly, denouncing the charges and likening them to Stalin's repressions of Red Army commanders in the 1930s. Grachev had been fighting these attacks since the fall of 1992, when he discharged several officers for illegal political activities. They challenged his action in court, and Grachev eventually conceded the dispute when the court questioned his authority.[47] Moreover, some of the charges about use of German currency from equipment sales in Germany to buy Mercedes limousines were substantiated, although the extent of Grachev's involvement remained ambiguous.

In truth, corruption among the senior military had become so widespread that for Grachev and his immediate staff to have remained wholly untouched by it would have been a miracle. In such circumstances, things are relative, and relatively speaking, Grachev warded off most of the attacks. Nonetheless, corruption remained a major obstacle to his restoring the Russian military to political reliability and operational readiness. Economic realities made competition for personal income among the military elites inevitable for a long time.

This brief survey is adequate to demonstrate the depths and seriousness of the problems facing Russia's manpower policy. Indeed, the problems were so severe that merely preventing the disintegration of the Russian military in 1992-94 was no mean achievement. In addition to coping with conscription shortfalls in the fall of 1993 and the spring of 1994, Grachev also had to deal with rising manpower needs for forces to control developments in the "near abroad," particularly in Central Asia and the Transcaucasus. Contract soldiers provided a barely sufficient source of recruits for the Russian army units in these areas in 1993. Arrangements with local governments for obtaining local manpower were worked out in some cases.[48] Nonetheless, the shift in foreign policy toward regaining military hegemony within the Transcaucasus and Central Asia created huge uncertainties for future military manpower needs.

Military Industry, R&D, and Procurement Policy

Because this subject has been widely analyzed in the West, and because there is the risk that treating it here takes us away from political and military affairs to issues such as economic reform and unemployment, only a few highlights will be offered. But to provide an appropriately comprehensive picture of Russian military affairs in 1992-94, military industry, R&D, and procurement policy must be at least briefly treated. These resource issues indirectly constrain the Russian military's activities in the CIS countries, especially in Central Asia and the Transcaucasus.

The Soviet ministry of defense only reluctantly cut back on procurement, and even then against enormous resistance from the military-industrial complex. The cuts were precipitous and rapid in 1992-93. The defense ministry tried to guide the process in some respects. When Andrei Kokoshin, a civilian analyst, formerly of the USA and Canada Institute, became deputy minister of defense for military-technical policy, he began a major effort to make the changes according to a rational scheme.

In principle, Kokoshin's strategy was simple. He wanted to cut procurement dramatically, reduce the number of models of weaponry by half or more, and let most of the military- industrial plants convert to civilian production. A select few plants with the greatest potential for building a future high-technology production base would be saved and supported as state-owned industry.[49] The same approach would apply to the scientific and R&D centers. Current procurement would be designed to support the new force structure, a much smaller one emphasizing mobility and employing a corps and brigade system in place of the old army division system.[50] Such a comprehensive strategy, of course, depended on controlling and directing more than procurement and R&D policies within the ministry of defense. Accordingly, an interdepartmental council for military-technical policy was created with Kokoshin as its chairman.[51]

This "military-technical plan 2000," as Kokoshin called it, was generally consistent with the views of military theorists at the general staff academy, who were inspired by the U.S. weaponry they saw demonstrated in the Persian Gulf War to present expansive speculations on the nature of future war. Yet their image of Russian military technical needs vastly exceeded even the best possible outcome of Kokoshin's plan. The plan also fitted the larger government policy of converting to civilian production and privatization as much military industry as possible. In fact, Kokoshin insisted that defense ministry ties to military industry would, where possible, be on a market contract basis, a break with the dense network of interlocking bureaucracies in the old Soviet system. Given the decision to keep nearly 400 firms as state-owned property, however, the conversion to a market basis faced limits.[52]

There were also difficulties with restoring a purely Russian military industrial base. Although Russia inherited the lion's share of the Soviet Union's military industries—estimates range from 60 to 80 percent of production facilities and from 90 to 100 percent of the R&D facilities—key ancillary production lay outside Russia, particularly in Ukraine and Belarus. The large rocket- and nuclear-testing ranges were in Kazakhstan, and even Tajikistan had an important laser-testing and space facility. Efforts were made to retain military-industrial ties within the CIS structure, and many survived. Whether order can be restored by the year 2000 following the chaos created by the breakup of the USSR and the collapse of the economic central planning system remains at best an open question. Whether most of it is really worth saving is also debatable if the aim is to have a modern high-technology base. That such a transformation can be achieved in a government-owned sector, impervious to market forces, is most dubious. Kokoshin understood that, but some of the key sectors he desired to save would not find the markets to ensure their financial survival without state procurements.

Schemes for saving the military industries through arms exports became popular among Russian industrialists in 1992-93, but foreign markets for arms of the quality produced in Russia were not large. China proved an exception. Holding an impressive foreign trade balance in dollars, China could pay for Russian weapons in hard currency. Thus the big sales in 1993 of SU-27 fighters and other weapons to China provided a modest outlet for Russian arms production. India also continued to purchase Russian military technology and weaponry. The Indian market, however, was changing; the previous emphasis on large weapons was giving way to an emphasis on technology. Hopes for scores of billions of dollars earned from exports of Russian weapons required a much broader foreign market than Russia could possibly achieve unless the United States dropped out of the international arms market.

On the whole, conditions and prospects within the military-industrial sector in Russia made the realization of official goals virtually impossible. Both the military industrialists' image of their own capabilities and the military theorists' fantasies about high-technology armed forces and their feasibility suggest that these groups were either out of touch with their own realities or ignorant of what is required to achieve the kind of military-industrial capabilities that exist in the United States.[53] A Russian free market economy could possibly produce them within the next decade or longer, but the old central planning structure could not be revived to achieve them except through forced allocations at the expense of the rest of the economy. The political power and organization for this latter alternative did not exist in 1994, although political developments in Yeltsin's government suggested that such a plan might be attempted. Yet, toward the end of 1994, the government was still pursuing a policy of stabilizing the ruble through holding down the state budget and especially allocations to military industries. Thus the final shape that the Russian military sector would eventually take was far from decided.

Command, Control, and Force Structure

The end of the Soviet Union marked the beginning of changes in the higher levels of the command and control system, not just in force structure itself. The highly centralized structure and process of Soviet military policymaking at the top gave way to new political realities. The Communist Party's Politburo and Secretariat, which had informally but completely dominated the government military and security structures, ceased to exist with the abolition of the party. The top state military policy institution, the Defense Council, disappeared. The Military-Industrial Commission under the Council of Ministers fell into limbo as central planning of the economy decayed. The KGB and ministry of interior, considered part of the Soviet Armed Forces until fairly late in Gorbachev's rule, also faced a series of changes. Notwithstanding the appearance of dramatic changes at the highest level, most changes were quite shallow; they failed to affect significantly the political, military, security, and military-industrial structures inherited from the Soviet system. Much change amounted to little more than renaming old institutions and shifting their subordination among higher-level authorities. Still, these changes reflected new political realities that would eventually penetrate deeper into the old structures.

Making sense of these processes requires exploration of the politics driving them and of the altering institutional topography. These processes are difficult to examine comprehensively, for not only are they extensive and complex, but changes continue to take place so often that any mere naming of institutions is soon out of date. Moreover, deterioration of the old Soviet force structure will continue into the late 1990s. At the same time, rebuilding efforts at the lower levels are difficult to assess both for the lack of specific information and for their complexity and variations. The main outlines of all these processes, however, can be elucidated.

Political authority over military affairs. The formal structure of political institutions at the top of the Russian Federation was prescribed in the new constitution, which was approved by referendum on 12 December 1993. It makes the president the supreme commander of the armed forces, gives him appointive and removal powers over the military "high command" as well as the right to confer military ranks, and requires that he approve "military doctrine." In the event of a threat of aggression against the Russian Federation, he has the power to impose martial law on the whole of the federation or in individual localities. The government, controlling the ministry of defense and other so-called power ministries, is the president's implementing arm for his military duties. In the parliament, the Federation Council (i.e., the upper chamber) has jurisdiction over questions of using military force outside the borders of the Russian Federation, and it must examine all laws adopted by the Duma (i.e., the lower chamber) concerning "questions of war and peace."

This allocation of powers and responsibilities leaves unclear a number of key questions. Presumably the Federation Council is the ultimate parliamentary authority in approving military actions by the president, but the Duma apparently has some role if it can pass laws concerning "questions of war and peace." More significant may be the lack of clarity in the constitution about ultimate power of the purse. The president and the government must propose a budget to the Duma, and the Duma may revise it, but because the president can still rule by decree, including decrees on expenditures of state funds, the locus of final fiscal authority remains unclear. Moreover, authority over taxation suffers the same ambiguity. As long as much of the military industrial capacity is controlled by the state, and while the private economic sector remains small, the locus of fiscal power for military spending is uncertain.

The constitution is supplemented by the earlier Law on Defense, signed into force on 24 September 1992, which provides a far more detailed outline of the powers and duties of the new Russian military establishment.[54] The president, as commander in chief of the Russian armed forces, not only has the ultimate say on operations in wartime, but during peacetime he must approve contingency warplans, mobilization plans, and plans for technical and scientific developments, conscription callups, and mobilization of industry and society in preparation for war. He is the ultimate authority on nuclear tests and weapons employment, and he conducts negotiations and signs international security agreements. He has military promotion authority and appointment authority for all high-level defense posts, subject to approval by the parliament. He must also present statements of military doctrine to the parliament for approval.

No working consensus on presidential appointive powers was reached during 1992-93. Must the minister of defense, his deputies, and the chief of the general staff be approved by the parliament? Although the law requires such approval, Yeltsin refused to request it before the election of a new parliament under the new Russian constitution. In the political climate of 1994, however, he is likely to ask for it.

The ministry of defense and the general staff are granted executive powers for implementing the president's decisions on military affairs. The law specifies several areas of such responsibility, none exceptional, although broader in dealing with civilian sector departments than is normal in Western defense ministries. Most of these powers are direct holdovers from those granted to the Soviet defense ministry.

The Law on Defense, like the constitution, leaves the budget process ambiguous. The ministry prepares it for parliamentary approval. In the Soviet system, the Supreme Soviet formally approved the entire state budget, including the defense sector, but this action was pro forma. The Politburo made the real decisions and had them made official state policy by the Defense Council and the Supreme Soviet. With the much-expanded participation of the parliament in the Russian system, parliamentary approval of the defense budget marks a fundamental shift and division of power—at least on paper. Because the government and the State Bank can apparently extend credits and print money with impunity, and because they did so with little concern for the deficit in 1992-93, the parliament's power of the purse remains in doubt. Moreover, the sense of fiscal responsibility vis-á-vis the currency and the State Bank was stronger in the government than in the parliament during 1992-93.

Yeltsin was nonetheless able to raise military pay virtually at will with little fear of a legislative check. Until the currency becomes stable, and until public sector funding has to be paid for largely by taxes raised from the private sector according to parliamentary laws, parliamentary power of the purse will remain more formal than real. Genuine progress toward parliamentary fiscal control, however, can be no greater than the overall progress toward a market economy and public-sector finance based on taxing the private sector.

In addition to approval of the budget, the Law on Defense gives the parliament more or less the same powers held by the United States Congress, for example making laws on ranks, on branches of services, and on pay and social welfare. The parliament also has the power to remove—or impeach—the minister of defense in accordance with the constitution. The Federation Council, or upper chamber of the parliament, must approve presidential decisions to call out the armed forces, to mobilize the country, and to use nuclear weapons. And, of course, it must ratify security and arms control treaties.

In one area the Russian parliament holds potentially larger formal powers than the U.S. Congress. It must approve "military doctrine." No American president could proceed very far with changes in U.S. national security policy without informal congressional support, but the Congress does not have to write that policy into law. The Law on Defense effectively makes the whole security and military policy area a formal legal matter.

At least two factors account for this Russian peculiarity. First, such legal formalism reflects the 1992-93 struggle between the Yeltsin government and his opponents in the parliament over the proper directions for Russian military and foreign policy. Unable to defeat

Yeltsin in elections and referenda, parliamentary leaders tried to defeat his security policy by legislation. Second, the heritage of the Soviet system prompts the penchant for writing down formally the details of military policy. Although such a law never existed during the Soviet period, military doctrine enjoyed a solid ideological basis and was expressed in general terms in party documents and authoritative articles by key military leaders. Soviet "military science," based on the official ideology, needed no "bourgeois" legal foundation. With Russia's official renunciation of Marxism-Leninism and the pseudo-scientific assumptions drawn from it, both military leaders and some parliamentarians felt an understandable compulsion to find a functional equivalent for grounding Russian military policy.

The old Soviet Defense Council gave way during Gorbachev's rule to a new Presidential Council, but this never fully replaced the Defense Council or developed a clear pattern of operation. It was evident that some organ at the very apex of the state system for managing military and foreign policy was needed, one that stood above all executive agencies and ministries to ensure coordination of security policy with domestic policy, much as the U.S. National Security Council was designed to do. Apparently to that end, Yeltsin created a Russian Security Council in July 1992.[55] He did so by decree, giving it broad coordination powers across the whole of the government ministries but with emphasis on the foreign, military, and military-industrial areas. At the time, more liberal observers in Moscow considered the Security Council to be without a sound legal basis; they saw it as a potential means for ignoring the parliament and as the de facto creation of dictatorial power.[56] The Security Council is mentioned nowhere in the Law on Defense, but it does appear in the new constitution, with the president designated as its head. Its functioning, however, left much to be desired. Following his resignation as the Commander of the CIS Armed Forces in June 1993, Marshal Shaposhnikov was appointed chairman of the Security Council. After nearly two months in that office, Shaposhnikov was complaining publicly that Yeltsin paid little attention to the Security Council and that it was not allowed to coordinate interministerial affairs of defense, security, and foreign policy.[57] In early August 1993 he resigned, citing his frustration with Yeltsin's handling of the council and also noting parliamentary opposition to his appointment.[58]

Thereafter, Yeltsin appointed several deputies to the Security Council, each heading an interdepartmental commission for a functional area; apparently each had not only a staff and coordinating power but also executive power, thus creating potential for conflict with government ministries as deputies exercised their executive roles.[59]

The ministries concerned with military and security affairs are next in the system of command and control. Under the Soviet system, the security and intelligence institutions were all militarized, uniformed, and staffed with personnel with military ranks. The ministry of interior (MVD) and the Committee for State Security (KGB) were large, complex, and deployed throughout the society. The ministry of defense embraced all the military institutions, including not only the military services and military districts, but also construction units, railroad units, and sponsorship over the largest public mass organization in the Soviet Union, the Voluntary Society for Assistance to the Army, Aviation, and the Fleet (DOSAFF). Military institutions also had tentacles in military-industrial and scientific institutions, although not direct command over them. The restructuring of this enormous institutional labyrinth—security, intelligence, and military—is an equally enormous and complex story unto itself, but the main outlines had begun to emerge by the end of the second year of the Russian Federation.

The security and intelligence establishment. Marked continuities between the old Soviet system and the new Russian security and intelligence establishment are to be expected. The MVD remains in operation both formally and substantively. Although the KGB has been formally abolished, all the KGB's subparts have survived, some now autonomous, most of them merely relocated.[60] What follows is a brief survey of some of the major institutions of the security and intelligence establishment.

The ministry of security, probably the most powerful of these institutions, was essentially the descendant of the old KGB, which had absorbed the majority of its directorates. It lasted only until January 1994. The ministry of security included internal counterintelligence (the KGB Second Directorate), military counterintelligence (the KGB Third Directorate), transportation security, surveillance, economic and industrial security, counternarcotics, security for key government buildings and command bunkers, as well as mail intercep-

tion, counterterrorism (formerly the KGB Fifth Directorate for political repression), and the old KGB Higher School.

Just before President Clinton's visit to Moscow in January 1994,
Yeltsin abolished the ministry of security, renaming it the Federal
Counterintelligence Service, and reducing its personnel from 137,000
to 75,000.[61] This reduction was accomplished in part by removing
subunits from its control. Its investigative arm was moved to the
office of the State Procuracy, and the Lefortovo Prison, notorious
for holding political prisoners, was moved to the ministry of interior.
Most of the personnel were not dismissed but merely transferred to
the Main Guards Directorate and the Federal Communications Agency
already directly under Yeltsin's control. The political motive for this
reorganization was related to Yeltsin's concern for control over the
security forces, and although the change was heralded as the genuine and final breakup of the residual old KGB, it merely split up that
structure and moved over 60,000 personnel to agencies directly under the president and hence outside parliamentary oversight.

The Border Troops, another KGB subcommand, were subordinate to the ministry of security. The troops were responsible not
only for Russian Federation borders but also for some of the CIS
states that still depended on Russia for border controls. With the
abolition of the ministry of security the Border Troops became an
independent command under the president. The old Border Troops'
structure has been maintained on the outer perimeter of the CIS,
with Russia paying most of the costs associated with maintaining
Russian control over these external borders. In Tajikistan, the civil
war and the involvement of Afghans has made the task difficult,
causing Russia to request assistance from Kyrgyzstan and
Uzbekistan. Both have sent battalions, but the troops have proven
too poorly trained to be of use, and the job remains in Russian hands.[62]
Kazakhstan, Kyrgyzstan, Turkmenistan, and Uzbekistan each have
bilateral arrangements for Russian Border Troops on the CIS frontier. Similarly, Border Troops have been kept in Armenia on the border with Turkey; in Azerbaijan they remain on the frontier with Iran.
Arrangements in Moldova and western Ukraine are cloudy. The
Border Troops, of course, have been displaced in the Baltic states,
sometimes with violence during 1992-94.

The External Intelligence Service (SVR), headed by Yevgenii

Primakov, is new as a separate agency and is concerned only with foreign-intelligence collection. It is, clearly, the old KGB First Directorate. Defections and reductions in resources have forced alterations in its activities, but it still runs most of its traditional operations with emphasis on Western states. Although the SVR publicly insists that it has abandoned "active measures," one observer notes that the active-measures part of the now defunct Central Committee Secretariat's International Department currently resides in the SVR.[63]

Another newly independent structure is the Federal Agency for Government Communications and Information. It consists of the old KGB Eighth Directorate (codes and ciphers) and the Sixteenth Directorate (signals intelligence), and its spokesmen declare it to be equivalent to the U.S. National Security Agency. In fact it is considerably different in that it has large domestic surveillance responsibilities and far less to do with support to the ministry of defense.

Yet another new organization is the Main Guards Directorate. Composed of the KGB Ninth Directorate and the KGB Seventh Directorate, it provides personal security for high-level government officials and foreign dignitaries, and it also includes the old MVD guard unit that now serves the Russian parliament. After the crisis with the parliament on October 3-4 1993, the parliament lost all control of its guards, and the new organization reports to the president alone.

Finally, the ministry of interior, or MVD, continues to function with only minor changes. A large institution consisting of all the police, central and local, as well as the Internal Troops (units organized on regular military lines up to the division level), it carries the primary burden of ensuring domestic law and order. After Yeltsin's close call with putting down parliamentary forces in October 1993, and in light of hesitancy among officers in the ministry of defense to respond vigorously in quelling outbreaks of violence, Yeltsin began beefing up the Internal Troops so that they alone can handle any such future crises. In many ways the ministry of security looked redundant to the MVD, especially its counterintelligence and several security missions. In fact, the only apparent reason for not folding most of these missions into the MVD would seem to be the political difficulty of completely abolishing a large part of the old KGB apparatus.

Because the MVD and several of the KGB's directorates, particularly the Second Directorate for civil counterintelligence, were organized on the old Soviet civil executive administrative territorial basis (i.e., Soviet republics, oblasts, and districts), they have experienced serious disruption with the breakup of the Soviet Union. Their components in the new states have been largely taken over by those governments, but their break with the Moscow center has varied from republic to republic. In the Central Asian states, relations with Moscow remain close if mutually suspicious, and most have been regulated by bilateral treaties. In the Transcaucasus, the rupture has been much greater, as it has been in Ukraine, Moldova, and most completely in the Baltic states. Belarus apparently retains close ties to Moscow, although they are, de jure, at odds with the Belarus constitutional declaration of neutrality. The breakup along CIS lines left many Russians, Belarusians, and Ukrainians as serving officers in non-Russian MVD and old KGB organizations. Again, this is most conspicuously true for the Central Asian republics.

The military establishment. Turning to the major part of the security establishment, the ministry of defense, the continuities with the old Soviet system are equally striking. For example, the following institutions still exist within the ministry of defense in spite of considerable restructuring:

- the general staff as the defense minister's working organ for control of all military organizations and their activities;
- the regional system of military districts, although now fewer in number through the loss of territory with the dissolution of the USSR;
- the system of five service branches;[64]
- the system of military schools and academies for training officers;
- the system of military commissariats at local levels to administer conscription and reserve affairs;
- paramilitary and preservice military training of the old DOSAAF public mass organization, now converted to ROSTO, but with essentially the same structure and activities;
- Civil Defense Troops, associated with the civil government

executive line from Moscow to oblasts and lower levels, continued as a disaster assistance agency;[65]
- Railroad Troops, which continue to function as in the past;
- Construction Troops, which although formally retained were apparently to be phased out.

The changes in Russia's military establishment, however, are no less striking. Beginning with the ministry of defense itself, the shift toward a market economy and market relations with military industries caused a dramatic rupture in the ministry's relations with the Military-Industrial Commission and its subordinate ministries. The nine defense-industrial ministries, controlling about 60,000 enterprises, are gone.[66] Only about 10 to 15 percent were to remain as government owned and therefore administratively related to the ministry of defense.[67] This figure will probably turn out to be too low, since privatization was slowing down in 1994. Nonetheless, the structure of the defense ministry was changing fundamentally as it lost most of the vast corps of "military representatives" of its procurement and R&D apparatus, which had helped to control and guide the old military-industrial complex. Undoubtedly, some of the apparatus survives and will continue to function, but the scale is being reduced radically. The new Law on Defense permits the appointment of a civilian defense minister, although the decision to use that authority has been put off at least through 1995.[68] One civilian deputy minister of defense, Andrei Kokoshin, was appointed, however, setting a precedent.

Grachev reported in the fall of 1992 that the central apparatus, including the ministry and the general staff, had been cut by 27 percent.[69] This included not just personnel but 41 directorates and 140 departments ("sectors," or subunits of directorates). Thus a considerable slimming of the military bureaucracy was occurring.

The *operational command structure* of the Soviet system included four "high commands" between the level of military districts (MDs) and groups of forces and fleets. These apparently were abolished. Two groups of forces remained in 1992-94, the Western Group in Germany and one in the Baltic region, the old Baltic Military District. The Western Group of Forces disappeared when all Russian forces left Germany in late 1994. The final date for closing out the group in the Baltic states remained a matter of negotiation in early 1994, but it has rapidly diminished as Russian forces left those states in the fall. The first echelon of military districts—Belarusian, Carpathian, and Kiev—were lost, and with it the most modern and combat-ready ground and air forces. The Odessa MD was also gone. In the Caucasus, the Transcaucasus MD broke up after futile efforts to save it, and the Northern Caucasus MD, on Russian territory, was in the process of becoming a "first-echelon" district in the spring of 1993.

The Central Asian and Turkestan MDs no longer exist because they are not on Moscow's territory, and thus their apparatuses have had to disband or adapt to new bilateral arrangements. Russian officers moved into key roles in the Uzbek defense ministry in Tashkent, where the Turkestan MD headquarters had been, and the small Uzbek military remained heavily dependent on Russian weapons and supply in early 1994.[70] Turkmenistan essentially gave its military defense to the Russian military on commission, making only long-term plans to handle that role by itself.[71] Kazakhstan struggled throughout 1992-93 to establish significant military institutions of its own, including air forces, ground forces, and a military schooling system.[72] Kyrgyzstan took only formal steps toward creating a military establishment in 1992; it has retained its dependency on the Russian military because, in the view of its president, the costs of creating its own forces were too high.[73] Tajikistan remained virtually a Russian military colony, engaged in civil war and dependent on the Russian forces there for its government's survival. After the losses of most of the old Soviet military districts, the Russian Federation was left with the Moscow, Ural, Volga, Siberia, Transbaikal, and Far Eastern Military Districts.

The loss of the Central Asian and Turkestan MDs was highly disruptive to several aspects of the old Soviet military structure. The air defense and space warning installations in Central Asia were integral to the all-union Soviet aerospace defense system. Not only strategic nuclear forces but key ranges for space, missile, and nuclear testing were located in Kazakhstan. Significant military aircraft industry was in Tashkent, and numerous Soviet officer and pilot training schools were in Central Asia.

Of the four fleets belonging to the *Navy*, the Northern and Pacific were the least affected by the dissolution of the USSR. The Baltic Fleet slowly rebased itself in Kaliningrad, St. Petersburg, and a few other ports still in Russian hands, although Russian negotiators continued to seek naval basing arrangements in the Baltic states. The Black Sea Fleet became the symbol of Ukrainian sovereignty in its dispute with Russia. How the dispute will finally be resolved is anybody's guess, but the fleet's combat utility, never very great, rapidly declined after the breakup of the USSR. Disputes arose over control of the Caspian Sea flotilla, but it was too small to be of significance for residual Russian naval power.

The breakup of the *Strategic Rocket Forces* led to disputes among Russia, Ukraine, Belarus, and Kazakhstan. Ukraine, the major opponent of returning these forces to Russia, showed signs of trying to become a nuclear power in its own right, but such an effort will require considerably more technical infrastructure and personnel than it now possesses. (Russian technicians remain essential to Ukraine-based weapons.) In any case, U.S. mediation and financial aid in 1993-94 appear to have produced a Ukrainian commitment to give up all nuclear weapons in return for U.S. cash and Russian nuclear fuel for Ukrainian power stations. This complex matter, which includes such issues as new kinds of nuclear weapons, reductions planned under START agreements, new ideas about policy for nuclear-weapons use in the discussions on military doctrine, and, of course, the continuing struggle between Russia and Ukraine over the control and disposition of nuclear weapons, deserves a separate study of its own and is, therefore, noted only in passing here.

As the defense ministry tried to impose new order on its nuclear forces, emphasis fell on the newer model ICBM, the SS-25, which is a mobile, single-warhead system. In February 1994, the Russian press reported that SS-25s and a follow-on variant would compose 30 to 40 percent of the missile force and would be deployed on about 900 mobile launchers (a number below the START limits).[74] The remainder of the ICBMs would be based in silos. The only mention of submarine-based missiles concerned their unreliability. Apparently, then, the Strategic Rocket Forces were using the START reductions to get rid of the older systems; placing primary reliance on the newer land-based mobile system, they were leaving the future of the submarine-based part of the force in question, or perhaps subject to a longer-term modernization aimed at greater reliability and a smaller number. Frequent mention of "third generation" nuclear warheads by the military theorists at the general staff academy also suggested that the Strategic Rocket Forces would continue a program of improved warhead design and performance. Given the defense ministry's obsession with remaining a world-class military power, emphasis on maintaining and modernizing the rocket forces was to be expected.

The *Air Defense Forces* (PVO) experienced major disruption as a consequence of the Soviet breakup. The Baku Air Defense District, never very modern, was lost. The Moscow Air Defense District, including the ABM site, was to undergo a 10 to 15 percent reduction in its capacity to handle attacks.[75] All these changes, however, were minor compared to the breakup of the network of radar warning systems, which included many sites on non-Russian territory, particularly in the Baltic states, Belarus, Ukraine, and Moldova in the west, but also in Central Asia. The early warning radar system for missile attacks also suffered the loss of several key installations in these regions.

The PVO issue is also related to the civilian air control system because it performed the lion's share of civil air control in the Soviet system. The breakup of the system came at a time when major modernization programs were in progress, aimed at bringing the air control system closer to international standards.[76]

The PVO was the service responsible for the Soviet ABM system, and, as such, was the "aerospace" service. Space programs fell almost entirely to the ministry of defense, although the Soviet Academy of Sciences was also involved in their oversight. A civil department, the Russian Space Agency, has now been established outside the defense ministry.[77] Intended to work with the Academy of Sciences as well as a number of ministries, it received R51 billion funding in 1992. The Russian military clearly will keep a strong hold on Russian space programs through the PVO, but the creation of a civil space agency could represent a significant change because it will probably limit programs through competition over funding.

The *Air Forces,* which depended on the PVO air-control system, faced many of the same problems as the Air Defense Forces in the breakup. Many of the most modern frontal aviation bases were in the western military districts; many of the aviation schools were also in the west, with some in Central Asia. The units Russia retained were woefully short on flying time because of fuel shortages, and they were further constrained in their operations by the poor availability of spare parts. In principle, Russia could move most of the aircraft to its own territory, but accommodating such redeployments would require large new investments in bases, support equipment, and family housing.

The *Ground Forces,* by far the largest component of the old Soviet military structure, have been rent asunder. Some 200 divisions and the controlling army, frontal, and high command structures declined rapidly following the breakup. The original requirement for this large force structure is obviously gone, and although published figures are difficult to find, considerably more than half the divisions must have been withdrawn, demobilized, or taken over by other CIS states.[78] Of the 37 large training areas for these forces, 16 were lost, and only one of the remaining sites can handle division-scale exercises.[79]

How to restructure ground forces in particular and the armed forces in general became a constant concern of the military theorists at the general staff academy. They had to consider severe limitations on defense spending, the disintegration of much of the old force structure, the dramatic technological changes in U.S. weaponry as demonstrated in the Persian Gulf War, and the new changed geographical situation after the USSR breakup. The following were among the commonly mentioned ideas for creating a new force structure:

- Creation of a strong mobile force that could move to any threatened sector of Russia's new frontiers. Only very limited forces, not adequate to throw back a serious invader, were to be kept near the frontiers.
- Creation of specially organized and trained peacemaking forces for use in maintaining stability within troubled regions of the CIS.
- Abandonment of the old ground-force structure based on divisions and armies in favor of a system of corps and brigades. Employing smaller units, this system would allow more command and control and be better suited to highly mobile operations.

- Creation of two or three regional joint commands in key areas, namely in the Far East and the North Caucasus. (The role of military districts, formerly combined arms commands on the level of a "front," remained ambiguous in this concept.)
- Shifting away from the historical dependency on tank units in large numbers capable of extensive offensive operations into the heart of Europe.

The rationale for this last concept is twofold. First, the mission of invading Europe has vanished. Second, views on the role of the tank changed as Russian theorists began to argue that high-technology weaponry made it possible to achieve the desired operational objectives with few or no large tank formations. The U.S. military experience in the Persian Gulf War, particularly U.S. air operations, was frequently cited to buttress this view, although the ground phase of the war should throw doubt on ideas as radical as those now being expressed by Russian theorists about the obsolete character of heavy ground forces.

Modest first steps in the creation of a strategic mobile force have reportedly been taken. The commander of the airborne forces in March 1993, Colonel General Yevgenii Podkolzin, said they were to be based in the Volga and Ural Military Districts and that the airborne divisions would compose 60 percent of the structure.[80] In other words, the airborne units would form the core of a mobile force, but heavier ground units and supporting arms would be added.

New "peacemaking" units were also included in the mobile force. In the spring of 1992, small units for "peacemaking" or "peacekeeping" were formed and sent to Yugoslavia (as part of the UN force there), to Southern Ossetia, and to the Dniester Republic in eastern Moldova.[81] Stripped of all artillery, tanks, and other large weapons, supported only with intelligence, communications, and engineering capabilities, these infantry units have armored fighting vehicles and trucks for transportation. They are indeed too lightly armed for more than peacekeeping missions. Composed only of volunteers, they receive large pay bonuses and two days' credit for each day of service on an actual mission.[82]

Clearly, the creation of a significant mobile force will take a long time, and it will demand a solution to the strategic lift problem. The old Soviet military air- transport fleet was generally estimated to be able to lift approximately one complete airborne division at a time. Many more modern transport aircraft will be needed to make this new mobile force deployable on an effective schedule in a crisis.

Pronouncements about changing the structure of ground forces from "army and division" to "corps and brigade" were numerous, but evidence about progress toward this transition is lacking. Likely that is because little or no progress was made in 1992-93. Such a major change would in the best of circumstances require several years to effect. It would require not only organizational change but also changes in weaponry in order to be effective. Many of the performance characteristics of Soviet ground-force weapons were designed specifically for the large, massed, armor formations assaulting NATO forces. Their adaptability to a more mobile corps-brigade structure and different tactics could prove limited because they would require such large airlift capacity for rapid deployment.

In the meanwhile, Grachev appeared bent on establishing a set of new, regionally focused, unified commands that would integrate all branches and kinds of forces within them for conduct of operations. He first mentioned this change during a visit to the Far East in April 1993.[83] Komsomolsk-na-Amure was named as the location for one such command, including the Pacific Fleet; another command, including all the forces in the Transbaikal and Siberian Military Districts, was to be at Ulan Ude. Both were to be operative by 1995. This change was a rational response to the fact that much of the old Soviet regional command structure was abolished or inappropriate for the new conditions. The general staff would be left to manage operations at fairly low levels with an enormous span of control. For the Far East and most of Siberia, that simply would not be practical.

Another such command appeared to be in the making in the Northern Caucasus. During a visit to the Military District headquarters in Rostov-na-Donu in February 1993, Grachev declared that this historically low-priority district must be made a "first-echelon" one. At least four factors were at work in this decision. First, the Transcaucasus MD was collapsing and was no longer viable as an institution on foreign territory. Second, the local violence and civil strife among non-Russian ethnic groups on Russian Federation territory, as well as in Georgia, Azerbaijan, and Armenia, were creating major security concerns. Third, forces previously deployed in the Transcaucasus that had survived "privatization" were moving to the North Caucasus MD,[84] and forces returning from Germany were being routed to the North Caucasus instead of planned destinations like Baltic garrisons. Fourth, of less importance for the command structure but potentially a troublesome force-structure development, Cossack units were being included in the forces of the Northern Caucasus MD.[85] In the course of 1993, during which Russia supported the Abkhazian insurrection against Georgia and pressed Shevardnadze to bring Georgia into the CIS and to allow permanent stationing of Russian military units on the Georgian-Turkish frontier, the strategic situation changed. As a result, the "first echelon" of Russian defense would be advanced once again to the border with Turkey if Georgia could be compelled to agree to permanent Russian military bases near the frontier.

Unlike other more advanced ideas on proper force structure for the high-technology world, these command changes were urgent, near-term, and probably attainable. Discussion of the end of the tank's relevance for modern warfare had arisen a few times before the collapse of the USSR, both in Russia and in the West. But reports of the death of the tank, especially in the Russian military, are greatly exaggerated. Large numbers exist and will remain on the scene for a long time. High-technology systems that might (or might not) make them obsolete simply cannot be produced in significant numbers, if at all, by Russian industry in the next decade. The tank is also likely to be a part of the most advanced Western armies as well.

A few other changes are worth noting briefly. The large military-education structure, consisting of over 162 college-level commissioning schools and higher-level academies, had to be radically reshaped. Forty-seven of them were located in other CIS states and were thus lost to Russia.[86] Their yield of new officers had to be cut back, and their curricula had to be revised to eliminate indoctrination in Marxism-Leninism. The system of preservice military training in secondary schools survived, if in poorer shape, and the fairly important preservice specialty training provided by DOSAAF clubs and schools was kept under the new name ROSTO (Russian Defense, Sport, and Technical Society).[87]

Surprisingly, *Civil Defense Troops* were retained, apparently because Yeltsin intervened in the drafting of the Law on Defense. Why he did so is not clear. They present an added cost that might have been eliminated by turning over their mission to the ministry of interior and its system of fire fighters.

Railroad Troops and *Construction Troops,* for a time slated to be abolished, survived, although in smaller numbers. What will eventually become of them is not clear, but public hatred of the Construction Troops because of their abuses of soldiers, especially ethnic minorities, makes them not simply unpopular but virtually impossible to staff with conscripts. Grachev suggested that they be allowed to die out as the remaining troops complete their service.[88] Perhaps they will.

Finally, the *military commissariats,* with offices at every local district level, still exist and conduct military conscription, sponsorship of ROSTO, preservice military training in schools, and reserve affairs. Their powers are now somewhat limited by dependency on local authorities, a reason given in some cases for their poor record in finding and drafting conscripts.

Russian Military Strategy

Military strategy is potentially a loose category, so being specific about what it includes is important. Here it means the use of military power, not only in wartime to defeat enemies, but also in peacetime to support diplomacy and strategic and conventional deterrence, and generally to exert influence outside one's borders. Decisions about weapons development, schedules, procurement patterns, and related issues are also a part of military strategy because they determine when, where, how, and to what degree a state will be prepared for war. Timing in these matters is central to effective military strategy. Finally, a state's military strategy should in principle be geared to support its foreign policy.

In light of this definition, what can be said of Russian military strategy? Does it exist? Is it geared to foreign policy? Do Russian military capabilities make its implementation feasible?

Warplans and contingencies. During the Soviet period, especially its last three decades, a complex array of warplans was developed and practiced. The European "theaters of military operations" (TVDs) had priority, but the Far East and the Southern TVDs also received intensive attention. Four "groups of forces" in East Europe played the key role in warplans for an offensive into Western Europe, and a smaller deployment of ground and air forces in Mongolia played a role in Far East warplans. While less is known about plans and strategies for Soviet use of ICBMs, SLBMs, and intercontinental bombers with nuclear weapons, highly developed operational plans were surely devised for these forces, not only to support contiguous theater warplans but also to strike noncontiguous theaters, namely the United States.[89] Naval forces also created a strategy underpinned by contingency plans. The navy's first priority was protection of the submarine fleet with SLBMs, that is, the strategic nuclear-missile capability based at sea. The Northern Fleet in the Barents Sea and the Arctic Ocean as well as the Pacific Fleet in the Sea of Okhotsk and the Sea of Japan carried this contingency mission. The Baltic and Black Sea Fleets were of much less importance, designed to protect the Soviet littoral and to assist ground force offensives in Central Europe and in Southern Europe. The Air Defense Forces (PVO), including Aerospace Defense Forces (VKO) that were never publicly acknowledged but were within the PVO, were designed and deployed to defend the entirety of the Soviet Union. Their operational plans were based on maintaining a high level of readiness for a U.S. attack, with no potential for offensive action.

Overall, Soviet warplans rested on the assumption that the Soviet Union would seize the offensive in all theaters from the beginning of conflict. Marshal Ogarkov, while he was chief of the general staff in the early 1980s, initiated attention to "multi-variant" warplans, meaning that some TVDs could be on the defensive initially, but in general the offense continued to dominate Soviet warplanning right up to the end of 1990.[90] The breakup of the Soviet Union and the withdrawal of the groups of forces from East Europe, the Baltic states, and Mongolia made most of the old warplans irrelevant. They no longer determined deployment of ground forces, which were not sufficiently ready to implement them. While the Northern and Pacific Fleets, unlike the Baltic and Black Sea Fleets, were not rent asunder by political struggles concerning territorial sovereignty over their bases, their drop in readiness made their old warplans difficult if not impossible to implement. The PVO and the air forces lost their coherence entirely, making them of marginal value for defensive contingencies. The same was true for a large part of the Strategic Rocket Forces that were deployed in Belarus, Ukraine, and Kazakhstan, although those in Russia were probably kept at usable readiness levels and still targeted according to the old warplans.

This new situation left the Russian military with virtually no implementable warplans other than hasty variants for defense of Russian territory itself. Progress in developing new warplans confronted several difficulties in 1992-94. First, the state of manning and readiness of residual ground and air forces was extremely low. The navy and the Strategic Rocket Forces probably suffered less degradation, but they too confronted readiness problems. Moreover, the PVO was broken up as a coherent system because of the loss of territory. Second, reorganization proceeded slowly while General Grachev redesigned the higher levels of the command structure. Third, there was no clear adversary against which to plan for war. Fourth, there was no official state military doctrine providing a legal basis for claims on resources for new military missions. Fifth, the resources available were limited and declining.

To infer the general directions of Russian warplanning with certainty is difficult, but the efforts to create new mobile forces suggest a defensive-offensive strategy. No longer could large ready forces be maintained in all contiguous TVDs. The most that could be done, apparently, was creation of forces that could be moved swiftly to any region of military action on Russia's border or into neighboring CIS countries. The struggle to create a CIS military system, i.e., a system treating the CIS as a "single military space," appears to have failed entirely by mid-1992. Yet six republics joined in a collective security treaty in May 1992, and Russian pressure to increase the number continued into 1994. As the defense ministry's preferences in foreign policy for the "near abroad" began to win support from the foreign minister in the summer of 1993, and with the formal promulgation in November 1993 of a new military doctrine stating Russia's strong interest in the ethnic-Russian population in other CIS republics and the Baltic states, an inchoate strategy became apparent. While a CIS armed forces had proven impractical to create, Russia did not give up on tying the CIS into a common military system.

The degree to which such a strategy was consciously conceived and followed in 1993-94 has been disputed. Some observers have insisted that Russian involvement in Tajikistan, the Transcaucasus, Moldova, Crimea, and elsewhere was not a coherent strategy but rather the consequence of "rogue" military commanders at local levels and the vicissitudes of CIS politics.[91] More careful and comprehensive analyses, however, have found evidence for a conscious and coordinated strategy aimed at restoring to Russian control most, if not all, of the old Soviet Union, including the Baltic states. One study, published in early 1994, found Russia "trying to recreate the former economic and military union it once dominated."[92] The analysis of Russian institutional and policy developments in chapter one strongly corroborates these judgments, making it difficult to explain Russian military strategy and foreign policy as benign, without imperial purpose, or merely the consequence of random developments and forces beyond the government's control. Random events and fortune were certainly in evidence, but as any student of war knows, even the most focused, strong-willed, and assertive strategies finally depend to some degree on unanticipated events, unexpected circumstances, and pure fortune for their outcomes.

Until mid-1993, it was possible to argue cogently that debate was taking place both on a range of foreign policies (as described in the earlier foreign policy section) and on a range of notions about proper military strategies (as described in the military doctrine section). To the extent that a set of actions by the Russian government adds up to a strategic gambit in one or another realm of military affairs, e.g., arms control, nuclear-weapons policy, threatening conventional-force deployments, or schedules for R&D and procurement of advanced weapons, it tilted heavily to the liberal side. The strategy's outward manifestations in Moscow's relations with the "far abroad" seemed more closely aligned with the aims set forth in the foreign ministry working document than with those contained in the document on military doctrine produced in the defense ministry. Conservative and reactionary forces slowed Russia's normalization of relations with Japan by insisting on no concessions on the Northern Territories, and they caused ambivalence in Russia's policy toward former Yugoslavia. Yet military aircraft were withdrawn from the Kurile islands, and a Russian battalion was sent to the UN peacekeeping force in the Balkans.

These small, symbolic steps reflected a determination by the Russian government to become part of the Western community of liberal industrial states. Even the conservative forces in the Russian parliament made no case for isolation, and their ideas about a special Russian development path were too vague for programmatic action. All sides agreed that Russia should have the most modern military possible, one on a technological level with that of the United States. How to get the industrial base required to equip such a military remained a matter of dispute; some of the old military-industrial complex bureaucrats believed that limited economic reform was needed, while the liberals were determined to introduce market forces broadly, even in most of the military-industrial sector.

The evolution of Russian policy in the "near abroad," specifically the Transcaucasus and Central Asia, and the increased role of the Russian military in many of the conflicts in these republics, have been described at length in chapter one. Beyond Central Asia and the Transcaucasus, Ukraine could also fall into this military trap of Russian imperial reassertion. The existence of separatists in Crimea, the Black Sea Fleet dispute, Russian dominance in the Transdniester Republic, the large Russian population in eastern Ukraine, and Ukraine's internal political fragmentation offer a host of opportunities for Russian forces to be inserted under the appearances of peacemaking. In January 1994, Belarus and Russia agreed to reunite their economies.[93] Already tied tightly to Russia in military relations, Belarus moved closer to outright annexation by Moscow. The price to Russia was not small; it granted Belarus concessionary energy prices and gave the Belarus state bank permission to create rubles. As a result, Russian inflation increased, and the Russian finance minister, Boris Fedorov, quit in protest. The driving forces behind this attempt to make Belarus part of the Russian Federation were military industrialists in both states who opposed privatization and the destruction of the command economy, especially for the military industrial sector. As of late 1994, however, the planned merger of the two economies had not occurred, although the idea was still very much alive.

Within the "near abroad," only the Baltic states were able to retain their independence from Russia and to remain outside the CIS.

Russian forces were withdrawn from Lithuania, and all but very small elements were withdrawn from Latvia and Estonia in early 1994. These withdrawals were made grudgingly, and were marked by sharp disputes and Russian threats as well as demands for retention of some naval- and air-defense facilities, but they were nonetheless carried out. Political instruments rather than military links became Moscow's primary means for trying to retain a foothold in these states. As the Russian foreign minister, Kozyrev, moved away from his earlier liberal foreign policy, he competed with reactionary Russian nationalists in defending the rights of Russian settlers living in the Baltic states, making threats against and intimidating Estonia and Latvia. Lithuania, having a much smaller Russian population than these two countries, was less vulnerable to that strategy.

Beyond the territories of the former Soviet Union, Moscow began to show its hand again in Eastern Europe in the fall of 1993. After Yeltsin told Poland and the Czech Republic in July 1993 that Russia would not object to their joining NATO, he promptly reversed himself. General Grachev was outspoken in his objection to an expanded NATO, declaring that Poland was a military threat to Russia. As the January 1994 NATO summit meeting approached, and as the Visegrad group of four Central European states[94] lobbied hard for admittance to NATO, Moscow faced the prospect that indeed they might be admitted. What role Moscow actually played in denying them membership is ambiguous. Several NATO states did not favor their admittance for reasons unrelated to Russia, but U.S. official statements included domestic Russian politics as a factor in rejecting them. Whatever the facts, Russian hardliners could claim afterwards that Russian resistance had prevented NATO expansion and kept Eastern Europe open for greater Russian influence.

In the latter half of 1993 and early 1994, then, Russian strategy, using a mix of diplomacy, economic instruments, and military forces that had not been withdrawn from several of the CIS countries, was taking a new and offensive shape. While not everyone in Moscow supported it, and some voices, including the deputy minister of defense, General Boris Gromov, occasionally warned that the involvement in Tajikistan could become another Afghanistan, the general political climate had swung in favor of expansionism. Opinion about what countries this policy ought to be applied to, however, remained divided, ranging from only the CIS to include the Baltic states, and perhaps even Eastern Europe.

Given Russia's objective military weakness, its successes by 1994 were impressive. They resulted not so much from renewed Russian military capabilities (although these contributed in the case of Grachev's continuing to maintain and support Russian forces in Tajikistan and the Transcaucasus) as from the internal weaknesses of the victim states. Left alone, these states would have had difficulties, including civil wars, but Russian meddling intentionally increased those conflicts. This is indisputably so in the cases of Abkhazia and Nagorno-Karabakh, but other civil conflicts were also probably worsened by Russia schemes for dividing and conquering. The Fergana Valley, where Kyrgyz and Uzbek populations live in mixed communities on both sides of the border, experienced a period of violence that Presidents Karimov and Akayev were ultimately able to suppress, but officials in both countries told the authors in December 1993 that the Russians had been guilty of provoking that violence. In Tajikistan, Russian policy has been not to reconcile the warring parties by forcing the regime to open political participation to the whole population but rather to back the government's policy of exclusion. That policy, of course, makes it imperative to maintain the Russian military presence.

Russian strategy for restoring military power in the form of new and modernized forces remains clouded. The evidence available on policies for military industry and for changes in force structure suggest a number of conflicting factors keeping it from taking a coherent shape. First, an intelligible strategy cannot be developed unless the overall Russian economy is put back on its feet. Whether that will be done by continuing the transition to a market system was thrown into serious doubt in the winter of 1993-94, when the new parliament convened and most of the market reformers left the government. A revival of parts of the old command economic system could have a number of possible results: it could deny the economy any serious technological improvement and therefore limit military modernization; it could produce hyperinflation, growing discontent, and another period of attempted market reforms; or it could produce a mixed system in which most heavy industry remained state-owned while light industry and commerce enjoyed a market arrangement—

a system similar to that of several Third World states including Egypt and Brazil. That variant, however, could not meet the demands of the kind of military modernization envisioned by the military theorists in the general staff academy.

In any case, the deputy defense minister for these matters, Andrei Kokoshin, was trying to reduce the size of the old military-industrial structure, saving its most advanced parts, reducing the redundancy in types of weapons, and clearing the way for serious progress in developing new systems toward the end of the 1990s. In the best event, a significant modernization of Russian forces is virtually impossible in the 1990s, and remains very unlikely even in the early 2000s.

Modernizing weapons and equipment, of course, requires large capital investments for R&D and procurement. The market reformers, in struggling to stabilize the currency, made strenuous attempts to hold down, even reduce, military spending in 1992-94. Nonetheless, pressures for higher military pay and compensation to discharged officers drove up military spending during this period. As was pointed out earlier, moreover, General Grachev announced that he would not reduce military manpower to 1.5 million as planned. He instead advocated a ceiling of 2.1 million, a level foreclosing the fiscal relief offered by the lower number. The conflict between maintaining a larger force structure and pursuing modernization, then, was far from resolved in early 1994.

The military theorists in the general staff academy were at this time advancing comprehensive ideas about the nature of future war, especially in light of the new military technologies displayed by U.S. forces in the Persian Gulf War.[95] Space-based weapons, advanced air forces, precision munitions, and information warfare systems bulked large in their writings. The implication was that Russian forces must have such technologies. Yet neither the Russian industrial base nor the necessary manpower skills were available, nor are they likely to be at any time in the 1990s.

This reality led to military thinking about how the Russian military might in the meanwhile compensate for the lack of such capabilities. Reequipping ICBMs with advanced conventional munitions and so-called third-generation nuclear warheads was one proposal.[96] New kinds of nuclear weapons in conjunction with a rejection of the no-first-use policy was another. More mobile conventional ground forces was yet another.

These areas of Russian strategy—force modernization and adaptation of weapons already available, size of forces, and readiness levels—were in serious disarray in early 1994 and were unlikely to be worked out completely in the near term.

Russian strategy concerning arms control was also somewhat confused, probably because no single approach had been devised during the first two years of the regime's existence. Moscow cooperated in implementing the START treaty but sought foreign assistance in the dismantling of its nuclear forces, apparently more interested in the cash than in the dismantling. START implementation, of course, involved serious political difficulties with Ukraine and Kazakhstan. Belarus, by contrast, cooperated fully with Russia. CFE proved far more difficult. The treaty was drafted on the assumption that the Soviet Union would continue to be a party to the agreement. When it broke up, the agreed geographical distributions of conventional forces left Russia disadvantaged, even as they permitted Ukraine and Belarus to retain what Russia considered unjustifiable levels of the most modern parts of the Soviet forces. After much fanfare about the destruction of the large inventory of Soviet tanks, little or nothing was accomplished to that end in 1992-93. General Grachev and other Russian military officials have repeatedly tried to get NATO to revisit the CFE treaty so that Russia can be freed of some of its constraints. The Russian defense ministry appears to find the limits imposed by CFE more painful than those of START or any other arms control treaty, and in the absence of formal relief, Russia may simply refuse to abide by CFE without admitting so.

In its military negotiations and diplomacy with Europe and the United States, Russia was highly cooperative in 1992 and most of 1993. Russia contributed forces to the UN peacekeeping effort in former Yugoslavia and was cooperative in the UN Security Council. In the winter of 1993-94, however, Moscow began to back away from this pattern of extensive cooperation, beginning in former Yugoslavia. Yeltsin and Kozyrev began to speak of Russian interests that would limit cooperation in the future. Yet given Russia's inherent weakness, there are limits on how far it can go in asserting such interests against strong Western objections.

As this broad sketch indicates, Russian military strategy is reasonably coherent in some areas, filled with contradictions in others, and only partly developed in yet others.

Although military establishments are generally expected to support and help diplomats in carrying out foreign policy, the defense ministry effectively usurped the foreign ministry's role in Russian policy toward the CIS. After two years, defense ministry views were prevailing with Yeltsin, and the foreign ministry was piping a wholly different tune, giving the impression that a consensus had indeed been reached on foreign policy and the requisite military strategy to back it. This is the most important finding about Russian military strategy for assessing the prospects for stability and peaceful development in Central Asia and the Transcaucasus, the main focus of this study.

Conclusion

The trauma and chaos induced in Russian military affairs by the breakup of the Soviet Union are difficult to exaggerate. A proud and ideologically indoctrinated officer corps witnessed the rapid decline and disintegration of the Soviet military during Gorbachev's *perestroika* policy. Unaccustomed and ultimately unable to act as a corporate political force, it did little to prevent this decline, and when the old Soviet military leadership did try to stem the forces of change, they often made the situation worse, especially with regard to relations with the Soviet public. In retrospect, it is puzzling that the officer corps sided with Yeltsin against Gorbachev as Yeltsin maneuvered in December 1991 to dissolve the Soviet Union. Anger at Gorbachev undoubtedly explains their decision in part, but they also believed, as a few later said, that the new CIS armed forces would be created simply by changing the sign on the old Soviet defense ministry. They saw the CIS as merely a new version of the Soviet Union, that is, as essentially a unified political entity with a unified military. By the spring of 1992, that illusion was destroyed, and the creation of a Russian military as a national institution had to be faced.

In the ensuing two years, the defense ministry's goals for force structure and territorial disposition evolved through a number of stages and variants, ranging from being driven back within the borders of the Russian Federation to full control of the former territories of the Soviet Union. Political struggles over the nature of foreign policy pushed these goals to and fro, but the defense ministry, assisted by conservative forces in the parliament and elsewhere, prevailed in reasserting Russian military influence in much of the former Soviet Union, particularly in the Transcaucasus and Central Asia. The formal measure of their success was Yeltsin's promulgation in October 1993 of the new Russian military doctrine in October, which asserted Russia's security interests not only in the rights of the Russian diaspora but also in the military affairs of all the CIS states. Given its statement of security requirements and interests, the Russian defense ministry had at last achieved a legal basis for its aims in restoring Russia to the status of a first-class military power.

The task of achieving that status, however, had only begun. Arrangements in the top institutions were taking clear, if not final, shape by late 1993, although vast force-structure issues remained unresolved. Marked, although not surprising, continuities from Soviet military institutional structures persisted, with many institutions undergoing no modifications at all. Manpower policy was still in disarray, although the new system of contract soldiers provided modest relief in the face of public resistance to conscription. New arrangements between the ministry of defense and military industries were inchoate at best, hostile and chaotic in many instances.

Under the circumstances, even these accomplishments were no mean feat. The military could have easily dissolved almost entirely. It could have become involved in civil war, with regionally deployed units going over to provincial governments opposed to Moscow's control. While such a scenario cannot be fully ruled out in the future, the great danger period appeared to have passed by the late fall of 1993. Yet the new parliament, largely hostile to President Yeltsin, demonstrated in several of its first acts (e.g., granting amnesty to those accused of the coup attempts in August 1991 and October 1993) that no consensus had been achieved among Russian political elites on the most fundamental issues of constitutionalism. The struggle over the form and control of the economy and property rights had merely grown more severe, not closer to resolution, although Yeltsin's privatization program continued, making the reversal extremely difficult.

The Russian military's institutional and policy achievements, however, introduced significant constraints on the directions Russia could take in both foreign and domestic policy. The new military doctrine entitled the military to a share of the state's resources that could not be fully met. Even partial attainment of such resource allocations would impose great industrial burdens on the economy and limit the degree of economic reform possible without abandoning these military commitments. Manpower requirements would continue to put the military at odds with Russian youth and their parents, or it would put great strains on the state treasury for paying contract soldiers.

In foreign policy, the Russian military managed to entangle Moscow in a new imperialism aimed at controlling Central Asia and the Transcaucasus at a minimum and, at a maximum, at bringing Belarus, Ukraine, Moldova, and possibly the Baltic states back into a unified military and economic relationship with Moscow. To the degree that the maximum goal is attained, Russia will also become more assertive in Eastern Europe.

But it is not clear that Russia will succeed in achieving even its minimum goal. The costs, both in resources and in political cohesion, might be greater than Russia could meet. And to attribute a new imperialism wholly to the Russian military would be wrong. Numerous political groups and leaders, not least the military industrialists, aided and encouraged the military and the security forces. Some political forces in Russia, as the earlier section on Russian foreign policy points out, were against imperial reassertion for fear that it would indeed bring a disaster, but they lost out in the course of the summer and fall of 1993. Their hope that a reform-minded parliament would be elected to redress the political balance in 1994 proved ill-founded.

Still, the military leaders deserve most of the blame or credit for the direction policy has taken. They resisted the rapid demobilization that the radical reformers demanded between 1989 and 1992. The parallels with the demobilization of the Red Army in 1921-23 are instructive in this regard. In two years a force of five or six million was cut to about 560,000, a reduction of about 90 percent, much against the will of most of its members. Lenin, Trotsky, and Stalin understood what failing to reduce it would mean: a fiscal burden that would prevent reconstruction of the economy and eventual modernization of the army. It would also create an additional political factor in Bolshevik struggles over power within the party and the direction for political and economic change. In many regards, Gorbachev and Yeltsin faced precisely the same predicament with the military. To carry through systemic political and economic change, they needed to reduce the military to a level that made it fiscally and politically insignificant. Neither was able to do so. Thus, by 1994, the Russian military had become a huge political factor in a way it had not been before. The civil leadership was fragmented and weak. The military, although still weak itself, was slowly regaining institutional coherence. Moreover, because Russia had taken the path of a new imperialism, the military had the justification and political power for claiming a larger and larger share of the resources of the state. Whether it can realize these claims, however, remained an open question at the end of 1994. Corruption in its senior ranks and open political process in the parliament and media were imposing significant constraints on what General Grachev and his commanders could reasonably expect to receive through the state budget process.

With an understanding of these dynamics within Russia, more light can be shed on the issues of war and peace, stability and instability, in Central Asia and the Transcaucasus. They explain Russia's interests in these regions and the forces in Russia that pursue those interests. Finally, they reveal much about the forces and methods Russia has brought to bear in those regions.

Notes

[1]"Yeltsin Reports on Economic Reform to Sixth Congress of People's Deputies," FBIS-SOV-92-068, 8 April 1992, 27.

[2]Stalin seized from Japan the southern half of Sakhalin Island and several smaller islands in the Kurile chain at the end of World War II. Four of the southernmost islands remain in dispute and as a result Moscow and Tokyo have not yet signed a peace treaty to end formally the state of war between them.

[3]See William E. Odom, *Trial After Triumph: East Asia After the Cold War* (Indianapolis: Hudson Institute, 1992), chap. 2, and G. F. Kunadze, "The New Thinking and Soviet Policy Regarding Japan," JPRS-UWE-90-012, 20 October 1990, 2-12.

[4]General Grachev, minister of defense, in August 1993 even called Poland a major military challenge to Russia.

[5]See Kozyrev's address to the UNGA, released by the Russian Embassy in Washington.

[6]While evidence for this school of thought can be found in editorial writings throughout 1992 and early 1993, the mood of editorial opinion began to shift in the United States after Foreign Minister Kozyrev's speech to the United Nations General Assembly in September. Within the U.S. intelligence community this view apparently retained considerable currency in early 1994. At a Ditchley Foundation meeting in January 1994, where numerous European (including Russian and East European) and North American experts gathered to discuss Russian affairs, this benign interpretation of Russian foreign policy was put forward vigorously, although not unanimously.

[7]A. V. Rutskoi, "Voennaya politika Rossii: soderzhanie i naprovlennost'," *Voennaya mysl'*, no. 1 (1993): 1-10.

[8]Sergei Blagovolin, "O vneshnei i voennoi politike Rossii," *Svobodnaya mysl'*, no. 18 (1992): 3-13.

[9]These terms arose in nineteenth-century Russia in the debate over Russia's proper development path. Westernizers insisted that Russia imitate Europe and become part of it; Slavophiles rejected that course, arguing that Russia inherently enjoyed its own special development path, morally superior to that of Europe.

[10]When one of the authors suggested as much to members of Rutskoi's staff in April 1993, they would not deny it, although neither would they confirm it.

[11]"Foreign Ministry Document Outlines Foreign Policy," FBIS-SOV-92-232, 2 December 1992, 3-5.

[12]See Thomas Goltz, "Letter from Eurasia: The Hidden Russian Hand," *Foreign Policy,* no. 92 (Fall 1993): 92-116, for evidence and hypotheses on this point. President Elchibey's former secretary of state, Ali Kerimov, asserted that Elchibey's refusal to let Russian forces occupy Azerbaijan while posing as international peacekeeping forces prompted Russian action to depose Elchibey.

[13]A senior Russian policy analyst made this argument to an audience at an off-the-record seminar in Washington.

[14]*Voennaya mysl'*, Special Edition (May 1992): 3-10.

[15]Rodionov's speech on military doctrine at a General Staff Academy conference late in May 1992 had these points from the typescript removed when it was published. The typed manuscript leaked widely, suggesting that Rodionov wanted it made public. General Grachev took a milder line, closer to the published draft doctrine, and that seems to

have set the limits on what could be called for in public debate among military officials.

[16]For detail on the final version of this Russian military doctrine, see "'Detailed Account' of Military Doctrine," FBIS-SOV-93-222-S, 19 November 1993, 1-11. Yeltsin's decree promulgating the doctrine was signed on 2 November 1993, after Security Council deliberations in October.

[17]One of the authors, during a visit to each of these countries in December 1993, heard Nazarbayev and Shevardnadze complain in private meetings about the implications of the doctrine. Talks with foreign ministry officials in the same countries and in Kyrgyzstan and Uzbekistan revealed equally deep anxiety that the document signaled a new Russian imperialism.

[18]RFE/RL Daily Report, no. 44, 5 March 1993, gives an example of deaths and maltreatment. Literally hundreds of such reports have appeared in the press since they began to surface in 1989, and they continue right into 1994.

[19]RFE/RL Daily Report, no. 125, 5 July 1993.

[20]"Yeltsin, Grachev Speeches at Defense Ministry," FBIS-SOV-92-228, 25 November 1992, 26.

[21]*Krasnaya zvezda,* 27 February 1993, provided the full text of the law. A translation to English can be found in JPRS-UMA-93-012, 7 April 1993, 8-30.

[22]"'Power' Ministries Extremely Worried by Draft Problems," FBIS-SOV-93-043, 8 March 1993, 28-29.

[23]"Fall Recruitment to Supply 27% of Needed Recruits," FBIS-SOV-93-069, 13 April 1993, 35.

[24]"Army Recruitment Problems Viewed," FBIS-SOV-93-061, 1 April 1993, 36.

[25]See RFE/RL Daily Report, no. 44, 5 March 1993, for an example of this problem in the Pacific Fleet as late as 1993.

[26]See William E. Odom, "The Soviet Military in Transition," *Problems of Communism* 39 (May-June 1990): 51-71.

[27]Ibid., 59-60.

[28]"Grachev Appeals to Khasbulatov on Draft," FBIS-SOV-93-108, 8 June 1993, 34-35.

[29]RFE/RL Daily Report, no. 68, 11 April 1994.

[30]RFE/RL Daily Report, no. 58, 24 March 1994.

[31]Ibid. Swedish military intelligence analysts judged the state of readiness in 1993-94 to be extremely low except in selected units; pilot flying time had plummeted, and naval units and regular ground forces almost never exercised.

[32]"Little Progress Seen on Yeltsin's Housing Pledge," JPRS-UMA-92-021, 10 June 1992, 16-18.

[33]Interview in *Krasnaya zvezda,* 9 October 1992.

[34]"Problems of Repostings From Hotspots," FBIS-SOV-93-053, 22 March 1993, 70-71.

[35]"Defense Ministry Holds First Conference on Troops," FBIS-SOV-93-037, 26 February 1993, 29-30.

[36]See discussion by Oleg Falichev in *Krasnaya zvezda,* 19 March 1993. He observes that 30,000 such repostings occurred in 1968 with no difficulty. The apparent inability of a paltry 2,500 in 1993 to make their new posts shows the degree of disintegration in the old officer personnel system.

[37]"Grachev Says Defense Ministry May Become Demilitarized," FBIS-SOV-93-024, 8 February 1993, 22.

[38]RFE/RL Daily Report, no. 111, 15 June 1993. Initially it was reported that 115 new generals had been promoted, but this figure was shortly changed to 80.

[39]FBIS-SOV-93-069, 13 April 1993, 49. RFE/RL Daily Report, no. 52, 17 March 1993, reports Yeltsin's signing a decree containing provisions on status and functioning of Cossack units in the army, MVD, and security ministry.

[40]See "More on Security Meeting," FBIS-SOV-93-041, 4 May 1993, 20-21, in which General Grachev is somewhat defensive on the issue of Cossack formations.

[41]RFE/RL Daily Report, no. 153, 12 August 1992.

[42]Boris Yeltsin, *The Struggle for Russia* (New York: Random House, 1994), 274-78.

[43]"Military Chiefs Face Internal Contradictions," FBIS-SOV-92-118, 10 June 1992, 25-26.

[44]"'Army Reform' Deputies Debate Army Problems," FBIS-SOV-93-040, 3 March 1993, 40-41.

[45]"Committee to Probe Defense Ministry Abuses," FBIS-SOV-93-025, 9 February 1993, 31.

[46]"Shaposhnikov Hits Back at Pravda," FBIS-SOV-93-079, 27 April 1993, 2-3, and "Grachev Implicated in Abuse of Official Position," FBIS-SOV-93-077, 23 April 1993, 35.

[47]RFE/RL Daily Report, no. 111, 15 June 1993.

[48]The authors learned of these from discussions with local officials during a visit to Central Asia in December 1993.

[49]According to a decree signed by Yeltsin in August 1993, nearly 400 military-industrial firms and research and design institutions were to be spared from privatization and retained as state industrial institutions.

See *Ukaz prezidenta rossiiskoi federatsii,* "Ob osobennostyakh privatizatsii i dopolnitel'nykh merakh gosudarstvennogo regulirovaniya deyatel'nosti predpriyatii oboronnykh otrastlei promyshlennosti," no. 1267, 19 August 1992.

[50]See Kokoshin's interview in *Krasnaya zvezda,* 22 July 1992, and RFE/RL Daily Report, no. 44, 5 March 1993.

[51]RFE/RL Daily Report, no. 44, 5 March 1993.

[52]RFE/RL Daily Report, no. 153, 12 August 1992.

[53]Mary FitzGerald, "The Soviet Image of the Gulf War," *Comparative Strategy* 10 (1991): 393-435.

[54]This law, "Zakon Rossiiskoi federtsii ob oborone," was published in *Voennyi vestnik,* no. 11 (1992).

[55]Stepan Kiselev, "Tikhii perevorot Borisa Yeltsina," *Moskovskie novosti,* no. 29, 19 July 1992.

[56]Ibid.

[57]RFE/RL Daily Report, no. 144, 30 July 1993.

[58]RFE/RL Daily Report, no. 153, 12 August 1993.

[59]See RFE/RL Daily Report, no. 161, 24 August 1993; no. 167, 1 September 1993; and no. 207, 27 October 1993.

[60]See J. Michael Waller, "Russia's Security and Intelligence Services Today," *National Security Law Report* 15 (June 1993): 1-2, 5.

[61]Amy Knight, "Yeltsin's KGB," *The Washington Post,* 13 February 1994, C5.

[62]"CIS to Deputy Battalions Along Afghan Border," FBIS-SOV-93-026, 10 February 1993, 4.

[63]Waller, "Russia's Security."

[64]"Five-Branch Structure to Be Preserved," JPRS-UMA-92-023, 24 June 1992, 51. The five branches are (1) Ground Forces, (2) Air Forces, (3) Air Defense Forces, (4) Strategic Rocket Forces, and (5) the Navy.

[65]*Krasnaya zvezda,* 5 March 1993.

[66]"Shaposhnikov Interviewed on CIS Military Issues," FBIS-SOV-93-078, 26 April 1993, 1-4.

[67]"Official Says Most Defense Enterprises to be Privatized," FBIS-SOV-93-092, 14 May 1993, 33.

[68]"Grachev Says Defense Ministry May Become Demilitarized," FBIS-SOV-93-023, 23 February 1993, 22.

[69]"Yeltsin, Grachev Speeches at Defense Ministry," FBIS-SOV-92-228, 25 November 1992, 24-27.

[70]Robert Karniol, "Uzbekistan Develops Communications Capabilities," *Jane's Defence Weekly* 20 (September 1993): 14.

[71]"Niyazov Lauds Military Cooperation with Russia," FBIS-SOV-93-079, 27 April 1993, 58.

[72]See "Commander of 'Combined Arms' Army Appointed," FBIS-SOV-92-074, 16 April 1992, 61.

[73]"Decree Signed on State Defense Committee," FBIS-SOV-92, 17 January 1992, 32.

[74]RFE/RL Daily Report, no. 28, 10 February 1994.

[75]"Moscow Air Defense to be Downsized," FBIS-SOV-93-069, 13 April 1993, 47-48.

[76]"PVO's Lt Gen Dubrov on CIS Air Space," JPRS-UMA-92-013, 14 April 1992, 30-31.

[77]"Space Agency Outlines Plans Until Year 2000," FBIS-SOV-93-025, 9 February 1993, 26-27, Moscow TV.

[78]See Sergei Rogov, Russian Defense Policy: Challenges and Developments, Center for Naval Analyses, January 1993, 32-36, for incomplete but considerable detail. He estimates from official data that 30 divisions, 72 brigades, 32 aircraft regiments, 9 helicopter regiments, and 412,000 weapons systems and vehicles must be moved back to Russia in 1993-94. Some of his sources say that 15 divisions, 23 missile and artillery brigades, and 36 aircraft and helicopter regiments were returned to Russia in 1992. Other sources give different numbers. In such chaotic conditions, it is doubtful that even General Grachev has more than rough approximations of the kinds and numbers of units and equipment moved and remaining outside of Russia.

[79]Ibid., 31.

[80]RFE/RL Daily Report, no. 45, 8 March 1993, and "Army Chiefs to Create Rapid Reaction Forces," FBIS-SOV-93-043, 8 March 1993, 28.

[81]"General Staff Chief on Role of Peace Forces," FBIS-SOV-92-173, 4 September 92, 24-25.

[82]Ibid. Bonuses of R8-12,000, indexed for inflation, are authorized.

[83]RFE/RL Daily Report, no. 76, 22 April 1993.

[84]"More on Grachev's 2 March Press Conference," FBIS-SOV-93-041, 4 March 1993, 22, and RFE/RL Daily Report, no. 52, 17 March 1993.

[85]Ibid.

[86]Rogov, "Russian Defense Policy," 31.

[87]"Article Examines Draft Shortfalls," FBIS-SOV-93-005, 8 January 1993, 16-17.

[88]"Defense Minister Interviewed," FBIS-SOV-93-109, 9 June 1993, 46.

[89]See Michael McGwire, Military Objectives in Soviet Foreign Policy (Washington, DC: The Brookings Institution, 1987), 117-212, for the best open-source elaboration of Soviet warplans.

[90]See Lothar Ruehl, "Offensive Defense in the Warsaw Pact,"

Survival 33 (September/October 1991): 442-50, for evidence of this in East German military documents.

[91]Not only was this interpretation widely expressed by Western media analysts, but it also held sway within U.S. government circles. Russian commentators in some cases encouraged that assessment.

[92]See Fiona Hill and Pamela Jewett, "Back in the USSR: Russia's Intervention in the Internal Affairs of the Former Soviet Republics and the Implications for United States Policy Toward Russia," *Strengthening Democratic Institutions Project,* Harvard University, JFK School of Government, January 1994, 3.

[93]Ibid., 28.

[94]Poland, the Czech Republic, Slovakia, and Hungary.

[95]FitzGerald, "Soviet Image," 393-435.

[96]Mary C. FitzGerald, "The Russian Image of War, *Comparative Strategy* 13 (1994): 177.

THREE

Central Asia and its Neighbors

In the Soviet era, the Central Asian nations, as republics of the USSR, did not have independent international relations. The Soviet state kept foreign influences out of Central Asia, restricting the interaction between Central Asians and foreigners. The yearly haj,[1] for example, which binds Moslems the world over, became an impossible journey for most of the faithful of Central Asia. Because few Central Asians were among the Soviet elite, few travelled abroad or met with Westerners. Consequently, when the Central Asian republics attained independence, it was difficult to guess what their international posture would be. Some observers thought that the new Central Asia would reestablish ties to the Moslem world, possibly under the influence of radical Islamists. Others speculated that China's influence might move westward to encompass the new republics. Still others believed that a new Turkic community could arise from the Turkestan of old.

These were the uncertainties confronting analysts as the USSR broke up. By 1994, the outline of Central Asia's international relations had become clearer. Russia remained the dominant power, with hegemony in military, political, and economic affairs. All other foreign countries were considerably less influential in the region, though all had seen their presence increase greatly since Soviet days. China built up economic ties to Kazakhstan and Kyrgyzstan, Afghans participated in the Tajik civil war, Iranians and Turks developed economic and cultural relations with Central Asians, and some visitors from the subcontinent arrived. Islam regained some of its post-Bolshevik visibility, though its political influence remained limited.

Though the presence of these new actors is smaller than Russia's, it represents a major change after seventy years of Central Asian isolation from the rest of the world. If Russia's star should wane, moreover, the role of these other players will rapidly increase. These countries will also contribute to creating new regions within Central Asia. In the Soviet epoch, membership in the USSR defined the geopolitics of the five republics. At present, however, a process of differentiation is underway, as individual republics (or districts within the large ones) interact with different foreign countries. China's weight, for example, will be felt much more in eastern Kazakhstan and in Kyrgyzstan than in western Central Asia, while Afghans will interact mostly with nationalities across the Amu Daryia, rather than with Kazakhs or Kyrgyz. Iran's ties will develop mostly with Turkmenistan and Persian Tajiks, and Turkey's relations will be stronger with Turkic peoples than with the Tajiks. Islam will have more relevance in the south than in the north of Central Asia. It is therefore possible that, if Russian power diminishes, the republics may in ten or twenty years gradually drift toward different regional systems, e.g. Turkmenistan to a Middle Eastern system and eastern Kazakhstan to a Chinese one.

China and Central Asia

Of all the countries on the periphery of the southern Soviet Union, the People's Republic of China (PRC) was the strongest and largest. In the aftermath of the breakup of the Soviet Union, China became the most powerful neighbor of the new states of Central Asia, overshadowing Russia and Iran in the size of its economy and population.

After the dissolution of the USSR, observers wondered if China would enlarge its sphere of influence and start a new version of the "Great Game" in Central Asia, this time pitting the People's Republic against the Russian Federation, with possible participation by India, Pakistan, Turkey, and Iran. The emergence of an independent Central Asia also raised questions about China's own Turkestani region, Xinjiang. Would the Central Asian republics' independence lead to a struggle for decolonization in Xinjiang? Or would Chinese control continue without difficulty?

By the end of 1994, China's presence and influence in Central

Asia had increased considerably. China had become a major trading partner for Kazakhstan and Kyrgyzstan[2] and opened embassies throughout the region. As a result of the continued preeminence of Russia, and hostility on the part of many Central Asians towards China, Beijing's influence in the region remained limited, however. China's activities did not challenge Moscow's supremacy in Central Asia. In turn, the birth of the independent Central Asian republics did not appear to undermine Chinese authority in Xinjiang.

As of late 1994, the most likely scenario was for a moderate expansion of the Chinese presence in Central Asia, especially in eastern Kazakhstan and Kyrgyzstan, which would not destroy regional equilibria. But two possible future developments could alter this assessment. China could adopt a more aggressive policy and take advantage of the turmoil in Russia to attempt domination of eastern Central Asia by force. On the other hand, the People's Republic could lose its grip on Xinjiang, forfeiting any influence in Central Asia. Both of these scenarios are improbable, but they should nevertheless be considered in any forecast of China's position in Central Asia.

China and Central Asia: Historical Background

Today's Central Asian republics occupy a region that belonged to the Turco-Mongol and Turco-Persian civilizations prior to the Russian conquest, but the Chinese empire sometimes exercised suzerainty over the local nomads. In the seventh and eighth centuries AD, Chinese rule in Central Asia reached as far as Tashkent.[3] Central Asia never belonged to the Sinic heartland, though, and it was generally free of Chinese control, especially when the Chinese empire was in turmoil.

In the nineteenth century, China's relations with Central Asia involved the remaining independent Moslem states of Central Asia and the Tsarist Empire. The Kokand ruler (one of the Central Asian emirs) supported Yakub Beg's rebellion in the Tarim Basin, which rocked Chinese Turkestan in the 1870s. Kokand assisted other uprisings, which sometimes had elements of religious struggle (jihad) in them, throughout the first three-quarters of the nineteenth century. Afghanistan and Ottoman Turkey also inspired some Chinese

Turkestanis in their anti-Chinese uprisings, but neither state had the wherewithal to intervene in the region.

Russia's influence in regional politics grew as the Tsars penetrated into Central Asia and the Moslem principalities faded away. In 1860, an unequal treaty[4] between Russia and China deprived China of its nominal suzerainty over 440,000 sq. km (an area about the size of Sweden or California) between Lake Bailkash and the current Sino-Kazakh frontier. In the aftermath of Yakub Beg's insurrection, Russian forces intervened through the Ili Valley and only withdrew after a 1881 Treaty awarded Russians extraterritorial rights in Chinese Turkestan and transferred the lower Ili Valley from the Chinese to the Russian Empire. The 1895 Anglo-Russian agreement demarcating the Chinese-Russian border between Turugard Davan and Afghanistan further affected the location of the frontier, in a pattern that China continues to reject. In the twentieth century, Central Asia stayed outside China's reach, firmly under Russian-Soviet jurisdiction.

Xinjiang

Xinjiang represents the domestic side of China's Central Asian question. Roughly the size of Alaska, with a surface area of 1.65 million sq. km (17.3 percent of the Chinese landmass), the region includes the Tian Shan range, the Dzungarian steppe to the north, the upper Ili Valley in the eastern central area, and the Tarim Basin, in which the large Taklimakan desert is located, to the south.

Because of its inhospitable habitat, Xinjiang is sparsely populated, averaging only 6 persons per square kilometer versus 168 per square kilometer for the rest of China excluding Tibet.[5] Its estimated 14 million inhabitants, only 1.2 percent of the Chinese population, are divided roughly equally between Turkic Moslem peoples and Han Chinese. The non-Han consist of approximately 6 million Uighurs, Turkic Moslems whose language resembles Uzbek; a million Kazakhs in the north; slightly more one hundred thousand Kyrgyz; and smaller numbers of other Central Asian peoples. Of the Han Chinese inhabitants, half a million are Moslems known as Hui or Dugan. Most Han settled in the province during the Communist era.

The province has oil fields, and its reserves may be as high as 3.5 billion barrels of recoverable petroleum products (comparable to the original North Sea finds) or even much higher.[6] There are also rich deposits of coal and metallic ores in the Tian Shan area. Xinjiang has no significant industry, but it is the site of the nuclear weapons test range at Lop Nor.

Though Xinjiang is a Chinese region, its bonds with the PRC are quasi-colonial. First, the area is only superficially contiguous with China. The eastern edge of Xinjiang is approximately fifteen hundred kilometers from the closest large city in China proper (Lanzhou), and the western frontier of the region is more than three thousand kilometers from the Chinese heartland. Second, as a result of these distances, Chinese control over the area has historically been sporadic. Because weak dynasties failed to assert their power in the region, it has not experienced continuity of Chinese rule. Third, Xinjiang is outside the Sinic cultural sphere. Its inhabitants were under the sway of Zoroastrian and Manichean dualist religions from the Middle East and later became Moslems; they never joined the world of Confucian philosophy. As speakers of Turkic languages who do not write in Chinese ideographs, they have no linguistic ties to China. Thus even under Chinese rule the region was part of the Central Asian cultural domain, and the emperors administered the law according to the Sharia rather than Chinese statutes.

The twentieth-century history of Xinjiang consists of two periods, with Mao's victory marking the transition between them. Until the Communist Revolution, Chinese rule in Xinjiang was tenuous. In the 1930s and 1940s, entire areas of Xinjiang became *de facto* Soviet protectorates, and other powers took advantage of the disorder in China to intrude into Chinese Turkestan. The British had an interest in the region because of its contiguity to Afghanistan and Tibet, where they had certain rights, and were thus active in the local politics of the region. Japan may also have been involved in anti-Chinese subversion in Xinjiang in the 1930s, and even Afghans may have supplied weapons to the Turkic Islamic Republic of East Turkestan in Xinjiang, while Chinese warlords used White Russian mercenaries against Moslem rebels in 1928-1934. Thus, until the Revolution, the Chinese state did not enjoy effective sovereignty in Xinjiang.

After the Revolution, the People's Republic eliminated foreign influences from the region; following the Sino-Soviet split, the USSR sought to subvert Xinjiang using the ethnic connections between it and Soviet Central Asia. In the 1960s and 1970s, Kazakhstan was a center for Soviet anti-Chinese propaganda. Although border clashes occurred and the USSR sent infiltrators to northern Xinjiang to spread propaganda among the Chinese Kazakhs,[7] Moscow could not reverse Beijing's growing authority in Xinjiang.

In the aftermath of the Revolution, Beijing overturned the demographic balance. Until the Communist Revolution, the Han Chinese population accounted for 5 to 10 percent of Xinjiang's residents, but the Communists brought millions of Han, who now make up almost half the population, to settle in the province. This colonization led to resentment on the part of the natives, but it solidified Chinese rule to an extent unknown in the pre-Communist period. The PRC also intervened more directly in the government of its Turkestani holding than the Chinese empire had. While the empire had often relied on local potentates, the PRC brought in Han to help rule the area.

There apparently were anti-Chinese incidents in Xinjiang in the early 1990s, but the security forces overcame the agitation,[8] and China's position in Xinjiang in 1994 is still strong, thanks to demographic parity with the Turkestanis and a willingness to repress dissent. Chinese rule is further strengthened by numerous fault lines—Kazakh-Uighur, urban-rural, sedentary-nomadic, and elite-masses—diving Xinjiang's natives. Moreover, the size of this province (three times that of France), strong traditions of localism, and easily controlled communications (only one road links the various oasis cities) hamper the task of potential insurgents. As long as the Chinese government remains decisive, Turkestani opponents will not defeat it, even if they obtain some foreign assistance.

China and the Independent Central Asian Republics

Central Asia is not a foreign policy priority for China. The republics are too weak to be either major adversaries or allies, and their economies are insufficiently developed to provide significant markets for Chinese products. To be sure, they could play a role in rivalry with Russia, but at this point China is pursuing a cooperative policy with Moscow.[9] Nevertheless, China has not totally ignored these new neighbors and has established relations and developed ties with them. In dealing with the Central Asian republics, China has taken into account the international implications of establishing ties with them, as well as the domestic implications for Xinjiang of their newly acquired freedom. At present, both foreign and domestic policy considerations explain China's conservative approach to Central Asia, an approach that supports the Soviet-style order in countries like Uzbekistan and Kazakhstan.

Because China could experience difficulties in controlling its own Central Asian population in Xinjiang, it has a stake in the domestic politics of Central Asia. Democratic or pan-Turkic nationalist governments could encourage rebellion in Xinjiang, or allow anti-Chinese guerrillas to use Central Asian sanctuaries. Thus the authoritarianism practiced by most Central Asian countries is more than acceptable to China. Nationalism in this region is confined within countries and focuses on disfranchising ethnic Russians and other non-titular nationalities.[10] Central Asian governments have shown no interest in anti-Chinese Turkestani nationalism or Moslem irredentism.

In light of these international and domestic considerations, China's policy in Central Asia in the aftermath of independence has been prudent, focusing on two axes, commercial and political.[11] Commerce with Central Asia has grown considerably. The PRC is now a major trade partner for Kazakhstan and Kyrgyzstan (its economic ties with Uzbekistan and Turkmenistan, which are not contiguous with the PRC, are less important). The Economist Intelligence Unit estimated that the PRC accounted for approximately 30 percent of Kazakhstan's and Kyrgyzstan's foreign trade with countries not previously part of the Soviet Union.[12] Thousands of Chinese traders have also moved into Central Asia to take advantage of business opportunities, and the markets of eastern Central Asia display Chinese goods.[13] On the political front, China made no territorial claims on eastern Central Asia, and it cooperated with the new states on border demarcation.[14]

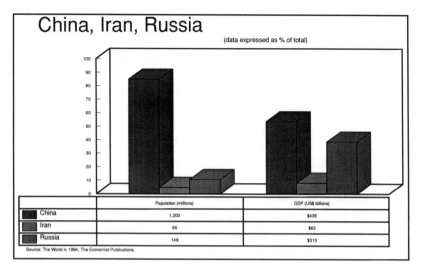

	Population (millions)	GDP (US$ billions)
China	1,200	$435
Iran	65	$65
Russia	149	$313

China, Iran, Russia
(data expressed as % of total)

Source: The World in 1994, The Economist Publications.

China and the Future of Central Asia

The Sino-Central Asian relationship, having started only as the Soviet Union broke up, was still relatively new in 1994. Recent developments, however, make it possible to speculate about the future course of this relationship. The most likely scenario is a continuation of present trends, with a significant but not overwhelming Chinese presence. Nevertheless, the possibility of either a more aggressive or a weakening China should not be discounted. A survey of these possible futures will yield a better understanding of the evolution of China's role in Central Asia.

A Continuation of Current Trends

The developing relationship between Central Asia and China is attractive to both sides and should expand gradually. For China, trade may increase leverage over Central Asian states, making it easier for the PRC to prevent these countries from adopting policies of which it disapproves. Trade also allows China to build up a position in Central Asia that it may use more forcefully if in the future Russia's hold on the region diminishes.

From the Central Asian perspective, the Chinese connection is also attractive. It provides an additional trade partner, and offers a counterweight to Russian influence. Even if Central Asia's rulers remain committed to a security relationship with Russia, they have an interest in avoiding isolation and in seeking ties with other nations. Central Asia's governments can also expect a friendly ear from China, which is concerned neither with human rights nor democracy issues that have soured relations between Tashkent and Washington. The April 1994 visit of Chinese Prime Minister Li Peng to Central Asia demonstrated that there is interest on both sides in strengthening the relationship.

There remain, however, significant obstacles to the development of stronger PRC-Central Asian ties:

- First, geography impedes commerce. There are no sea lanes of communication, and ground transportation between China's industrial regions and Central Asia requires covering thousands of kilometers of barren territory with (inevitably) poor infrastructure. Using China as an outlet for Central Asian oil and gas, for example, would require laying a pipeline across half of Asia.
- Second, many Central Asians, especially Kazakhs and Kyrgyz, fear China, and are uneasy about the growing Chinese presence.[15] Their dislike of China is grounded in concerns that a billion plus Han Chinese might take over their sparsely populated countries. Moreover, as Turkic peoples they empathize with Xinjiang's Turkic nationalities, and as Turco-Mongols of nomadic background they have a history of hostility with the sedentary Chinese.[16]
- Third, for the past century, Central Asia's infrastructure and cultural development have been oriented towards Russia rather than China. Its elites are at home in the Russian world and very removed from the Middle Kingdom. In the future, if they diversify away from Russian cultural influences, it will be by learning English and sending students to the West rather than by assimilating into Chinese culture.

Starting from a very low base in Central Asia, Chinese activity has in a few years grown considerably. With its focus on Central Asia's eastern regions, it can be expected to continue doing so. Nevertheless, it is unlikely that China's role will radically change the existing strategic balance, which Russia dominates.

An Aggressive China

A more aggressive China could result from developments in Russia, combined with historical factors that could push China towards dominance in Central Asia.

This study has detailed the continued power of Russia in Central Asia and the Russian Federation's assertion of its "rights" in the region, including limits on the role of outside powers in the "near abroad"; but Russia's politics are unpredictable and its economy is weak. Political turmoil and economic crisis could therefore render Russia incapable of controlling Central Asia. Even if Russia grows healthier at home, Russian politicians might decide that the nation cannot afford the burden of quasi-colonies and withdraw from Central Asia. In the context of a Russian retreat, a far more assertive China could surface, its aggressiveness reinforced by its unique history.

China did not evolve in a balance-of-power environment. Until the nineteenth century, China was the sole superpower in, and the cultural center of, its universe. After the western and Japanese onslaught, it became an object of power politics rather than a participant in diplomatic intercourse. Thus prior to 1949 it had no experience of the moderation that the balance-of-power realities often imposed on western nations, and since the Revolution it has been ruled by communist dictators for whom coercion, both at home and abroad, has been the key instrument of politics.

In the nineteenth century, the Western powers and Japan imposed upon China the unequal treaties that deprived it of territory and sovereignty. The People's Republic restored China's sovereignty, ending a century of humiliation, but it did not regain the territories that had been formally ceded to outside powers in the nineteenth century. The reversion of Hong Kong will mark the first time that China has regained control of land lost through unequal treaties. (The UK leased Hong Kong's Northern Territories for 99 years, but China relinquished Hong Kong Island and Kowloon to Britain in 1842 and 1860). It is possible that this event could whet the appetite of Beijing's masters for the abrogation of other agreements that forced China, no less unequally, to give up territory to "barbarians."

Thus China's history as first a supreme civilization-state and then a semicolony may generate a desire to revert to the glorious past and wipe out prior humiliations. In particular, the recovery of lost lands might tempt a strong China.

In Central Asia, Beijing could attempt to regain the districts in present-day Kazakhstan and Kyrgyzstan that it lost to the Tsars. Even without formal annexation, it could use military threats and the absence of countervailing forces to make Central Asia a virtual protectorate of Beijing. Such a course could serve China's natural resources policy. Because the PRC is now a net importer of oil, control over Central Asia might give it access to new oil resources, either in Central Asia itself or in the Persian Gulf. In Central Asia, it could seek to stretch its influence as far as western Kazakhstan's oil fields. In the Gulf, it could attempt to link up with Iran via Central Asia; in such an arrangement, admittedly highly unlikely, China would dominate the eastern part of Central Asia, while Iran would become the foremost influence on Turkmenistan.

Chinese power in Central Asia could take a more benign shape than annexation. In the case of Russia's retreat from the scene, China's economic presence would further increase, and the PRC might pressure Central Asian republics to alter certain policies. For example, it might ask them to end the (small) presence of anti-Chinese Uighur organizations that operate in Central Asia, such as the Free Uighurstan Party, and to stop opposing Chinese nuclear testing in Xinjiang.[17] China could also assist the local governments with internal security to help them survive without Russian help. As a result, its role in Central Asian internal affairs would assume a greater dimension.

A Debilitated China

If Chinese expansionism lies at one end of the spectrum of possibilities, Chinese weakness lies at the other. There are signs of administrative chaos, economic difficulty, and political instability in China, where the government is losing control over the provinces and a frail 90-year old remains as paramount leader.[18] In a few years, the PRC could face secessionism, social unrest, and a fight for Deng's succession. Under such circumstances, China would be unable to undertake any aggressive policy in Central Asia, and might lose control of Xinjiang. There are several developments that could lead to the latter possibility:

- The existence of officially independent Central Asian nations could, in spite of the problems they now face, tempt Xinjiang's Turkestanis to imitate Central Asia and seek independence.
- Though most Central Asian governments remain authoritarian, in some areas the press has been partly freed from censorship. China's Turkic population might tune in to Central Asian (or Turkish) satellite broadcasts, videos, and radio programs. Greater access to foreign media could help rouse the Xinjiang natives and cause problems for the PRC.
- Because of the lack of discipline in some Russian army units, as well as the civil wars in Afghanistan and Tajikistan, millions of guns are now available for sale or theft in Central Asia. Some observers claim that these weapons and explosives have already found their way across the borders to "counterrevolutionary elements" in Xinjiang.[19]
- After seventy years of atheist Soviet colonization, Islam is gaining visibility in Central Asia. With the PRC as another godless occupier, rising religious sentiment might fuel anti-Chinese agitation in Xinjiang.[20]
- The escalating drug business creates new opportunities and financial resources for armed gangsters in the region. A "New Colombia" on the other side of the frontier could spur banditry in Xinjiang. Though such criminals may not necessarily oppose the government, the ability of its colonized peoples to acquire arms and money would represent another challenge for the PRC.

If it managed to leave China's embrace, Xinjiang could become the sixth Central Asian republic, though given its ethnic diversity and size it might form more than one entity. In any event, the end of Chinese control in the province would undermine Chinese influence in Central Asia. China would lose its common border with Central Asia, and decolonization in Xinjiang would more generally indicate domestic turmoil and a concomitant weakening of Chinese power.

Conclusion

These scenarios represent different main paths for the future of Sino-Central Asian relations. (It is not necessary to enumerate each of many possible permutations of each one.) The most probable development in the next decade will be a gradual increase in the Chinese presence in Central Asia, especially in the eastern regions, without changing present-day equilibria radically.

Afghanistan and Central Asia

Afghanistan is in the middle of a multisided civil war, and when Central Asia's republics attained independence, some pundits thought that the Afghans, many of whom have coethnics in Central Asia, would spread violence and turmoil north of the frontier. Indeed, after the dissolution of the Soviet Union, Afghan Tajik fighters helped antigovernment groups in Tajikistan. The impact of the Afghan guerrillas on Central Asia, however, has been limited. Preoccupation with their own civil war, limited offensive power, and stable governments in Central Asia (except for Tajikistan) have combined to minimize Afghans' role in Central Asian politics. In fact, as of 1994, Central Asian rulers support certain Afghan factions inside Afghanistan, and may have a greater leverage in Afghanistan than Afghans do in Central Asia. Should Central Asia become less stable and Russia's power diminish, Afghan influence in Central Asian affairs may rise, but it is unlikely to become a critical factor in regional affairs.

Afghanistan's links to Central Asia are the product of geography and ethnicity. The limits on Afghans' power are due to the poverty of Afghanistan and to the atomization of Afghan society. To grasp how Afghans could play a role in Central Asian politics, it is useful to understand both the nature of the ties between Afghans and Central Asians and the situation inside Afghanistan.

Afghanistan's Links to Central Asia

Afghanistan has strong links to Central Asia. It borders Tajikistan, Uzbekistan, and Turkmenia, and the presence of the same ethnic groups on both sides of these borders reinforces the effect of this proximity. There are approximately 4.1 million Tajiks, about one million Uzbeks, and some four hundred thousand Turkmen in northern Afghanistan, the area bordering on Central Asia. The balance of Afghanistan's 16 to 17 million people consists of Pushtuns (about 40 percent of Afghans), Hazaras (Mongoloid Shias), and other peoples.[21] The use of Persian dialects as the lingua franca throughout Afghanistan reinforces the links between Afghans and Tajiks.

Table 1
Population (estimate, thousands)[22]

	Tajiks	Uzbeks	Turkmen
Afghanistan	4,100	1,000	400
In titular republic	3,200	14,100	2,500
CIS outside republics*	1,000	2,600	200

* Mostly in Central Asia

Soviet policy expanded relations between Afghans and Soviet Central Asians. For example, Soviet officials utilized Soviet Central Asians, especially Tajiks, as interpreters and liaison staff in Afghanistan, and they brought Afghans to study in Tajikistan. The USSR encouraged feelings of ethnic solidarity in order to draw northern Afghans toward the Soviet Union. Thus contacts and ties across the Soviet-Afghan frontier developed rapidly after World War II. The Afghan-Soviet War further accelerated this process by increasing the Soviet presence in Afghanistan and by improving the communication facilities between Afghanistan and the USSR.[23]

There are, however, limits to the bonds produced by ethnicity in Afghanistan. For Afghans, the parameters of group identity and collective action are fluid, involving tribes, towns, Sufi orders, and other networks unrelated to ethno-linguistic bonds.[24] According to Olivier Roy, these language-based "macro-ethnic" groups (i.e. "Tajik" or "Uzbek") have gradually acquired increasing importance in the consciousness of Afghans.[25] Nevertheless, ethnic tags such as "Afghan

Tajik" or "Turkmen in Afghanistan" do not constitute the primary focus of loyalty and identity for all those they apply to, and there are thus limits to these peoples' cohesion and power as ethnic groups. This is particularly true in the case of the Tajiks, whose sense of nationhood is very weak.[26]

Afghanistan and Central Asia

The political factors that allow the linkages between both sides of the Amu Daryia to affect Central Asia are the simultaneous upheavals in Tajikistan and in Afghanistan. In Central Asia, because of the dissolution of the USSR and the civil war in Tajikistan, the border is porous. In Afghanistan, where internal fighting and the availability of weapons have created a pool of armed fighters, Afghans can intervene in Central Asia's conflicts. The relevance of Afghanistan to Central Asian security became clearer when thousands of Tajik refugees fled to Afghanistan in 1993 and Afghans helped them set up antigovernment training camps inside Afghanistan. As the Tajik civil war unfolded, however, it became apparent that Afghans were not at the center of the events in this former Soviet republic. As discussed in chapter 1, the war in Tajikistan was the product of internal disputes and of Russian and Uzbek meddling, not of Afghan or other non-CIS intervention. Outside of Tajikistan, there have been no reports of Afghan involvement in either Uzbek or Turkmen affairs, and in fact Afghanistan's power in the region is severely limited for several reasons.

Afghanistan has never been rich, and the prerogatives of the state have always been limited by the frailty of government institutions and the power of tribes, clans, families, and similar groups. Afghanistan today is even poorer than it was in the past, its economy having been shattered by the war (in which an estimated 9 percent of the population perished). Continued fighting between factions precludes any economic recovery.

The Afghans are fierce warriors, as demonstrated by their 10-year battle against the Soviet Army. The ability of Afghans to undertake offensive actions into Central Asia, however, is circumscribed by military and political considerations. On the military side, though the fighters are well supplied with ground weapons, they lack large armored and helicopter or air forces, command and staff structure, and logistics support, not to speak of an industrial base. Since the end of the Soviet invasion, they have lost the superpower support that supplied them with hardware, training, and intelligence data. On the political side, Afghanistan's absence of national unity allows temporary alliances between groups but prevents the formation of a national Afghan army under a single commander. Furthermore, the civil war within Afghanistan forces Afghans to focus on fighting other Afghans rather than on taking part in foreign conflicts.

On the other hand, Central Asian governments may have more impact on Afghanistan than Afghans do on Central Asia. As Roland Dannreuther writes in *Creating New States in Central Asia,* "If the 'Great Game' is being played anywhere, it is not in former Soviet Central Asia, but in Afghanistan."[27] Uzbekistan has been helping an ethnic Uzbek Afghan general, Rashid Dostum, to promote Uzbek interests in the Afghan civil war.[28] Because the Central Asian states, with the exception of Tajikistan, are stronger and more cohesive than Afghanistan, they find it easier to influence Afghanistan than vice versa.

Conclusion

Afghanistan has never had strong governments, and it has often been plagued by internal fighting. The violence and destruction resulting from the war against the USSR further debilitated traditional sources of authority and increased the potential for anarchy and the breakup of the country.[29] Consequently, Afghanistan will remain a zone of conflict, some of whose combatants can be expected to cross the border into Central Asia; in turn, some Central Asian governments will support factions within Afghanistan. But the limited offensive power and disunity of Afghan groups will restrict their impact on Central Asia. Moreover, the Afghans can participate in the conflicts in Tajikistan because of cross-border ethnic ties and the demise of the Tajik state. Afghans are far less likely to affect developments in Uzbekistan and Turkmenistan. The former is a stronger and more populated country than Tajikistan, and shares fewer ethnic ties to Afghanistan, while the latter is protected from Afghan interference by an unpopulated desert and lack of roads. Kazakhstan and Kyrgyzstan, which have no common border with Afghanistan, are beyond the reach of Afghans.

Afghanistan's influence on the future of Central Asia will be limited to Tajikistan. Even in Tajikistan, Afghans' role in the country is not as prominent as that of Russians or Uzbeks. Only if there is a total collapse of Russian power and political order in Central Asia, culminating in civil wars throughout the region, might Afghanistan play a greater part there. Some observers have noted the possibility of pan-Tajikism leading to the creation of an enlarged Tajikistan encompassing the Tajik Republic, northern Afghanistan, and possibly areas of Uzbekistan. Such a new country could seriously upset the regional balance of power. The limited organization of Tajiks, continuing internal rivalries, and the greater power of Uzbekistan and the Russian army, however, make such an outcome highly unlikely. Fighters in Central Asia's wars may seek sanctuary in Afghanistan and bring in Afghans to fight with them (repeating the story of the Basmachis, the anti-Soviet rebels who fought the Bolsheviks in Central Asia after the Revolution, but with weaker opponents). Even under these circumstances, however, Afghanistan's increased relevance to the region would be the result of domestic upheavals in Central Asia, not of Afghan intervention.

Iran and Central Asia

Iran shares a long border with Turkmenistan, and Persia has been a great cultural influence on Central Asians. The great cities of the region, such as Samarkand and Bukhara, are historically Persian-speaking. When the Central Asian republics became independent, some analysts thought they would become the prey of an Iranian Islamic conspiracy. By 1994, however, it was apparent that concerns over Iran's influence in Central Asia had been exaggerated. Iran has not been aggressive, nor has it made Central Asia the focus of its foreign policy. Although Iran's relations with Central Asia have developed since the Soviet period, the Islamic Republic has not become a major power in that region. To understand Iran's policies in Central Asia, we should first survey its ties to the area and then analyze its actions there.

Iran's Ties to Central Asia

There are important cultural ties between Central Asians and Iranians. Tajiks speak Persian, and throughout the southern areas of Central Asia, Persian was the language of high culture. In many areas of life, Turkish and Iranian influences in Central Asia blended over the centuries to create a Turco-Persian world.[30] But there are also differences between Central Asians and Iranians. Except for the Tajiks, Central Asians speak Turkic dialects, which have acquired a significant addition of Russian vocabulary. Moreover, Persian itself had been losing ground to Turkish in Central Asia since the late nineteenth century. Central Asian Moslems are also less pious than Iranians and come from a Sunni background.

Iran and Independent Central Asia

Iran's foreign policy in the twentieth century did not take Central Asia into account because it belonged to the Soviet Union and had almost no interaction with Iran. The establishment of independent republics in the region forced Iran to pay more attention to Central Asia and created new opportunities in foreign policy as well as new dangers.

The Central Asian republics offered Iran the opportunity to broaden its international relations by acquiring new friendly neighbors. The landlocked position of these republics represented a commercial gain to Iran, which could offer them transit rights to the sea or to Turkey. But the new independence of the Central Asian states also presented Iran with the possibility of ethnic agitation among the approximately nine hundred thousand Turkmen tribesmen of northeastern Iran.[31] (In the 1920s, Iran suffered from a Turkmen rebellion, in which Soviet propaganda contributed to antigovernment agitation among Iranian Turkmen.[32]) Furthermore, with the internationalizing of the Tajik civil war in 1993, Iran risked finding itself involved in the conflict, either because of its cultural ties to Tajikistan or because of its religious links to fellow Moslems. Given Iran's precarious economic situation and diplomatic isolation, it had a strong incentive to develop relations with these new republics, but to do so in a manner that would neither create new entanglements for the

Islamic Republic nor generate the hostility of the new regimes and Russia.

Iran has been developing its economic activities in the region. It has joined the Economic Cooperation Organization (ECO), whose other members include Turkey, Afghanistan, Pakistan, and the Central Asian nations. It has promoted the transportation of Central Asian commodities through Iran to either Turkey or the Iranian coast. A railroad to link Turkmenistan to the Iranian rail system is being planned,[33] for instance, as is a $5 billion pipeline to move Turkmen gas to Europe through Iran and Turkey.[34] In the political field, Iran has established diplomatic relations with all the Central Asian countries, and is training Tajik diplomats in Iran.[35] It has been careful to stay clear of activities the rulers of Central Asia find subversive. For example, conservative Sunni Moslems, rather than Iranians, have been the main providers of funds to Islamists in Central Asia.[36]

The progression of Iranian influence in Central Asia will be slowed not only by Iran's prudence, but by geographic, economic, and political realities. The infrastructure in Central Asia was originally part of the Soviet Union's, and it remains oriented northward, towards Russia; it is therefore unlikely that Iran will divert much transport away from Russia. Moreover, the continued tensions between Iran and the U.S. diminish Iran's attractiveness as an alternative route for Central Asian oil and gas because investors are loath to fund projects that Washington opposes. Russian pressure to continue to develop pipelines through Russia rather than through Turkey or Iran (see the discussion of Russian-CIS economic relations in chapter 1) compounds the impact of U.S. pressure. Beyond transportation, there is little potential for Iranian-Central Asian exchange. Iran's principal exports are petroleum products, which Central Asia does not need from Iran.[37] Iran's imports are mostly manufactured products bought from industrialized nations.[38]

Conclusion

Iran's relations with Central Asia have grown since the independence of the former Soviet republics. Because they started from nil, however, they remain relatively undeveloped compared to the ties Russia enjoys with the former SSRs. Iran's policy of moderation in the region, in contrast to the expected Islamist agitation, has served it well. At first wary of Iran, Central Asian rulers have become pragmatic about establishing ties with that country and about cooperating in transportation and infrastructure.[39] These relations will probably continue to develop. Because of its long border with Iran, Turkmenistan will be the Central Asian state most involved with Iran, while Tajikistan, because of cultural affinities, will be most open to Iranian influence. The other Turkic Central Asian states will have far fewer reasons to raise the level of their interaction with Iran.

This situation is unlikely to change in the foreseeable future. Iran's goals and ambitions are focused on the Persian Gulf and the Arab world, and its limited resources prevent it from attaching too much importance to Central Asia. If they wanted to break free of Moscow's embrace, the Central Asian regimes could conceivably seek Iran as an ally against Russia, but such a policy would not be realistic unless Russia were destroyed by internal conflict. Besides being unable to take on new challenges, Iran puts more value on its relationship with Russia than with the former SSRs. Russia, and possibly Ukraine, rather than the Asian republics, are the sources of manufactured products and advanced weaponry that Iran wants. Furthermore, an isolated Iran does not wish to incur the wrath of Russia, a country with troops on its borders and a permanent seat on the UN Security Council, which might one day vote on embargoes or other anti-Iranian measures. As proof of Iran's support for Russia's role in Central Asia, it has ignored Russia's actions against the Moslems of Tajikistan.[40] The end of Russian power in Central Asia would also endanger Iran by opening the door for Turkestani nationalists who might claim the loyalties of Iranian Turkmen.[41]

Turkey and Central Asia

The independence of the Turkic nations making up Central Asia created excitement in Turkey about establishing ties with thirty million Turks in the middle of Eurasia. By 1994, most of the initial euphoria had vanished. Turkey had new economic and cultural ties with the region, but they fell short of the grandiose dreams of the early 1990s. Geography, economic reality, and political obstacles had placed severe limits on the development of these relations. As of 1994, Central Asia was still firmly in the Russian orbit, and Turkey's priorities continued to be the development of its links with the European Union, the management of its economic crisis, and the Kurdish insurgency.

Turkey's Historical Links with Central Asia

The Turkic peoples, now scattered from Bulgaria to Xinjiang, have evolved along different paths over the centuries. The Turks of the Turkish Republic are the successors to the Ottoman Turks, who conquered Byzantium in 1453. The Turks of Central Asia were never part of the Ottoman Empire and developed separately from the eastern Mediterranean Turks. During the Ottoman period these two Turkish populations were separated by the Persian Empire and relations between them were distant, but at the end of the nineteenth century, Ottomans had some influence over the Central Asian jadids, or modernizers, who looked to Turkey for inspiration. In the short interlude between the downfall of the Tsar and the establishment of Soviet dominion, Central Asians unsuccessfully sought Turkish assistance. Enver Pasha, the Young Turk leader, fought along the Basmachis until his death in 1922, but his was the act of an isolated man, not the reflection of Turkish policy. After the victory of Communism in Central Asia, contact between Turkey and Turkestan ceased.

Turkey and Post-Independent Central Asia

In the immediate aftermath of Central Asia's independence from Moscow, there was considerable Turkish activity aimed at Central Asia.[42] The year 1992 culminated with a summit in Ankara of Turkic-speaking nations. Turkish initiatives in 1992 included offering $1.5 billion of credits and ten thousand scholarships for Central Asians at Turkish universities. Turkey also resurrected the Economic Cooperation Organization (ECO) to include Central Asia, Turkey, Iran, Afghanistan, and Pakistan in a regional economic organization, and it set up a satellite television network to broadcast in simplified Turkish to Turkestanis.

By 1994, Turkish influence in Central Asia had made some progress, but it remained below the expectations of the early 1990s.

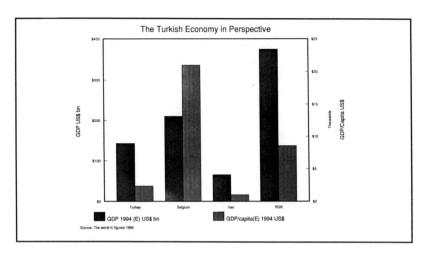

In the political sphere, the Central Asian republics have remained within Moscow's orbit, and Turkey has continued to focus on European and Near Eastern issues rather than on Central Asian ones. In the economic field, Turkish businessmen have been active in the region, but the major deals have been signed by large American or West European corporations. Chevron of the U.S. has taken the lead on the Tengiz oil field in Kazakhstan, and two large non-oil foreign investments in the region came from Philip Morris and BAT (formerly British American Tobacco). South Korean conglomerate Daewoo plans to produce cars in Uzbekistan.[43] According to published trade statistics, Turkey is still only a minor trade partner for the Central Asian republics.[44] There are nevertheless projects, such as a gas pipeline from Turkmenistan to Turkey via Iran, indicating that some opportunities for increased Turkish-Central Asian interaction existed.[45] In the first eight months of 1993, Turkish exports to Uzbekistan rose to US$177 million, though commerce with the entire CIS (mostly Russia) still represented less than 5 percent of Turkish exports, versus more than 60 percent for sales to the OECD countries.[46]

Reasons for Turkey's Limited Progress in Central Asia

Turkey's inability to become the new leader of a Turkic bloc stretching from the Great Wall of China to the Aegean is due to economic, geographic, cultural, and diplomatic factors.

Turkey is a small economy with medium per capita income (see graph above), whose economic power is further diminished by the current economic crisis. Turkey is unable to provide markets for Central Asia's products, contribute large amounts of economic assistance to this region, or give jobs to surplus Turkestani workers. Central Asia's small economies are in turn too poor to provide significant opportunities for Turkey.

The political influence of Turkey will also be limited by geography. There is no contiguity between Central Asia and Turkey, making physical communications between them dependent on Iran or on Russia's poor transportation networks and on its political goodwill.

Culture and history are another barrier to closer relations between Central Asia and the Turkish Republic. While Anatolian Turks acquired an Islamic-Imperial identity, their Central Asian brethren developed differently. (In fact the groups no longer even look alike—today's Turks look European or Middle Eastern, whereas many Central Asians have mongoloid features). In southern Central Asia, the cultural world bears the imprint of centuries of Iranian influence. Persian was the language of the cultural centers of Bukhara and Samarkand, and the Turkestani elites were generally equally at ease in Chagatay Turk and Persian. In northern Central Asia, shamanistic rituals are still strong, and Islam is far weaker than in Turkey. This region's local languages are more distant from Turkish than the southern Central Asian idioms.[47] Furthermore, the elites of Central Asia have been Russified, and almost half of the residents of the region are Slavs or Persians who are outside of the Turkish realm.

In the area of culture and education, Central Asians offered the opportunity to study abroad prefer North America, western Europe, and Japan or South Korea to Turkey, which is not perceived as possessing leading-edge educational facilities. Moreover, the attraction to western popular culture and products (from MTV to Coca-Cola) should not be underestimated.

There are also foreign policy considerations on both sides that limit Turkish-Central Asian relations. Central Asians continue to have strong ties with Russia, which is their most important foreign partner. Ankara, on the other hand, makes western Europe its priority, and it cannot afford to be distracted by Central Asia from its European ambitions and more pressing regional crises in Kurdistan.[48]

Conclusion

During the Soviet era Turkey was absent from Central Asia, but its presence today can already be considered significant. Because of cultural ties and the potential for some infrastructure projects (such as the Turkmen gas pipeline), relations between the Central Asian republics and Turkey are likely to increase. Though Turkish companies cannot compete for large-scale developments with western multinationals, western businesses may use Turkish subsidiaries in their dealings with Central Asia. For smaller transactions, Turkish businessmen may find that their linguistic ties and understanding of the Orient give them an advantage over western or East Asian competitors. Consequently, it is probable that Turkish commerce will continue to develop in the region. On the other hand, Central Asia will not become part of a new Turkic realm, and Turkey will be only one of several new partners for these new republics.

The Indian Subcontinent and Central Asia

The historical links between Central Asia and the subcontinent are strong, especially among Moslems. Islam arrived in India via Central Asia, where the Moghul dynasty originated. Babur, the last Timurite from Central Asia, founded the Moghul dynasty in 1526. In the nineteenth century, Central Asia and the subcontinent bifurcated. Russia colonized Central Asia, and Indians became part of the British Empire. The Turco-Persian traditions that had bound Central Asians to Indians (particularly Moslem ones) receded into history, especially in predominantly Hindu India. In the twentieth century, the Bolsheviks cut the remaining links between Central Asia and the outside world.

Following the USSR's breakup, both Pakistan and India established commercial and diplomatic relations with the Central Asian republics. Trade with the subcontinent and the possible activity of businessmen from India and Pakistan will diversify Central Asia's economic relations. Overall, because Central Asia is a priority for neither Islamabad nor New Delhi, the subcontinent is unlikely to have a significant role in Central Asia's evolution.

Pakistan and Central Asia

Thanks to the collapse of the Iron Curtain around Central Asia and Afghanistan, Pakistan now has ties to Central Asia. Some Pakistani clerics have been involved in religious work in Central Asia, and Pakistani businessmen have been active in the region.[49] Pakistan might also provide Central Asia with an outlet to the sea. One alternative to the Russian route for Turkmen gas, for example, is through Afghanistan and Pakistan to the Arabian Sea.[50]

Central Asia, however, is not the focus of Pakistan's international relations because its feud with India dominates its foreign policy.[51] Pakistan does have vital interests at stake in Afghanistan.[52] First, it does not wish to see a pro-Indian government in power in Kabul. Second, some ethnic groups, primarily the Pathans (or Pushtuns) and the Baluchis, straddle the Afghan-Pakistan border. It is therefore in Pakistan's interest to prevent the emergence of Pathan or Baluchi movements that would unsettle their kinsmen in Pakistan.

Given this situation, Pakistani leaders (or at least some elements within the national security apparatus) support factions in the Afghan civil war. This could give rise either to Pakistani collaboration or tensions with Uzbekistan, which has also been involved in the Afghan fighting by supporting Rashid Dostam. There have, however, been no published reports of Pakistani-Uzbek interaction in Afghanistan as of late 1994. Because Uzbekistan is more attentive to northern Afghanistan and Pakistan more to the south, there are no reasons for Pakistani and Uzbekistani interests to clash in Afghanistan.

In the future, it is probable that Central Asian-Pakistani ties will continue to develop in certain areas. Pakistani traders and investors, who are accustomed to Third World bureaucracies, may have an edge over businessmen from the developed world. If a modicum of order is restored in Afghanistan, some Central Asian imports and exports could transit through Pakistani ports. In the spiritual realm, men of religion from Pakistan may rekindle historical ties between Moslems from Central Asia and the subcontinent. Sunni Moslem Pakistanis are also a logical missionary conduit for the money of Saudi Arabia and other wealthy Sunni nations. Overall, the development of a stable Moslem hinterland is a desirable outcome for Islamabad, and one in which it will attempt to exercise some influence.

Several factors, however, will restrict Pakistani-Central Asian relations. First, the instability and devastated infrastructure of Afghanistan hamper trade between the former Soviet Union and Pakistan. Second, Pakistan is a poor country without the capital, in either the public or private sector, to assist economic development in Central Asia. Third, Pakistan's diplomacy is focused on India, and Islamabad's most important interlocutors are the US, China, and the Gulf countries. Central Asia's relevance to Pakistan's security is minor. Russia and perhaps one day China are the key to Central Asians' security concerns. Although Pakistani-Central Asian relations may expand, therefore, they will not be of strategic importance for either side.

India and Central Asia

Central Asia is not a region crucial to Indian security. The British Raj was involved in the areas to its north as part of the containment of Russian and later Soviet power, leading to British intervention in Afghan affairs and in Tibet. Partition, however, transformed New Delhi's imperial perspective into a more parochial one, which generally rejects a continent-wide strategic vision in favor of the more focused question of how to confront Pakistan.[53]

There are, nevertheless, several reasons for India to pay attention to Central Asia:

- By establishing ties with Central Asia, India denies strategic depth to its Pakistani rival.
- Kashmiris may feel emboldened by the end of colonialism in Central Asia[54] and seek assistance from Central Asian Moslems. India, like China, must be concerned about the effect on its Moslem region of the end of Soviet hegemony and the proliferation of weapons and armed groups in some parts of Central Asia (though Pakistan, rather than Central Asia, is currently the main foreign actor in the Kashmir insurgency).
- An Islamic grouping that included Central Asia, Afghanistan,

Pakistan, Iran, Kashmir, and Xinjiang would disturb India deeply.[55] Although the likelihood of such a divided group of peoples achieving political cohesion is slim, India, as a Hindu country often invaded by Moslems, may take very seriously the possibility of an Islamic commonwealth.

• The former Soviet Union was an important trade partner for India. Though Russia is the principal successor state, it makes sense for India to establish ties with the other former Soviet republics.

These considerations justify some Indian interest in Central Asia. India's credits of $10 million to Uzbekistan in 1993[56] indicate that India is willing to develop relations with Central Asia. In the future, Indian-Central Asian relations may grow in certain areas. For example, Indian entrepreneurs may be attracted by new opportunities in Central Asia. Some trade relations may expand, and a diplomatic dialogue could start on some issues of common concern, such as Chinese policy or what is commonly termed Islamic fundamentalism. But, at least in the 1990s, relations between India and Central Asia are not going to be a priority for either India or the Central Asian nations.

Islam

One of the issues confronting analysts when the Soviet Union broke up was the role that Islam would play in the domestic and international politics of the Moslem republics of the former USSR. Many feared—or hoped—that after decades of godless oppression, the Central Asians were ready for radical Islam. The proximity of Iran and the presence of millions of Persian speakers in Tajikistan and Uzbekistan[57] left open the possibility of the extension of Iranian Islamism's reach into the former Soviet Union.

As of late 1994, however, Islamism had not conquered Central Asia. There has been an increase in the visibility of religious practice, and foreign missionaries (mostly Sunnis rather than Iranian Shias) have been proselytizing, but Islamic politics has not made significant gains. It remains possible that economic failure, combined with a spiritual vacuum, could lead to powerful Islamic movements, but these would grow out of domestic issues rather than foreign manipulation.

Less than six years ago, the late Ayatollah Khomeini advised CPSU General Secretary Mikhail Gorbachev to convert to Islam and forswear seventy years of rotten communism.[58] At the time, it seemed a preposterous gesture, but in the early 1990s the situation was different. God and his prophet (with American missiles) crushed dialectical materialism in Afghanistan and helped bury the Soviet Union, indicating the political relevance of Islam. The Afghans' liberation, coupled with continued concern over Iranian actions abroad, created fear over the "Islamic threat" to Central Asia. Headlines about Afghan and Tajik "Islamic fundamentalists" fighting the Dushanbe government illustrate this point. (The modern form of politicized Islam as seen in Iran is better labeled "Islamist" than "fundamentalist"; the latter word is more accurately applied to conservative traditionalism of the Saudi type.[59]) To some observers, a decade after militant Islam deposed the shah and a few years after the Afghan War, it seems that Islam is again on a war path, this time in the former USSR. This section focuses on southern Central Asia, which is more profoundly Moslem, more than on Kazakhstan, where Islam's roots are shallower.

Soviet Rule and Islam

The Soviets were the only western colonizers who tried to eradicate Islam. The "Islamophobia"[60] (and general aversion to religion) of the regime expressed itself in the liquidation of most places of worship and the mobilization of a vast antireligious apparatus. There were twenty-seven thousand mosques in the Russian Empire on the eve of the Revolution; by 1941, the number in the USSR had dropped to "just over a thousand."[61] The propaganda effort directed at eradicating religion was enormous: for example, in the small republic of Kyrgyzstan alone, there were, in 1982, 27,500 antireligious propagandists[62] for its 4 million souls (these agitators were 74 percent more numerous than physicians![63]).

The Soviet regime closed mosques and seminaries and preached atheism, but Islam remained the core of the people's identity in Moslem regions. As an analyst wrote, "Many Central Asians even today [early 1970s] appear to feel that it is precisely Islam that contains the essence of their cultural tradition."[64] Recent opinion polls of the population in Uzbekistan confirm that "Islam remains intimately connected with their national identity, way of life and understanding of the meaning of life."[65]

Soviet atheism also failed at the level of the political leadership. All accounts of life in the post-Stalin era agree that Soviet Moslem red potentates continued to condone Islam and followed the ritual requirements of circumcision, Islamic wedding, and religious burial.[66] Furthermore, Soviet propaganda was counterproductive with the younger generation, members of which were reported, in the 1980s, to be more religious than their elders.[67] (The same situation occurred in the Christian regions of the late Soviet Union.)

An increased visibility of religion in Central Asia does not necessarily indicate the success of the Islamic political agenda. It reflects a return to tradition after seventy years of monstrous rule by a power dedicated to destroying Islam. For example, the consecration of new mosques is often the public display of previously underground prayer houses, not a statement of fanaticism.

To understand the security implications of religion in Central Asia, one should consider that although Islam has provided a religious and cultural framework to the region, it was never the basis for political unity. Historically, competing khanates and emirates—all Moslem— were often at war with each other. More recently, violence within the region and in Afghanistan has been between Moslems rather than along sectarian lines. Bernard Lewis's comment that "Pan Islamic solidarity was a matter of grave—and indeed exaggerated—concern to the Allies in the First World War"[68] is still relevant in the last years of our century. Since World War I, over thirty Moslem-majority polities have gained independence. From the Moroccan-Algerian-Polisario conflict to the Indonesian-Malaysian "confrontation," their relations have been marred by violence. Moslem Bangladesh sought "Hindu" assistance to remove the yoke of Moslem (West) Pakistan. Saddam Hussein erased a Moslem nation-state from the map and gassed thousands of Moslem Kurds. Even Islamic radicals generally end up as Islamo-nationalists rather than universalists.[69] Islam has not been more successful at generating internal unity: coups d'etats, revolutions, and assassinations have been as prevalent in

Moslem states as in other underdeveloped countries. In the foreign policy arena, Moslem cooperation has been ineffective beyond the verbal realm. The Star of David over East Jerusalem and India's hold over most of Kashmir are but two reminders of the impotence of Islam as an international political movement. Its victory in Afghanistan owes more to the commitment of the United States, initiated by President Carter, a born-again Baptist, than to the actions of international Moslem organizations. Even in the field of humanitarian relief, in places such as Somalia, Christian nations, rather than Moslem ones, have taken the lead in saving Moslem lives.

The participation of Afghans in the Tajik civil war has been portrayed by some as an Islamic onslaught. It should be remembered, however, that in spite of political labels, the conflict in the Tajik Republic stems from complex clan wars and Russian activity and is not an ideological confrontation. Some Afghan fighters may be "Islamists" but their participation is more reflective of regional and kinship affinities than of a coordinated effort at jihad. Moreover, even to refer to the Afghan War as a great jihad is misleading. Islam provided a unifying force in Afghanistan, and was reinforced by the assistance provided by foreign Moslems; the occupation of the country by godless creatures induced the faithful to take up arms. But even Islam could not unify the Afghans. During the war they remained highly competitive with each other and were sometimes fratricidal. Additionally, defense of land, freedom, and traditions was another motive that was not directly tied to Islam itself and would not apply to offensive actions by Afghans in Central Asia.[70] The civil war that followed the Soviet retreat across the Oxus demonstrated the lack of unity among Afghanistan's Moslem fighters.

This is not to deny that Islamism has had a major impact in certain regions of the world. But to portray it as a force capable of unifying many countries distorts reality. It can be extremely powerful within a country when merged with revolutionary fervor and organization, as Iran and Algeria, for example, have shown us. But because political Islam is rooted in the domestic specifics of every individual society and is divided into sects and schools of interpretation, it does not have the centralized organization that made Soviet Communism an international force. Moslem groups, in spite of claims of universalism, are in fact often

nationalists.[71] Iran has been cited by some as the great manipu-
lator of Islamic movements, posing a threat comparable to Mos-
cow-directed Communism. Iran has sometimes helped Islamic
opposition movements, but Iran's ability to exert control over
foreign Islamists, especially if they achieve power and get access
to the resources of the state they rule, will be limited by two
critical factors. First, unlike the USSR, Iran is a medium-size
Third World nation without the ability to project military power
or the industrial-technological base to become a great power.
Second, Soviet Marxism-Leninism was a centralized system
whose command center, like the brain of an octopus, was able to
control far-flung tentacles. Islamism does not fit this model. Many
Islamist movements have roots that predate Khomeini's revolution[72] and have no reason to bow to Persian Shias if they achieve
power in their own countries. Islam also lacks the centralization
of the Roman Church, which allowed Pope John-Paul II to play
an important role in the endgame of the Cold War.

Finally, in the context of policy analysis, it should be remembered that religious Moslem regimes have not necessarily
been anti-American. For example, the Saudis and the late president of Pakistan General Zia ul-Haq have been more pro-Ameri-
can than many "secular" Arab governments, Christian liberation
theologians, and atheist Marxists. Militant Islam in the Middle
East, such as Iran's and Hizbolah's, is anti-American for reasons
that are to a considerable extent peculiar to the region. These
issues are at best secondary to Central Asians and Afghans. Religious, ecological, cultural, and physical persecutions by the
Soviets ensure that America is unlikely to be Central Asians'
"great Satan,"[73] unless Washington sides actively with Islam's
foes.

Conclusion

As it has in the Middle East, Islam in Central Asia could possibly become the crystallizing force of those opposing both the
socioeconomic failure of the local regimes and the continued influence and presence of Russian neocolonial forces. Since left-
wing ideology has been discredited, and nationalism is still in-

choate in Central Asia, Islam is the only belief system with the potential to appeal to the masses across regional and clan lines. In Egypt and Algeria, where socialism, Third Worldism, and Arabism failed, Islam has managed to become the focal point of opposition to the governments. Such Islamic militancy in Central Asia may enjoy support from Afghans and possibly other foreign Moslems, but it will be generated primarily by the internal problems of the local regimes and Russian intervention rather than by foreign Moslem subversion. Poverty, increasing inequalities, corruption, and a spiritual void provide a fertile ground for Islamists. In this context, propaganda and actions aimed at rooting out "fundamentalism" may help political Islam in the region by convincing the population that their rulers are nothing but communists under Russian influence and afraid of the faith of their forefathers. Nevertheless, Islam's political emergence in Central Asia will be slowed by the divisions along national, linguistic, clan, regional, and other lines that are more significant than those in Egypt, Algeria, or Iran, countries that are further along the road to nation-state cohesion.[74]

The "fundamentalist threat" provides a very good justification for the Russians and neo-Soviet rulers to stay in power[75]; it legitimizes political repression and the presence of the Russian military. Invoking such a threat has the advantage of excusing Russian actions in the eyes of western democracies, which fear Islamism more than they support democracy (as indicated by their efforts in Haiti to uphold a [suspended] Roman Catholic priest compared to their silent blessing of the coup d'etat that robbed the Algerian Islamic Salvation Front of its electoral victory). This tactic was used by Foreign Minister Kozyrev when he warned of "extremist" forces to justify the invasion of Tajikistan.[76]

Russians who support a continued presence in Central Asia also cite the Moslem "danger" in order to justify their policies to the Russian people. Given the negative image of "fundamentalism" and Russia's own problems with Moslems inside the Federation, Russians might support an "antifundamentalist" struggle, whereas they would oppose the same actions if described as neo-Soviet imperialism financed by Russian taxpayers.

Conclusion

The shape of the international relations of Central Asia is not yet mature. The former republics have enjoyed formal independence for less than three years, and they remain tied to Russia through a web of relationships. Their future as independent nations is still in doubt, and therefore, the patterns of their interaction with the "far abroad" remain inchoate. Nevertheless, a few facts were already apparent as of late 1994.

First, no single non-CIS foreign country has become the dominant actor in Central Asia. Depending on geography, language, and culture, different countries have acted in different areas in the region.

Second, at this stage, the combined presence of all these foreign nations remains much smaller than Russia's. Russia's links to Central Asia, as described in chapter 1, are quasi-imperial, involving Russian control in military, police, and economic affairs. The other countries' relations are limited to diplomatic and commercial intercourse.

Third, foreign countries (with the possible exception of Afghanistan) have been a source of stability in Central Asia. They have brought economic opportunities to the region in the form of trade and cooperation. If these ties continue to develop, they will contribute to Central Asia's prosperity and continued stability.

Finally, geography is a factor that should not be overlooked. All Central Asia's republics are landlocked. All are a significant distance from the sea and have access only to poor infrastructure leading to the sea. This will put severe restrictions on Central Asia's international relations because it will slow the development of trade and communications with the outside world.

Notes

[1] The haj is the pilgrimage to Mecca that Moslems are enjoined to undertake once in their lifetime, should their means permit it.

[2] Economist Intelligence Unit, *EIU Country Reports* (Transcaucasus and Central Asia), 1st quarter 1994, 13, 15.

[3] René Grousset, *L'Empire des Steppes* (Paris: Payot, 1939), 168-69.

[4]The term *unequal treaty* refers to the agreements that China was forced to sign with the stronger European powers and Japan in the nineteenth century. These accords deprived China of land or of sovereign rights, such as jurisdiction over foreigners on Chinese soil.

[5]Population data is from *The Kazaks of China: Essays on an Ethnic Minority,* ed. Linda Benson and Ingvar Svanberg (Uppsala: Almqvist & Wiksell International, 1988), 21-26, 35-36, 41; *Statesman's Year-Book 1992-1993,* ed. Brian Hunter (New York: St. Martin's Press, 1992); Rajan Menon and Henry J. Barkley, "The Transformation of Central Asia," (*Survival,* Winter 1992-93): 81; Robert L. Worden et. al., *China: A Country Study* (Washington D.C.: U.S. GPO, 1988), 84. Despite minor differences, these sources are in general agreement.

[6]Carl Goldstein, "Final Frontier," *Far Eastern Economic Review,* 10 June 1993, 54-59. According to the "Energy Survey" in *The Economist* (18 June 1994, 12), the Tarim could have 70 billion barrels in reserves, with 70 billion barrels in Karamay to the north, making China's oil reserves second only to Saudi Arabia's.

[7]Ingvar Svanberg in *The Nationalities Question in the Soviet Union,* ed. Graham Smith (London: Longman, 1990), 203.

[8]See William Peters, "Central Asia and the Minority Question," *Far Eastern Economic Review,* 9 Jan. 1992, 14, and Isabelle Maltor and Dongfang Ouyang, "Nouvelle donne régionale pour le Xinjiang," *Le Monde Diplomatique,* November 1993, 22. The findings of these sources were confirmed at an off-the-record meeting with a sinologist in France, November 1993.

[9]See Steve LeVine, "Li Peng tip-toes along the old silk road," *Financial Times,* 29 April 1994, which mentions the PRC's desire not to create Russian suspicion. The importance of Russian-Chinese trade is another reason for China to avoid provoking Russia. For the growth of PRC-Russian trade, see RFE/RL Daily Report, no. 82, 29 April 1994.

[10]A titular nationality in the USSR was the nationality after whom the territorial unit was named (i.e. the Kazakhs are the titular nationality in Kazakhstan). The non-titular nationalities are other, generally minority, ethnic groups.

[11]See Roland Dannreuther, *Creating New States in Central Asia* (London: IISS, 1994), 63-65.

[12]Economist Intelligence Unit, *EIU Country Report* (Transcaucasia and Central Asia), 1st quarter 1994, 13, 15.

[13]Authors' observations in Bishkek, Kyrgyzstan, in December 1993.

[14]In RFE/RL Daily Report, no. 80, 27 April 1994, Liz Fuller reports the signing by the PRC and Kazakhstan of an agreement defining the last disputed stretch of their 1700-kilometer border.

[15]The authors learned as much in meetings with government officials and political scientists in Kazakhstan and Kyrgyzstan, December 1993, and in an off-the-record conversation with a Central Asian foreign minister, May 1994.

[16]Mongolians have a similar attitude toward the PRC.

[17]For Lop Nor tests and "Eastern Turkestan" movement based in Almaty, see *Izvestiya* (Moscow), 19 Oct. 1993, morning edition, 3, in FBIS-SOV-93-201, 29 Oct. 1993, 84. See Robert Karniol, "Beijing faces challenges from reawakened ethnic interests," *Jane's Defence Weekly,* 9 Oct. 1993, 19 on Uighur movements in Kazakhstan. See also Dannreuther, *Creating New States,* 64.

[18]See, for example, Richard Hornik, "Bursting China's Bubble," *Foreign Affairs* 73 (May-June 1994); Gerald Segal, "Beijing's Fading Clout," *The New York Times,* 25 May 1994, A21; Michael Vatikiotis et. al., "Gunboat Diplomacy," *Far Eastern Economic Review,* 16 June 1994, 22-28; Lincoln Kaye, "Labour Pains," *Far Eastern Economic* Review, 16 June 1994, 32-33; and Lincoln Kaye et. al., "Disorder Under Heaven" and following stories, *Far Eastern Economic Review*, 9 June 1994, 22-30.

[19]Guacang Huan, "The New Relationship with the Former Soviet Union," *Current History*, Sept. 1992, 254.

[20]See Ahmed Rashid, "The China Factor," *Far Eastern Economic Review,* 13 Jan. 1994, 12-13 on Chinese concern about the spread of fundamentalism.

[21]CIA map 724842 (R00434) 4-92 released to the public, using 1992 U.S. Bureau of Census data; and 1992 estimate of Economist Intelligence Unit, *EIU Country Reports* (Pakistan and Afghanistan), 2nd quarter 1993, 6.

[22]Data is from CIA map 724842 (R00434) 4-92 of Afghanistan. Figures are slightly different for Tajiks (3.5 million) and Turkmens (100,000) in Richard F. Nyrop and D.M. Seekins, *Afghanistan: A Country Study* (Washington D.C.: U.S. GPO, 1986), 105-6, and Robert L. Canfield, "Ethnic Regional and Sectarian Alignments in Afghanistan," in *The State, Religion and Ethnic Politics: Afghanistan, Iran and Pakistan,* ed. Ali Banuazizi and Myron Weiner (Syracuse, NY: Syracuse University Press, 1986), 78. See CIS section of *The Statesman's Year-Book 1992-93* for CIS data.

[23]See Alexandre Bennigsen, "Mullahs, Mujahidin and Soviet Muslims," in *Problems of Communism,* Nov.-Dec. 1984; Muriel Atkin, *The Subtlest Battle: Islam in Soviet Tajikistan* (Philadelphia: Foreign Policy Research Institute, 1989); Graham E. Fuller, *Islamic Fundamentalism in Afghanistan* (Santa Monica, CA: Rand, 1991);

Robert L. Canfield, "The Collision," in *Afghanistan and the Soviet Union: Collision and Transformation,* ed. Milan Hauner and Robert L. Canfield (Boulder, CO: Westview Press, 1989); and Milan Hauner, Introduction, ibid.

[24]For Afghan identity see Charles G. Cogan, "Shawl of Lead," in *Conflict* 10 (1990); M. Nazif Shahrani and Robert L. Canfield, *Revolutions and Rebellions in Afghanistan: Anthropological Perspectives* (Berkeley, CA: Institute for International Studies, 1984); Canfield, "Ethnic Regional"; G. Whitney Azoy, *Buzkashi: Game and Power in Afghanistan* (Philadelphia: University of Pennsylvania Press, 1982); Olivier Roy, *L'Afghanistan: Islam et modernite politique* (Paris: Le Seuil, 1985); and Amin Saikal and William Maley, *Regime Change in Afghanistan: Foreign Intervention and the Politics of Legitimacy* (Boulder, CO: Westview Press, 1991).

[25]See Olivier Roy, "Ethnic Identity and Political Expression in Northern Afghanistan," in *Muslims in Central Asia: Expressions of Identity and Change,* ed. Jo-Ann Gross (Durham, NC: Duke University Press, 1992), 74. Also off-the-record discussion with a Central Asia specialist, Paris, Nov. 1993.

[26]Off-the-record discussion with a Central Asia specialist, Paris, Nov. 1993.

[27]Dannreuther, *Creating New States*, 66.

[28]Bess Brown, RFE/RL Daily Report, no. 25, 7 Feb. 1994, 3.

[29]Cogan, "Shawl," 192, and Amin Saikal and W. Maley, *Regime Change,* 139.

[30]See *Turko-Persia in Historical Perspective,* ed. Robert L. Canfield (Cambridge: Cambridge University Press, 1991).

[31]The nine hundred thousand figure is from *Atlas of the Middle East,* ed. Moshe Brawer (New York: MacMillan Publishing Co., 1988), 89.

[32]Robert Olson, "The Turkoman rebellion in Eastern Iran in 1924-25: the Soviet Union's reaction," *Central Asian Survey* 12 (1993): 525-26.

[33]Economist Intelligence Unit, *EIU Country Report* (Iran), 1st quarter 1994, 21.

[34]Itar Tass 1750 GMT, 5 April 1994 and TRT TV Ankara 2100 GMT, 5 April 1994, in FBIS-SOV-94-066 6 April 1994, 46.

[35]Off-the-record meeting with a U.S. diplomat, Washington, D.C., May 1994.

[36]Dannreuther, *Creating New States,* 63. In a conversation with a journalist having significant Middle Eastern experience, one of the authors was told that the Saudis, who condone sending fanatical religious missionaries abroad to buy domestic peace, are more active than the

Iranians in sponsoring fundamentalism in Central Asia.

[37]The republics use oil from Central Asia or import it from Russia.

[38]Economist Intelligence Unit, *EIU Country Report* (Iran), 1st quarter 1994, 3, cites the figure 82 percent manufactured goods.

[39]Dannreuther, *Creating New States,* 61-62.

[40]See Patrick Clawson, "Alternative Foreign Policy Views Among the Iranian Policy Elite," in *Iran's Strategic Intentions and Capabilities,* ed. Patrick Clawson (Washington D.C.: National Defense University—INSS, 1994), 45-46. In *Iran's National Security Policy: Intentions, Capabilities & Impact* (Washington, DC: Carnegie Endowment for International Peace), 7, Sharam Chubin points out that "Iran's top priority in the north remains its relations with Russia."

[41]See chapter 4 for a discussion of Iran's ethnic makeup and its security implications.

[42]See Dannreuther, *Creating New States,* 58-61, for an excellent summary of Turkey's role in Central Asia.

[43]"Daewoo unveils big expansion plan," *Financial Times,* 19 Oct. 1994, 7.

[44]Economist Intelligence Unit, *EIU Country Report* (Transcaucasus and Central Asia), 1st quarter 1994. Trade statistics listing the major trade partners do not even mention Turkey.

[45]Itar Tass 1750 GMT, 5 Apil 1994 and TRT TV Ankara 2100 GMT, 5 April 1994, in FBIS-SOV-94-066, 6 April 1994, 46.

[46]Economist Intelligence Unit, *EIU Country Report* (Turkey), 3, 24.

[47]1994 conversation with U.S. State Department analyst on Kazakh, Kyrgyz being more difficult for Turks to understand.

[48]See Philip Robins, "Between Sentiment and Self-Interest," *Middle East Journal* 47 (Autumn 1993) on limits to Turkish reach in Central Asia. See also Eric Rouleau, "The Challenges to Turkey," *Foreign Affairs* 72 (November-December 1993): 115. In RFE/RL Daily Report, no. 199, 19 Oct. 1994, 3, Bess Brown reports that many documents signed in 1992 have yet to be implemented.

[49]Khalid Durán, "Rivalries Over the New Muslim Countries," *Aussenpolitik,* IV/1992, 378-379. For a good account of Pakistani policies and activities in Central Asia, see Dietrich Reetz, "Pakistan and Central Asian Hinterland Option: The Race for Regional Security and Development," *Journal of South Asian and Middle Eastern Studies* 17 (Fall 1993).

[50]International Monetary Fund, *Economic Reviews: Turkmenistan* (1994/3) (Washington D.C.: IMF, 1994), 5.

[51]Off-the-record seminar, Washington D.C., May 1993.

[52]For Pakistan's relations with Afghanistan and Pakistan's ethnic

problems, see Marvin Weinbaum, "Pakistan and Afghanistan" in *Asian Survey*, June 1991; John Tsagronis, *Pakistan: Prospects for Democracy* (Washington, D.C.: Hudson Institute, 1992); Louis Dupree, *Afghanistan* (Princeton, NJ: Princeton University Press, 1973), 488-508, 540, 557, 758; Selig Harrison, "Ethnicity and the Political Stalemate in Pakistan" in *The State, Religion and Ethnic Politics: Afghanistan, Iran and Pakistan*, ed. Ali Banuazizi and Myron Weiner (Syracuse, NY: Syracuse University Press, 1986); and Graham Fuller, The "Center of the Universe:" *The Geopolitics of Iran* (Boulder, CO: Westview Press, 1991), 228. See also Selig S. Harrison, *In Afghanistan's Shadow: Baluch Nationalism and Soviet Temptations* (New York: Carnegie Endowment for International Peace, 1981), 39, 51, 81.

[53]Stanley Wolpert, *A New History of India* (New York: Oxford University Press, 1993), 412-13.

[54]*The Economist*, "Kashmir," 10 Apr. 1993, 43.

[55]Milan Hauner, *What is Asia to Us: Russia's Asian Heartland Yesterday and Today* (Boston: Unwin Hyman, 1990), 90, cites a similar idea by Amir Amanullah of Afghanistan. Robin Wright, "The West is looking at South Asia," *Los Angeles Times*, 4 August 1992, H3, sees such a possibility in the wake of the Soviet breakup. See Gail Minault, *The Khilafat Movement* (New York: Columbia University Press, 1982), 72, on Hindus' "primordial fears" of Moslem hordes from the Khyber pass.

[56]Liz Fuller, RFE/RL Daily Report, no. 98, 25 May 1993, 3. In RFE/RL Daily Report, no. 147, 4 August 1994, Liz Fuller reports that India opened the first of two $10 million credits to Uzbekistan for joint-venture financing.

[57]There is a Tajik minority in Uzbekistan, and Tajik is widely spoken in some major centers.

[58]Graham Fuller, "The Emergence of Central Asia," *Foreign Policy* 78 (Spring 1990): 54-55.

[59]Graham Fuller, *Islamic Fundamentalism in the Northern Tier Countries* (Santa Monica, CA: Rand, 1991), v, 2, and Roy, L'Afghanistan, 16.

[60]Gregory Gleason, "The Political Economy of Dependency," *Studies in Comparative Communism* 24 (Dec. 1991).

[61]Cyril E. Black et. al., *The Modernization of Inner Asia* (Armonk, NY: M.E. Sharpe Inc., 1991), 281.

[62]Bennigsen, "Mullahs," 40-41.

[63]According to *The Statesman's Year-Book 1992-93*, 429, there were 15,800 doctors in 1989.

[64]Ethel and Stephen P. Dunn, in *The Nationality Question in Soviet*

Central Asia, ed. Edward Allworth (New York: Praeger, 1973), 55.

[65]USIA Opinion Research Memorandum, 30 Sept. 1992. For the role of Islam in Central Asia, see Azade-Ayse Rorlich, "Islam and Atheism" in *Soviet Central Asia: The Failed Transformation,* ed. William Fierman, (Boulder, CO: Westview Press, 1991), 187, and Paul B. Henze, *Impressions and Conversations in Uzbekistan and Kazakhstan* (Santa Monica, CA: Rand, 1990), 33.

[66]Rorlich, "Islam and Atheism," 189, 194; William Fierman, *Introduction, Soviet Central Asia: The Failed Transformation,* ed. William Fierman (Boulder, CO: Westview Press, 1991), 5; Bennigsen, "Mullahs," 42; and Paul Henze, Impressions 33.

[67]Rorlich, "Islam and Atheism," 190; James Critchlow, *Nationalism in Uzbekistan: A Soviet Republic's Road to Sovereignty* (Boulder, CO: Westview Press, 1991), 175-76; and Anthony Hyman, "Moving Out of Moscow's Orbit," *International Affairs* (1993), 293.

[68]*The Emergence of Modern Turkey* (London: Oxford University Press, 1968), 343.

[69]See Marie-Lucie Dumas, review of *L'echec de l'islam politique,* by Olivier Roy, *Politique Etrangere* 57 (Winter 1992): 954-5.

[70]Chantal Lemercier-Quelquejay ("Muslim Minorities," in *Soviet Nationalities in Strategic Perspective,* ed. S. Enders Wimbush, [New York: St Martin's Press, 1985], 52) says the Basmachis fought for their traditions rather than jihad.

[71]See Richard P. Mitchell, *The Society of Moslem Brothers* (London: Oxford University Press, 1969), 264-66.

[72]For example, Sayyid Qutb in Egypt, according to Gilles Keppel, *Le Prophete et Pharaon* (Paris: La Decouverte, 1984), 56-57.

[73]See Roy, *L'Afghanistan,* 17 for a similar analysis concerning Afghanistan.

[74]See Olivier Roy, "Nationales et sovietiques," in *Le Monde des Debats*, March 1994, 21, on the weakness of Central Asian political Islam and its divisions.

[75]"Moslem countries support 'holy war' in Tajikistan," *Izvestiya Moscow,* 24 Feb. 1993, 5, in FBIS-SOV-93-038, 1 March 1993, 18-19.

[76]Stephen Foye, RFE/RL Daily Report, no. 147, 4 Aug. 1993, 3. See also "Tajikistan: The empire strikes back," *The Economist,* 7 Aug. 1993, 36, and Kozyrev's remarks at the signing of the Israel-PLO Declaration on the White House South Lawn.

F O U R

The Transcaucasus, Turkey, and Iran: The New International Environment of the Transcaucasus

In the Soviet era, both Turkey and Iran faced a Soviet monolith on their northern border. Neither country had influence in the Caucasus, and both sought to defend themselves against Soviet expansionism. The appearance of three small republics on Turkey's and Iran's border transformed the local environment, leaving Turkey and Iran with weak neighbors to their north. The post-Soviet situation in the Transcaucasus has potentially grave implications for both countries. Although at this time Russian hegemony seems guaranteed, and conflict between Turks and Iranians is unlikely, the potential for disorder and violence in the region remains.

This chapter looks at the internal and foreign policies of Iran and Turkey in some detail because they have considerable significance for Transcaucasia—far more significance than the policies of Central Asia's neighbors have for Central Asia. Central Asia's neighbors—China, Afghanistan, Pakistan, India, and Iran—have either little at stake in the region or little ability to influence developments there. On the other hand, Transcaucasia is of great importance to Iran and Turkey. Ethnicity and geography make it a region that neither country can ignore. Moreover, Transcaucasia is a more violent region than Central Asia. With the exception of Tajikistan, Central Asia has been relatively free of major conflict, but from the Black Sea to the Caspian, Transcaucasia and the Northern Caucasus have been the scene of wars. An understanding of the prospects for regional stability in the Transcaucasus requires an in-depth analysis of Turkish and Iranian developments.

Turkey and Iran could have used the decolonization in

Transcaucasia to extend their influence over Georgia, Armenia, and Azerbaijan. Because of simmering disputes between Ankara and Tehran, the expansion of Turkish and Iranian activities in Transcaucasia had the potential to lead to a confrontation over control of the region. The proximity of Kurdistan, along with other sources of Turkish-Iranian conflict, might have fueled a wider conflagration. Finally, Russia could have fought the emergence of Turkish and Iranian power in Transcaucasia, causing friction between Moscow on the one side, and Ankara and Tehran on the other.

By the end of 1994, Turkey's and Iran's influence in Transcaucasia remained well behind Russia's. Both countries had raised their profiles in the new republics, but neither had overshadowed Russia, which rapidly regained its hegemony in Transcaucasia. Relations between Turkey and Iran continued to be difficult, although they did not reach the brink of war, and developments in Transcaucasia were not the main reason for tensions between them. There was also some distrust between Russia and Turkey, but because Turkey acknowledged Russian supremacy in the former Soviet Union, there were no signs of an impending clash between Ankara and Moscow. Iran continued to enjoy good relations with Russia.

This chapter consists of two sections. The first describes the policies and activities of Turkey and Iran in Transcaucasia, including their relationship with Russia. The second analyzes the complex interaction between Turkey and Iran. The review of both countries' policies goes beyond their activities in Transcaucasia to include other aspects of their interaction, because these have important implications for the region.

Turkey

Turkey is a Janus among nations, facing both east and west. Neither fully European nor truly Asian, it is the only Moslem nation to have adopted western legal and political norms. Since its creation, the Turkish republic has looked to the West in search of political and economic ideas rather than to the Moslem or communist East, but it has not escaped the consequences of its location next to Iran, Iraq, and Syria. In the early 1990s, Turkey established diplomatic relations with the new republics and helped Azerbaijan, but Ankara continued to pay more attention to its ties with the European Union (EU) and the U.S. than to developing links to the Transcaucasus. As the Russians reasserted their supremacy in Transcaucasia in 1993, Turkey, which had gained a small foothold in Azerbaijan, saw its influence recede.

The upheavals in the USSR, culminating in its dissolution and that of the Warsaw Pact, had repercussions in Turkey that went beyond its border with the former Soviet Union. In the Cold War era, Turkey had a secure position in the West's organizational charts as a frontline state. In the aftermath of the demise of the Soviet Empire, Turkey's role in the western alliance became less clear, though Ankara remained committed to a western orientation. To understand Turkey's current predicament, a brief historical survey is useful. The Ottoman Empire failed to keep up with the industrial and military progress of Europe, leading the Porte (the name given to the Ottoman government) to borrow western methods to survive European expansionism. The rulers were only partly successful in modernizing the country; they imported modern technology and exposed their elites to western science and education, but, in the end, the Great War of 1914-1918 destroyed the multinational, half-reformed empire.

By the end of the First World War, the Allies stood ready to partition their Ottoman foe and to dispatch it, like the Moghul Empire and Persia, to the cemetery of Moslem kingdoms humiliated by Christian nations. Instead, a fully sovereign Turkish republic emerged from the debacle of the war, and having transformed itself into a strong, modern nation-state, Turkey is today the most successful Moslem country in the world.[1]

Mustafa Kemal, who latter renamed himself Kemal Ataturk (father of the Turks), rescued the Anatolian remnants of the empire from the bankruptcy of the Porte. His foreign policy achievements were impressive: he expelled the foreign armies from Turkey and built a sovereign Turkish republic. His domestic accomplishments were unique in their utter transformation of the country. The Ataturk regime launched an unprecedented westernization-modernization program. Ataturk attempted to replace the traditional identities of the people, based on sectarian or regional bonds, with a secular Turkish nationalism on the European model. Henceforth, Turks would be a nation composed of Turkish speakers who lived in Turkey. This change was revolutionary because in the Ottoman Empire, the realm was held together by Islam and military conquest rather than ethnicity. (The term Turk was a pejorative word reserved for the uncouth peasants of Anatolia). The government also abolished the caliphate, replaced the Arabic script with the Latin alphabet, purged the lexicon of its Arabic vocabulary, and adopted European legal principles in place of the Sharia. The republican government also took the symbolic actions of banishing the fez cap, the (relatively new) symbol of Moslem Ottoman Turkey, in favor of western headgear, and forced all Turks to adopt first and family names like Europeans. Overall, the Turkish republic went beyond the changes imposed by such modernizers as the Meiji reformers in Japan, who upheld many traditions, including the monarchy and use of Chinese characters. As a result, Turkey underwent a massive sociocultural transformation, and its elites became more Europeanized than any other Moslem people,[2] though the weight of pre-Kemalist customs endured in the countryside. The resulting friction between old and new, religious and secular, persists to this day in Turkey.

After World War II, Turkey joined NATO, assuming several roles in the defense of the West. It was a frontline state bordering two Warsaw Pact states, Bulgaria and the USSR, and it also served as an anchor for stability in the eastern Mediterranean. The Gulf War demonstrated that bases in Turkey could be used for operations in the Persian Gulf. Thanks to its NATO membership, Turkey made significant progress in cementing ties with the West. Its forces participated in joint exercises, and it hosted several U.S. naval and air facilities. In the political arena, however, Europe and the United States did not reciprocate Turkey's embrace. The European Union has consistently rejected Turkey's application to join, even though it admitted Greece and continued to fund that country while it blockaded Macedonia and menaced Albania with "drastic measures."[3] In the US, the government has often acceded to Greek pressure to trim its assistance to Turkey. Thus, in spite of over seventy years of westernization, Europeans and Americans still treat Turkey as an Islamic nation that does not belong in Europe.

The Post-Cold War Situation

The breakup of the USSR rid Turkey of its major adversary. The Warsaw Treaty Organization, stretching from Bulgaria through the Black Sea to the Transcaucasus, crumbled, and was replaced by a half a dozen destitute states with fragile governments. Peddlers and prostitutes from the former Soviet Union now substitute for yesterday's threat of invading Soviet soldiers.[4]

Ironically, the end of the Cold War deprived Turkey of its role as a pillar of NATO on the southern flank, and therefore its allies pay less attention to it. As a consequence of the breakdown of the eastern bloc, the European Union can now include the European Free Trade Association (EFTA)[5] and possibly Central Europe, thus diminishing its already low interest in Turkish membership. Turkey could have found a new role as the western representative to the Turkic republics of the ex-USSR, channelling European and American aid and political influence to these new countries. American and European interest in supporting Turkey as a western proxy in the former Soviet Union, however, waned because (a) the Iranian peril, which Turkey was meant to fight, did not materialize, and (b) western policymakers chose not to challenge Russian reassertion in the "near abroad." Thus, Turkey today finds itself more isolated than it has been since 1947, when President Truman pledged the U.S. to its defense.

Despite these changes, political and economic integration into the West remains the cornerstone of the country's foreign policy. In 1992, the member states of the OECD[6] absorbed 63.5 percent of Turkey's exports, and tourists, most of them from the EU, brought in $3.6 billion to the Turkish economy.[7] Companies in Western Europe also employ millions of Turks, who remit billions to relatives at home, and whose jobs abroad lower domestic unemployment. Consequently, Turkey's foreign policy is centered on Western Europe, as its accession to associate membership in the Western European Union in 1992 indicated. The 1996 customs union with the EU will be another step toward what Turkey hopes will be eventual membership. Beyond its economic weight, the West also plays a crucial role in defending Turkey. Only the U.S. can protect Turkey if it needs assistance against Iraq, Iran, Russia, or other foes. Participation in

NATO also helps the peaceful management of its perennial crises with Greece.

In fact, Turkey has no alternatives to its western orientation. Other regions cannot replace the Euro-Atlantic world for Turkey. The ex-Soviet Union has only limited economic attractiveness (in 1992, only 4.7 percent of Turkish exports went to the CIS[8]), and it cannot offer political support to Turkey. The Middle East is unstable, and its minuscule, oil-based economies—Saudi Arabia's GDP is barely more than half of Switzerland's,[9] and its economy is in poor shape—cannot become an alternative source of wealth for Turkey. In addition, Turks may be Moslems, but they have few affinities for their former Arab subjects. On the domestic stage, a western orientation serves the goals of Turkey's elites. As Samuel P. Huntington wrote, Turkey is the "prototypical torn country,"[10] split between the West and the Middle East. The poorer and rural segments of Turkish society are rooted in a Moslem outlook, while the ruling classes are European. A link with the West thus strengthens the secular elite against the countervailing pull of traditional Turkey. The more closely Turkey is attached to European institutions and commerce and to Euro-American military institutions, the more difficult it will be for the forces which never accepted Ataturk's revolution to return Turkey to its oriental roots. Because markets and investors are located in the West, ties to the West are also essential for the government's attempts to raise the Turkish standard of living, because they allow it to show that westernization is economically good for them. For the pro-western forces, strengthening links to the West is also particularly relevant in light of the success of the Moslem-oriented Welfare Party in the municipal elections of March 1994.

While Ankara may focus on Europe, however, it cannot escape from Turkey's geography and must pay attention to events unfolding in the Transcaucasus and, more generally, to its east.

Turkey and the Transcaucasus

The predecessors of the Turkish republic had been involved in Transcaucasia, but the region had been shut to Turkish influence since the Bolshevik conquest in the 1920s. Since the collapse of the USSR, the history of post-Soviet Turkish-Transcaucasian relations is divided into two periods. In the wake of the dissolution of the Soviet Union, Turkey moved forward in establishing ties with the new republics, especially with Azerbaijan. In the next stage, Russia reasserted its domination of Transcaucasia, reversing the moderate increase in Turkish influence. In general, though the Turkish presence in Transcaucasia will in the near future remain greater than in Soviet days (when it was admittedly nil), it will pale in comparison with Russia's presence.

Prior to the twentieth century, Byzantium and the Ottoman Empire ruled parts of the Transcaucasus, in competition with Persia and the Caucasian principalities. The nineteenth century marked the decline of Ottoman power in the region and the concomitant ascendance of Russia, but Turkey retained cultural ties to Azerbaijan until the Russian Revolution. Although Russia's defeat in World War I and the ensuing civil war gave Turkey a temporary foothold in the region, Ataturk's Turkey, fighting its own war of liberation against the western powers, could not defend Turkey's position in the Transcaucasus. Soviet Russia conquered the Transcaucasus and obstructed relations between Turkey and the region. Soviet rule in Transcaucasia thus had the advantage, for Turkey, of preventing Transcaucasian troublemakers, such as Armenian irredentists, from destabilizing the border area. (Turkey had to fear Soviet subversion, but these subversive elements were controlled by Moscow, not by Transcaucasian movements.)

The breakup of the USSR altered the situation by creating three new states to Turkey's northeast. Rather than deal with the Kremlin, Turkey had to relate to countries whose ties with Turkey had historically been very different from one another: Christian and non-Turkic Georgia was friendly, Armenia was hostile, and Moslem Azerbaijan was eager for Turkish backing.

Turkish relations with **Georgia** were good because Georgia needed Turkey as an alternative to Russia.[11] Tbilisi did not rekindle claims on Turkish territory made by Stalin after World War II, and Turkey, looking forward to good relations with Georgia, did not press Georgia to return the provinces lost by Ottoman Turkey to the Tsars. Georgia's Abkhaz (who have coethnics in Turkey) and Moslem Ajars could have asked Turkey for support against Georgians, but they have not done so. In any case, Turkey would have rejected such appeals because it does not desire to participate in another Eastern Orthodox-Turkic Moslem conflict in the region, and pan-Islamism is anathema to the secular-nationalist Turkish elite. In the volatile and sometimes unpredictable environment of the Transcaucasus, however, the admittedly remote possibility of Georgian-Turkish dispute cannot be ruled out. The surfacing at some point of territorial claims and counterclaims also cannot be excluded. There is in addition the possibility that Russia could attempt to foment anti-Turkish incidents in Georgia by manipulating some elements in the region. Such activities could serve Moscow by creating a fear of Moslem Turkey among Georgians, thus making domination by Orthodox Russia more acceptable.

Overall, as Russia reconstitutes its dominion over Georgia, Turkey's role as a partner for the Georgians is likely to recede because Ankara cannot compete with Moscow for hegemony in Georgia. Border commerce and small-scale economic interaction, however, are likely to continue unless the Russians close the border completely.

Turkey's relations with **Azerbaijan**[12] are different. Azerbaijanis are a Turkish people, but unlike the Sunni Turks, they are of Shia heritage and have been much influenced by Persia. Their long experience under Soviet rule further differentiates them from today's Anatolian Turks.

In the disorder following the Russian Revolution and the end of World War I, Ottoman forces, under the banner of the Army of Islam, fought for the Azerbaijanis in Baku. Azerbaijan rapidly succumbed to the Bolshevik invasion, however, and until a few years ago there were no contacts between Turkey and Azerbaijan. In the wake of Azerbaijan's temporary independence, Turkey's involvement in Azerbaijan grew considerably. President Elchibey was a strong proponent of a Turkish rather than an Iranian Islamic model to replace the Soviet one. Turkey thus brought Azerbaijani students and officer cadets to Turkey and provided Azerbaijan with some military assistance. Private Turkish entrepreneurs were active in the country, setting up shops and small businesses.

After Aliyev deposed Elchibey, Azerbaijan moved much closer to Russia and improved relations with Iran, to the detriment of Turkey's influence in the country. Though Turkey's presence in

Azerbaijan will remain greater than it was in Soviet days, it will be small compared to Russia's, as long as the Moscow-backed regime of Aliyev rules in Baku. If a more independent-minded regime takes power, however, Turkish influence could increase. But in addition to political obstacles, geography will limit Turkish relations with Azerbaijan. Azerbaijan is not contiguous with Turkey except for the Nakhichevan sector, which is separated from the rest of Azerbaijan by Armenia and borders Turkey for only a few kilometers. Because of the conflict with Armenia and the anarchy in Georgia (which borders both countries), there are currently no unimpeded land routes between Turkey and Azerbaijan in Transcaucasia.

Armenia's relations with Turkey are highly charged.[13] Yerevan demanded formal recognition by Turkey that the massacre of Armenians in 1915 constituted an act of genocide, and some Armenians harbor claims on Turkish territory. Turkey refused to consider the 1915 events as genocide, arguing that the Armenians provoked them by siding with the Ottomans' enemies during World War I. The terror campaign mounted by the Armenian Secret Army for the Liberation of Armenia (ASALA) against Turkish targets in the 1970s and 1980s has also contributed to Turkish-Armenian tensions, as have reports of Armenian collusion with the PKK (the anti-Turkish Kurdish Workers' Party insurgents).[14] Nevertheless, as tensions between Armenia and Azerbaijan grew, Turkey had no desire to get involved in a conflict with Armenia, which would be a public relations blow in the West and damage its hopes for closer ties to Europe and the US.

Thus, Ankara preferred to see Armenia and Russia defeat Azerbaijan rather than risk a war on Azerbaijan's behalf. Bilateral relations could have improved if Armenia had dropped its demands for acknowledgment of the genocide in exchange for better economic and political ties, or if Turkey conceded that the Ottomans had perpetrated a genocide. The former scheme was attractive to Turkey because it would have improved relations across its border and its image in the West, and would also have allowed Armenia to free itself from Russian influence, but extremist elements in Armenia prevented President Ter-Petrossian from moving along such a road.[15] In 1994, with the continuing fighting in Nagorno-Karabakh and Russia's renewed grip on Transcaucasia, this opportunity has been missed, and Turkish-Armenian relations will likely stay unfriendly.

Relations between Turkey and **Russia** are another aspect of Turkey's ties to the post-Soviet Transcaucasus. Though Russia does not border Turkey, it has remained a formidable force in Transcaucasia. In Russia, some circles took a dim view of the resurfacing of the dreaded Turk in Transcaucasia. Russia opposed the use of Turkey, instead of Russia, for pipeline routes from the Caspian to Europe, and Moscow helped to depose the pro-Turkish president of Azerbaijan, Abulfez Elchibey (though it did so not only because of his Turkophilism). The Russian Army newspaper, *Red Star,* warned readers of the nefarious "neo-Osmanism" of Turkey, defined as the alleged buildup of forces in eastern Turkey, activism in Cyprus, Syria, and Iraq, and a desire to side with Azerbaijan. The former head of the CIS armed forces predicted the outbreak of World War III if Turkey got involved militarily in the Caucasus. The presence in the Russian Federation of Turkish peoples (Tatars, Bashkirs, Kalmyks, and Yakuts), who have pushed for greater autonomy from Moscow, also accounted for uneasiness on the part of some Russians.[16] Some of the warnings about "neo-Osmanism" may have been only a pretext for reasserting Russian rule, but they had the potential to heighten tensions with Turkey.

There is indeed a conflict between the desire of Russia to rule the Transcaucasus and Turkey's wish to develop a presence there and erect a *cordon sanitaire* between itself and the Russians. In reality, however, Turkish interests can accommodate continued Russian dominion in Transcaucasia.

Turkey lacks the resources to confront Russia on its own or to restore order to the Transcaucasus. Given these facts, Russian domination in the region mitigates the crises with which Ankara must deal. First, Russian rule may prevent the uncontrolled expansion of the Nagorno-Karabakh War. Second, Russian occupation denies the area to Iran, a country ideologically hostile to Turkey. A zone of healthy and peaceful buffer states between itself and Russia is the ideal situation for Turkey, though from Turkey's standpoint, Russian control is an acceptable second-best outcome. The Russian reconquest of the Transcaucasus, especially Azerbaijan, has hurt Turkey's prestige by demonstrating its inability to support the Turks of Azerbaijan. The events of 1920-21, when Turkey accepted the Sovietization of Azerbaijan, show that there is an historical precedent for Turkey's accepting Moscow's domination of Transcaucasia. Turkey is stronger today than in the 1920s, but it is not a great power, and Russia is still a military force to be reckoned with, especially in light of recent NATO actions that may cause Turkey to doubt the alliance's credibility.[17]

A conflict between Russian and Turkish forces could emerge as a result of Turkish involvement in the Azerbaijani-Armenian War or the Azerbaijani civil conflict, or possibly as a result of Turkish support for Georgia against Russia. Because Turkey is not going to challenge Moscow's hegemony in Transcaucasia, however, there is almost no probability of a Russian-Turkish conflict materializing. The lack of command authority on the part of Moscow or the Transcaucasian states over some smaller military units in the Transcaucasus, which act in effect as glorified gangsters, creates the possibility of uncontrolled battles. But this possibility remains slight because marauding gangs have no incentive to challenge the Turkish army, and if Ankara and Moscow both wish to avoid conflict, they should be able to deal with localized incidents.

Conclusion

One could imagine scenarios that would lead to greater Turkish involvement in the Transcaucasian clashes, but the chance of their coming to pass is slim. For example, popular outrage over the fate of Azerbaijan, or one day Georgian Moslems, could force Turkey to defend Moslem Transcaucasians, but the Turkish government opposes nationalist calls from within Turkey and Azerbaijan for an activist pro-Azerbaijani or pro-Elchibey policy. Turkey has provided some military assistance to Azerbaijan, and may continue to do so, but according to most reports, this assistance involves only a limited number of men and equipment.[18] Because Turkey is a democracy, public pressure could make Ankara more adventurist in the future. Having watched the slaughter of Bosnians, Turks may demand action in Azerbaijan, where, as in Bosnia, Orthodox Christians are killing secularized Moslems with ties to Turkey. Turkey has generally been cautious in military actions, however, and the influence of hotheads on military policy is circumscribed by the role of the leadership of the armed forces in policymaking. The only precipitate action on the part of Turkey since Ataturk has been the 1974 invasion of Cyprus, a crisis that was more intense for Turkey than the current Transcaucasian one. The Turkish Cypriots were Turks living on a neighboring island rather than Turkic people who had been separated from Turkey for ages. Moreover, Cyprus had been formally Turkish until 1914, and the Turkish Republic was one of the signatories to the agreements the Greeks had violated.[19] Thus Turkey is likely to remain cautious toward the conflicts of the Transcaucasus, and although economic exchanges might grow, they will do so without permitting the Turkish-Transcaucasian relationship to challenge Russia's hegemony.

Iran

Iran lies next to Azerbaijan and Armenia, and it has cultural and ethnic links to Transcaucasia. Unfortunately, Iran's policies have been distorted by analysts who concentrate on the rhetoric of the mullahs and on bloody repression and terrorism by the regime. Evil though this murderous regime is, it needs to be understood in historical context to anticipate patterns of Iranian policy in the region in the mid- and late 1990s.

The Islamic Republic's conduct of international relations has been influenced by its rejection of Iran's Pahlavi past and its embrace of a new Islamic foreign policy. From the beginning, however, Islamic Iran kept some of the policies of the shahs and continued to take into account its secular national interests, whose weight in framing policy has increased as the excitement of the revolution has waned. These interests put a premium on stability to Iran's north, in Transcaucasia and Central Asia, to allow the country to focus its power on the Persian Gulf and the Arab world. Iran must also conduct its diplomacy from a position of weakness. Its revolution has failed to overthrow its foreign foes, and being locked in an anti-U.S. posture, it has shut itself off from its former ally, the world's only superpower. Consequently, Iran's policy in Transcaucasia is to eschew entanglements and to prefer Russian domination to either Turkish influence or Azeri nationalism.

Iran's foreign policy

Iran's foreign policy blends xenophobia and fanaticism with an acceptance of the realities of power politics. The Islamic republic added a new "Islamic" aspect to Tehran's foreign policy but also continued to pay attention to the traditional national interests that had guided the late shah and his father. As a result of the diminished fervor at home for revolution, the failure of Islamists to overthrow neighboring regimes, and a severe economic crisis, the role of Islamic precepts in guiding foreign policy has gradually been overshadowed by nationalism.[20] Continued economic hardships and its inability to export its revolution in the Gulf[21] may lead Iran to a drastic reversal of policy, in which it tries to parlay moderation for economic assistance and better relations with the West. Conversely, it might be tempted to revert to more extreme actions to try to prevent the revolution from dying. Regardless of Iran's evolution, the country will face severe difficulties in continuing a revolutionary foreign policy. So far the mullahs have paid a heavy price for their Americanopohbia. Allied to the US, Iran is the natural anchor of western interests in southwest Asia and the great power of the Gulf. Against America, it is a third-rate country with almost no allies. Moreover, in spite of all the headlines generated by Islamist "fundamentalism," Iran has failed to export its brand of Islamist revolution to all its major targets, namely Saudi Arabia, Iraq, and the Gulf emirates.

The memories of the defeats of the past two centuries have had much influence on Iranian behavior. In the nineteenth century, Russia (in the Caucasus) and Britain (through Afghanistan and British India) encroached on Persian sovereignty. By the eve of the First World War, Persia was a de facto Russo-British condominium, with Russia paramount in the north and the UK supreme in the south. The war and its aftermath transformed parts of the country into a battleground for foreign armies.

After taking power in 1921, Reza Khan (later Reza Shah) restored Iranian independence.[22] At home, he strove to improve the terms of oil concessions with Britain. Abroad, he sought German assistance to balance British and Soviet influence.

Through the 1937 Sadabad Pact with Turkey, Iraq, and Afghanistan, he tried to add diplomatic weight to Tehran, but his attempts failed. His refusal, after the German invasion of the USSR in 1941, to accede to allied demands to transship equipment to the Soviet Union through Iran displeased the allies, who proceeded to invade Iran to make it a bridgehead to the USSR. At the end of World War II, Iran was again in a feeble position. The USSR occupied the north, Britain controlled its oil fields, and a young, inexperienced Reza Pahlavi (son of Reza Shah) sat on the Peacock Throne.[23]

Iranian revolutionaries maligned Reza Pahlavi, claiming he was subservient to America. Contrary to these accusations, he actually increased his country's power and was not a puppet of the West. He lifted Persia from semicolonial status to the rank of a regional power. His foreign policy axes can be summarized as follows:

- Enlist the support of a third player as a counterweight to the USSR and the UK. The shah allied himself with Washington, to get superpower backing to remove the Soviet Army from northern Iran and to link up with U.S. industry, which challenged Britain's historical dominance of Iran's oil wealth.
- Secure the northern border through the U.S. alliance and establish normal relations with Moscow. Protecting the northern front gave Iran more opportunity to focus on domination of the Persian Gulf.
- Gain control of the country's petroleum resources, utilizing them to increase its economic, diplomatic, and military strength.

These policies were typical of a medium-size power. The shah sought support from the strong to dominate the weak and protect himself from the powerful. He did not export any particular ideology, but enjoyed good relations with Chinese communists and Israeli socialists, and bought billions of dollars of weapons from Nixon's America. Shia Islam was the state religion, but neither proselytization nor support for Islamic causes were on Reza Pahlavi's agenda.

The Islamic Revolution

A key weakness of the shah was the popular charge that he was a tool of foreigners. This was a potent accusation because of Iran's past humiliations at the hands of outsiders. Like the 1905 Constitutional Movement and the nationalist leader Mohammed Mosaddeq in the 1950s, the Islamists built upon resentment of perceived alien subjugation. The shah's westernized style, cooperation with Americans and Israelis, and lack of attention to the clergy and the bazaar gave him the image of a ruler estranged from his land, culture, and faith. It was these ties to foreigners and foreign mores that the Iranian revolution sought to overturn.[24]

Since the revolution, competition between rival power centers has created inconsistencies in Iranian foreign policy. Nevertheless, the main thrust of its goals and methods can be discerned, and separated into two components. The first is an Islamic revolutionary break from the past. The second is a pursuit of nationalist goals, in continuation of Iran's imperial foreign policy. It should be noted that "new" methods, for example Islamic agitprop, are often used to further "old" aims, such as hegemony in the Gulf.

Islamist foreign policy

The Islamic revolutionary movement represents a watershed in the Moslem world. From the beginning of the nineteenth century to the end of World War II, many Moslems approved of westernization because it seemed to rescue their countries from destruction by strengthening them with European efficiency. Anti-Western Moslems were reactionary old-timers rather than revolutionaries. Khomeini offered an alternative, and transformed the Iranian Shia faith into a revolutionary Ceasaropapism[25] that resorted to methods of revolutionary organization for Islamist ends. The hatred of compromise displayed by the Iranian Shias' movement was reinforced by a Manichean world view inherited from Iran's ancient dualist religions, which stressed the separation between the path of "God and belief" and that of "Satan and disbelief."[26]

A politicized theology provided the background for the foreign policy of the late *faqih* ("jurisprudent"), Khomeini's title as interpreter of the law. The policy included opposition to the US, "which is by nature the master of international terrorism [and] has created misery the world over, and whose natural ally is. . . international Zionism," the "atheistic East," the "oppressor Kafir [unbeliever] West," and Jews (a "cancer" for Iran). These diplomatic guidelines enjoyed the benefit of originating from the Islamic government, a "divine phenomenon."[27] Their implementation has led Iran to base its revolutionary diplomacy on the following precepts:

- Opposition to the United States. Though at times the Islamic Republic has collaborated with the US, its foreign policy consistently opposes the United States in deeds and propaganda.
- Enmity to Israel and the Arab-Israeli peace process. Although revolutionary Iran has dealt with Israel, hatred of that country and opposition to Arabs involved in the peace process are key elements of its foreign policy.
- Denial of neighboring Arab governments' legitimacy. Like many revolutions, Iran's has openly challenged the credentials of neighboring rulers. Tehran considers that, in separate but equally vile ways, almost all Arab governments have been unfaithful to the Koran's teachings. Given the fragile basis of Arab governments, Iranian propaganda concerns them greatly, especially because violent clergymen and terrorists often back Iran's fighting words. Iran's ideological warfare has been directed at conservative religious regimes (Saudi Arabia), moderate "secularists" (Egypt), and "radical secularists" (Iraq, Algeria). Iran's conflicts with the Arab countries have varied in intensity and scope but the fact remains that, to the ruling mullahs, the Arab kings and presidents are no more legitimate than bourgeois regimes were to the Bolsheviks.
- Widespread recourse to terrorism and political assassination as a normal method of implementing foreign and domestic policy objectives.

Persian foreign policy

The "Government of God" did not alter geography, geology, or demographics. The basic facts that underlay Iran's analysis of its interests remained the same after the revolution. Moreover, Iran still has a strong perception of its pre-Islamic greatness, and it is infused with Persian nationalism independent of its Islamic faith.[28] Its status as the only Shia-controlled country also separates it from the other Moslem nations and sharpens its sense of uniqueness.

Consequently, in certain areas, religious zeal did not supplant Iran's national interest. Because Islamist ideology opposes secular nationalist oppressors of Moslems and abhors atheist communism, Iran might have been expected to condemn the Syrian regime, which ruthlessly repressed Islamist opponents and is based on the Alawite community of doubtful Moslem credentials, just as it has condemned almost all other Arab regimes. Yet Syria, which happens to support Iran because of Syrian rivalry with Iraq, has been exempted from Tehran's condemnation. Khomeinist Iran's passivity regarding the 65 million Moslems under godless yoke in the Soviet Union and Afghanistan was particularly telling. Such tolerance continued in the post-Soviet period, as Tehran failed to take Russia to task for killing Tajik Moslems and supporting Serbs in Bosnia.[29] In these cases, then, Iranian national interests enjoyed primacy over Islam. The theological justification for such tolerance of evil may be that only a strong Iran can fight for Islam, and that short-term compromises are needed to fulfill long-range goals. In practice, however, Iranian policy has been selectively revolutionary and has remained tame in many areas in a pattern that suits its national interests as a secular regime would define them.

In spite of the difference between Pahlavi and Khomeinist foreign policy, Shia activism must be understood in part as a violent continuation of the shah's regional ambitions. Pahlavi Iran cast its shadow on the Gulf statelets through its stronger demographic and military base and cowed Iraq by virtue of its superior military power and the manipulation of Kurdish proxies. Revolutionary Iran uses its anti-Israeli zeal to weaken the Arab states in the Gulf and the eastern Mediterranean. The successes of the Iranian-backed Hizbolah against Israel demonstrated to the Arab peoples that while their leaders palavered, Islam fought.[30] Iran may be unwilling to fight Israel, but its strident anti-Zionism and support for anti-Israeli fighters in Lebanon allows it to embarrass Arab regimes and expose their failure to defeat Israel.

If Iran's foreign policy retains some similarities with the shah's, the methods at its disposal to implement that policy have changed. Having broken its relations with the West and in particular with the United States, Iran has lost its traditional sources of military equipment. Alternative suppliers from communist East Asia and the former Soviet Union have sold Tehran weapons, and some of these countries have proved willing suppliers of equipment to build nuclear weapons and delivery systems. In the conventional realm, however, these heterogeneous manufacturers of varying technological prowess have not enabled Iran to construct a large conventional military force. Moreover, Iran's current economic crisis puts limits on its ability to buy foreign goods and services.

There are also economic factors constraining Iran's power. After a murderous war with Iraq, sanctions by the leading oil industry power (the US), the exile of many skilled professionals, and 2 million refugees from Afghanistan, Iran's economy is in poor shape. Its oil sector is in need of considerable repairs, and its economy, which is expected to contract in 1994 and 1995, must absorb a population that grew by almost 2 million souls in 1993 alone.[31] Oil, which represents 89 percent of Iran's exports,[32] does not generate enough revenues to buy social peace with subsidized goods (as the Gulf monarchies do).

Thus because of its isolation and limited resources, Iran's military programs focus on both extremes of the spectrum, seeking nuclear weapons while relying on unconventional warfare (terrorism, subversion) to pursue diplomatic aims.[33] Consequently, it cannot confront directly large military powers, such as the US. It has, however, great nuisance value, especially because many neighboring states are vulnerable to political subversion and covert operations. Indeed, Iran remains a power to be reckoned with for several reasons.

First, Iran is a nation of more than 60 million people and possesses oil fields that, even with low prices, generated hard currency revenues in excess of $14 billion,[34] giving Tehran cash for military purchases.

Second, none of the contiguous states presents a clear and present danger to Iran. Pakistan has a larger population and 580,000 men under arms, but it faces severe domestic challenges as well as problems with India, and is not threatening to Iran. Turkey may compete with Iran in the region but faces other challenges that are more important to it than Iran (first and foremost the Kurdish insurgency). Besides, their common border consists of mountains higher than 2,000 meters with a poor road network, creating obstacles to offensive operations. Iraq has survived the Gulf War, but is much weaker. Russia has a de facto border with Iran through the CIS in Transcaucasia and Turkmenistan, but Russia's military power has waned since the Soviet era. All of Iran's other neighbors, i.e. former Soviet Republics and Gulf Arab countries, are weaker. At this point, therefore, Iran does not have a single neighbor that represents a credible danger to its territory.

Third, many Arab regimes are fragile and suffer from internal dissent. Iranian covert action, including terrorism, propaganda, and subversion, is thus a potent weapon against them.

In conclusion, Iran is not a major conventional threat, especially as long as the U.S. remains committed to the region. On the other hand, its subversive actions are real dangers to many of its neighbors. Moreover, if the U.S. reduces its commitment to the region, a weak Iranian army might prove stronger than many of the even less well-performing armed forces of the oil states.

Iran's internal composition

Iran has achieved a relatively strong degree of national cohesion, but only 45 to 65 percent of the Iranian population of 65 million is Persian,[35] and of these approximately five hundred thousand are non-Moslem Bahais, Jews, and Zoroastrians. Because the non-Persians are concentrated along borders that often straddle ethnic groups, the threat of discontent degenerating into separatism poses a grave danger to Iran's security. As a result of the economic crisis and political problems faced by the government, some observers report that Tehran's hold on the non-Persian populations is weakening.[36] Because several minorities are close to the Transcaucasus, these ethnic issues are relevant to Iran's outlook on Transcaucasia.

Azerbaijanis, who inhabit northwestern Iran, are the most important non-Persian group. Like their brethren north of the border, they speak a Turkish language and are Shia Moslems. They represent from 20 to 30 percent of the Iranian population and are well assimilated into Iranian society, including the revolutionary movement.[37] Nevertheless, in periods when Iran was vulnerable, Azerbaijanis sought to gain autonomy, often with foreign assistance. In the aftermath of both world wars, Moscow set up Soviet republics in Iranian Azerbaijan, and used Soviet Azerbaijan to spread Soviet influence and subversion in Iran.[38] Though Iran's Azeris may be better integrated today than in the past, the historical precedent of Azerbaijani secessionism must be present in the minds of Iran's rulers.

Kurds, who speak Indo-European languages related to Persian but unlike other Iranians are Sunni, compose Iran's second largest minority. Representing an estimated 9 percent of Iran's population, they are less integrated into Iranian society and its elite than Azerbaijanis. Foreign powers have also manipulated the Kurds against Tehran. The Soviet leaders backed the Mahabad Republic established in Iranian Kurdistan in 1945-46 in their bid to rule northern Iran, and Iraq made extensive use of Kurdish rebels against Iran in the war between Iran and Iraq, as did Iran against Iraq. Nasser reportedly supported Kurdish aspirations to forge a "land bridge" between the Syrian sector of the United Arab Republic (of Egypt and Syria) and the USSR.[39] The insurgency in Iranian Kurdistan continues to this day, with varying levels of intensity and violence, making the Kurds Iran's most problematic minority population.

Other ethnic minorities include Shia **Arabs**, of whom half a million reside in the oil-rich province of Khuzestan, **Turcomans**, along the border with the eponymous republic, **Qashqai** tribesmen, **Baluchis**, and other groups. There are also numerous **Afghan** refugees, who may be causing the "Sunnitization" of Khorasan province in eastern Iran (Afghans, except for Hazaras, are Sunni Moslems), but Iran is sending some of them back to Afghanistan.

Because of Iran's multinational nature, Shia Islam, rather than ethnicity, has defined the Iranian state since the Safavid Dynasty embraced this sect in 1501, and the Islamic Republic has accentuated this orientation. As an authoritarian state in the late twentieth century, where ethnicity and nationalism are far more salient than they were under the Safavids, it has an interest in stressing religion, which unites 90 percent of the population, and opposing ethnic autonomy.

The integration of minorities in Iran has progressed, and divisions along ethnic lines are not so deep as in most other multinational polities. At least for the Shia, a nation-state that goes beyond Persians to include other Iranian citizens now seems to exist.[40] The cohabitation of several ethnic groups within the Islamic Republic, however, hinders liberal political development. In the context of multiethnicity, the government is likely to repress opposition as representing a treacherous attempt to destroy the state's territorial integrity. Authoritarian rule is thus likely to remain entrenched because the government will always fear for the state's unity.

Iran's ethnic structure explains why Tehran regrets the dissolution of the USSR. Some of the new states of the former Soviet Union are based on ethnic groups that encompass millions of Iranian citizens, i.e., Azeris and Turkmen. These new ethnic states, by their very existence, are thus a challenge to Iran's national unity.[41] With Azerbaijanis and Turkmen in the former Soviet Union enjoying statehood, their kinsmen in Iran may ask themselves why they to cannot live in ethnically homogenous nations rather than in a Persian-dominated empire. This vulnerability is one of the reasons for Iran's discomfort with events in the Transcaucasus and Central Asia.

Iran's policy toward the Transcaucasus

Any understanding of the Transcaucasus must take Iran into account because of its geographic location, cultural affinities, and economic resources (compared to the even poorer ex-SSRs). As mentioned, Iran faces severe problems, both at home and abroad. The revolution is moribund, and as a growing number of Iranians become disillusioned with the revolution's promises, the stability of the regime and the continuity of its revolutionary policies are in doubt.[42] Iran is thus not seeking involvement in the region, but rather hopes to protect itself from the wars and disorders north of its border. As in the case of Turkey, however, Iran cannot ignore a contiguous region.

The history of Persian involvement in the Transcaucasus bears similarities to Turkey's. Until the beginning of the nineteenth century, Persia was a Transcaucasian power. The Shia faith provided close ties to the populations of Azerbaijan, and Iran also had influence in Georgia, some of whose nobles converted to Islam and served the shahs in the seventeenth century. Following Russia's victories over the Ottomans and Persians in Transcaucasia, Persia lost its formal suzerainty over northern Azerbaijan, but it retained its cultural connection until the Soviet occupation. In the twentieth century, the Soviet Union excluded Iran from the Transcaucasus, and Persia was forced to defend itself against Soviet encroachments.

The independence of Azerbaijan put Iran in a difficult situation. This new republic is important to it because (a) it has ethnic ties to northern Iran, and (b) as a link to the former Soviet Union's ground transportation network,[43] it provides an alternative route for Iranian commerce that is not vulnerable to a naval blockade. Unfortunately for Tehran, when Azerbaijan became independent, Iran's ability to establish strong relations with Baku were limited. As a secularized people, Azerbaijanis were repulsed by Tehran's ideology, and they were unwilling to align themselves with Iran because of its economic failure. Oil-rich Azerbaijan had no interest in Iran's petroleum, and in sectors where Azerbaijan needed assistance, such as its oil industry, it preferred to deal with first-rate multinationals rather than with Iran's backward companies. Moreover, Elchibey was pro-Turkish and felt no sympathy toward the blackrobes of Tehran. The war with Armenians also helped to weaken Tehran's position in Baku because Iran was friendly to Armenia. As Armenians ravaged large areas of Azerbaijan, Iran started to oppose Armenian actions because of the risks posed by Azerbaijani refugees fleeing toward Iran,[44] but it did not seek confrontation with the Armenians, and its assistance to Azerbaijan seems to have been limited to helping refugees.

The defeat of Elchibey and his replacement by Gaidar Aliyev improved Iran's position in Azerbaijan. Whereas Elchibey was pro-Turkish, Aliyev was an old-style communist ruler. Like the Russians, he sought good relations with Iran, and his Soviet-era thinking was less threatening than the nationalism of Elchibey. The risk that a government in Baku would support Azeri nationalists in Iran receded as Azerbaijan was reintegrated into the Russian fold.

Iran, Russia, and Transcaucasia

Russia has voiced concern over Iran's activities in the Moslem areas of the former USSR. Foreign Minister Kozyrev, for instance, has warned against extremist Islamist forces in Iran and Pakistan.[45] Regardless of whether Russians have actually been worried about Iranian Islamism, Moscow wishes to exclude Iran—and all foreigners—from the Transcaucasus. At the same time, Moscow wants to maintain good relations with Iran, which is the only country that breaks the U.S. monopoly in the Gulf, and is a purchaser of Russian weapons.

As in the case of Turkey, the Russian reconquest could serve Iran's own goals.[46] The Russian reassertion in Azerbaijan has already diminished the risk of Azerbaijani agitation against Iran, and Russia's weakness and interest in economic relations with Iran ensure that it will not condone anti-Iranian activities from Azerbaijan. Russian rule in Transcaucasia also denies the area to Iran's Turkish rival. Moreover, as a weaker country than Turkey, let alone Russia, Iran cannot block the recolonization of the Caucasus by Russia.

Conclusion

In conclusion, Iran's ambition in the Transcaucasus is to exert influence, but at a minimum price. Iran has an interest in fostering a peaceful settlement of the Armenian-Azerbaijani conflict to solve the refugee crisis on its border. On the other hand, Russian hegemony in Transcaucasia limits Tehran's ability to influence the outcome of the war in the Transcaucasus. Economic relations between Iran and the Transcaucasus may develop, and contacts between Iranian Azerbaijanis and the Azerbaijani Republic will be greater than they were in the Soviet era, but Iran's presence will remain secondary to Russia's. If Russia's position weakens, Iran's relative importance in Transcaucasia will increase, but even under such circumstances, the limited resources available to Iran combined with its domestic problems will continue to restrict its ability to extend its reach into the former Soviet Union.

The Transcaucasus and Turkish-Iranian Relations

In Kurdistan and Transcaucasia, Turkey and Iran face the consequences of the disintegration of the USSR and the defeat of Iraq,
as well as attempts by Moscow and Baghdad to reconquer their lost
territories. The dislocation resulting from these events could make
relations between Tehran and Ankara even more complex. In particular, the Kurdish issue, whose parameters have changed since the
Gulf War, could possibly generate Turkish-Iranian tensions.

Iran's and Turkey's strong interest in avoiding war with one
another reduces the possibility of an armed confrontation between
them. In fact, the prospects of such a conflict are highly improbable.
It is nevertheless useful to analyze Turkish-Iranian relations because
doing so uncovers sources of instability in the region, such as the
situation south of the Transcaucasus, which is precarious and fraught
with dangers. The most sensitive area of Turkish-Iranian competition is Kurdistan because both Turkey's and Iran's vital interests are
at stake in this region, which is the scene of several insurgencies.

With as many as 12 million citizens of Kurdish descent[47] in its
population of 61 million, Turkey's "Kurdish question" is its major
security issue. An estimated eleven thousand PKK fighters[48] tie down
a large fraction of the army and gendarmerie (the paramilitary internal security force) in southeastern Turkey, and Kurdish terrorists
have attacked targets in western Turkey as well as Turkish interests
abroad. It is estimated that the annual cost of the 150,000 troops
fighting the insurgency is $6 billion, and the rebellion has also forced
Turkey to extend the length of conscription.[49] The fight against the
insurgents also hurts Turkey's relations with the West, with some of
its partners accusing it of human rights violations.

Settling the Kurdish question would remove an important weakness in Ataturk's legacy. The father of modern Turkey claimed that
the new Turkey was a Turkish Anatolian homeland, but in reality
millions of its inhabitants were Kurds. In a nationalist state based on
the Turkish ethnolinguistic group, the Kurds, who neither spoke
Turkish nor identified with the new nation, were a serious challenge
for Ankara, evidenced by the frequent uprisings in the Kurdish regions of southeastern Turkey. In its quest to solve the Kurdish question, Turgut Ozal, the former prime minister and president, recog-

nized that the "Mountain Turks," as Ankara called its Kurdish citizens, were indeed Kurds by any other name. Such a willingness to accept reality was the result of the impossibility of winning a war of repression in southeastern Turkey while simultaneously attempting to strengthen liberal democracy and stay in the Euro-Atlantic community of nations.

Unfortunately, recognizing the existence of a Kurdish question will not be sufficient in itself to solve Ankara's problems. Some Kurds make unacceptable demands on Turkey, and the animosities that plague Kurdish-Turkish relations will take years to lessen. Hence the road to a settlement of the Kurdish problem will be arduous. In fact, since the death of President Ozal in 1993, there has been a recrudescence in the fighting with the PKK and a lessening of the Turkish government's commitment to a political settlement.[50]

The Kurdish question has international implications because "Kurdistan" comprises areas of Turkey, Iran, Iraq, and Syria. President Ozal stated during the Gulf War that the border splitting Turkey's Kurds from fellow Kurds in Iraq was "artificial." He might have added that beyond this line lie the oil fields of Mosul, which Ataturk claimed for the Turkish republic. Because Iraq is currently enfeebled, Turkey extends a de facto protectorate over northern Iraq,[51] using Iraqi Kurds against the PKK, establishing ties with the local chieftains in northern Iraq, and supplying the zone with electricity from Turkey. Moreover, the UN protection force operates from facilities in Turkey, giving Turkey leverage over developments there. The disunity of the Kurdish people, who do even not share a common language (Kurds speak several mutually unintelligible dialects with large regional variations) and whose independence movements have always been faction-ridden, facilitates Turkish dominion in the area.[52] Therefore Turkey's rivals, such as Iran, may be worried that Turkey is realizing Ataturk's dream of a southeastern enlargement of Turkey's domain. At the same time, the consequences of the Gulf War in northern Iraq create new burdens and problems for Turkey, and some Turkish officials believe that Turkey would benefit from ending the operation of western forces in Kurdistan.[53]

Because the Kurdish issue is also vital to Iran for domestic reasons, the Kurdish insurgencies constitute a potentially explosive situation for the region. More than 5 million Kurds may live in Iran, and they have an estimated 10,500 active guerrillas opposing Iran's government.[54] Furthermore, because of their location in northwestern Iran they can link up with Iran's foes in Iraq or Turkey. Thus the rise of Turkish influence in Kurdish areas of Iraq significantly affects Iranian security by strengthening the hold of a regional rival over Iraq's Kurds.

To complicate the Kurdish issue further, Iraqi activity in the region also affects the local balance of power. Iraq has potential sources of friction with Turkey in the damming of the Euphrates, Turkish support for the Gulf War coalition, and the Turkish (Turcoman) minority in northern Iraq.[55] The triangular relationship of Iraq, Iran, and Turkey is unstable. It mixes issues of international rivalry, internal security, and natural resources at the crossroads of the three nations, all with incompatible political systems and each heir to an empire. In this context, the steps that could conceivably push Iranian-Turkish relations into a downward spiral include disputes arising from Iranian and Turkish actions as well as from the behavior of other countries in the region.

One possible catalyst for an Iranian-Turkish conflict would be an increase in Iranian actions against Turkey. For example, Iran could provide more assistance to the PKK, as it reportedly did in 1993.[56] (The Kurdish revolts of 1925 and 1929-30 previously created friction between the two countries.) The alleged support of the PKK by Armenia,[57] which borders both Turkey and Iran, adds to tensions in the Turkish-Iranian frontier region. Iran could also provoke Turkey further by supporting Islamists and engaging in other low-intensity activities. In 1992 and 1993, for example, there were several reports of Iranian involvement in terrorism on Turkish soil.[58]

An attempt by Turkey to further extend its rule over Iraqi Kurdistan, either in terms of the level of control it exercises or the size of the area it oversees,[59] could similarly elevate tensions between Iran and Turkey. At some point, Iran could consider Turkish hegemony over the Kurds to be a mortal threat because it might lead Iran's Kurds to gravitate toward Turkey.

Beyond the immediate Turkish-Iranian border area, Syria could be another source of Turkish-Iranian confrontation. Syrian support for the PKK and Dev Sol (extreme left-wing Turks)[60] irritates Turkey. Syria in turn has grievances against Turkey over the Euphrates, which the Turks, who see water as a resource they should wield as the Arabs have wielded oil,[61] are damming to increase the water flows retained in Anatolia. Hatay, a Turkish province claimed by Syria, is another bone of contention. Syria restricts the discharges of its main river, the Orontes, whose upstream areas are in Syria, and refuses to accept Turkish sovereignty over this province. Because Syria is allied with Iran, a Turkish-Syrian conflict could involve Iran, though Syria's current movements toward peace with Israel and its attempts to improve relations with Ankara make a Syrian-Turkish conflict currently unlikely.

The former Soviet Union is also an area that could foster Iranian-Turkish confrontation. The emergence of Azerbaijan, for instance, added a new source of friction between Turks and Iranians. The Azerbaijani Republic could, in the future, appeal to Greater Azerbaijani sentiment among Iran's Azeris, endangering the territorial integrity of the Islamic Republic.[62] Irredentists could seek "enosis" (merger) with the south and precipitate a conflict resembling the Cyprus imbroglio, possibly involving Russia and Turkey. Concerns in Turkey over Iranian incursions into Azerbaijan demonstrated the potential for rivalry between Turkey and Iran in Azerbaijan.[63] Moreover, within Iran, the Kurdish issue is linked to Azerbaijan because the regions are contiguous, and there are territorial disputes between Kurds and Azerbaijanis in Iran that could lead to clashes between them; the resulting conflict on the Turkish border could draw in Kurds from Turkey and Iraq. As of late 1994, however, it appeared unlikely that Azerbaijan could fuel a Turkish-Iranian confrontation. Both Iran and Russia have an interest in good bilateral relations and, with Azerbaijan under Moscow's influence, the Azeri issue is currently under control, but circumstances could change rapidly.

Central Asia could provide an additional arena for Turkish-Iranian confrontation. Agitation within the Turkmen community, which is not well integrated within Iran, could lead to suspicion in Tehran of Turkish manipulation of Iran's Turkic peoples.[64] More to the east, war between Persian-speaking Tajiks and Turkic Uzbeks could generate another area of Turkish-Iranian conflict, though this is, at the present time, implausible.

Finally, the religious and ideological fault lines that divide Turks from Iranians, namely the Shia-Sunni and the Islamist-secularist chasms, enhance mutual misunderstanding and fuel conflict between Ankara and Tehran. The Shia-Sunni split goes back many centuries. During the Ottoman period, opposition to the Shia heretics was an important aspect of the sultan's policy. As Selim I wrote Shah Ismail in 1514:

> The Ulema and our teachers of the law have pronounced death upon thee, perjurer and blasphemer as thou art.[65]

Though the orthodox sultan of Constantinople has been replaced by a secular ruler in Ankara, the presence of Shias in Turkey (the Alevis), whom Iran might wish to manipulate,[66] could revive sectarian tensions between Turkey and Iran. Greater influence by Sunni Moslem political groups in Turkey could heighten the importance of this religious issue.

To this historical religious discord, one must add a more current ideological one. Ataturkism is anathema to Iranian clerics,[67] while the Turkish elites abhor Islamist obscurantism. This combination of both ancient (Shia/Sunni) and modern (Khomeinist/Kemalist) splits between Turks and Persians contributes to mutual dislike.

All the above-mentioned causes for conflict between Iran and Turkey could be exacerbated by the nature of the Iranian regime and by the general environment of Middle Eastern politics.

First, paranoia plays a key role in Iranian affairs.[68] Iran could interpret events in Kurdistan, the Transcaucasus, Central Asia, and other areas as a Turkish-Israeli-Russian-American-Saudi plot against the Islamic Republic, and feel compelled to wage war against Turkey. The isolation of revolutionary Iran has increased the paranoid pathologies of the Iranian rulers, as well as their capacity for faulty judgement.

Second, though the leaders of Islamic Iran are anything but "mad" fanatics, they combine burning religious fervor and nationalism with a violent streak, both at home and abroad. Their murder campaign against British novelist Salman Rushdie illustrates their standard operating procedures.

Third, the Middle East comprises numerous countries and organizations with extremist aims and weapons, and harbors the planet's most important mineral treasures. In such an environment, peace is the exception, never the rule.

In conclusion, though there are risks of conflict, Iran and Turkey have overwhelming reasons not to fight each other. Turkey wants to join Europe and prepare for the 1996 customs union with the EU rather than sink in Third World quagmires. Its Kemalist army takes a dim view of adventurism and must, prudently, consider the dangers that loom in the Transcaucasus, Cyprus, Greece, and the Balkans. As for Iran, it has nothing to gain in taking on a NATO army and everything to lose in a war that could break its national unity and the regime. The reported recent lessening of Iranian support for the PKK and a willingness to cooperate on infrastructure projects in Central Asia show neither country is currently eager for a conflict.[69] Furthermore, the two nations have no territorial claims against one another to spark a dispute.

In any case, a Turkish-Iranian war could occur without engulfing the Transcaucasus. With Russian forces on the border, both Tehran and Ankara wish to avoid confrontation with Russian power. Fighting between Iran and Turkey would probably reinforce Russia's hold over the region for two reasons. First, Russia would fear that a withdrawal from the Transcaucasus would bring Iranian or Turkish forces inside former Soviet territory. Second, more Transcaucasians may support a Russian presence on their southern borders if they think that it will protect them from disorders from the south. In the absence of Russia, however, the Transcaucasus could become involved in the fighting.

All in all, the practical effect of the myriad issues that stimulate hostilities between Turkey and Iran seems to be concerted effort by both parties to avoid them. Both have too much to lose from the unleashing of forces of instability. At the same time, all these contentious issues limit cooperation between Turkey and Iran, cooperation that could increase their ability to restrict Russian influence in the Transcaucasus.

Conclusion: Turkey, Iran, and the Transcaucasus

This analysis highlights the centrality of Russia in Transcaucasia. Iran and Turkey are peripheral to the situation. Even if they were to fight one another, itself a relatively unlikely scenario, a strong Russia could easily block any attempt to extend the conflict to the

Transcaucasus. It is Russia that has forced Georgia to join the CIS and has armed its internal enemies and assisted the former communists in returning to power in Azerbaijan. In spite of reports of meddling in the region by Turkey and Iran, their influence has been minor. Indeed, both Turkey and Iran have been factors for stability. Turkey provided a useful role model for Azerbaijan during the Elchibey period and was looking forward to developing its ties with Georgia, and Iran has provided assistance to Azerbaijani refugees and has tried to settle the Nagorno-Karabakh war.

In principle, a conflict between Iran and Turkey in which Russia actively supported one side is conceivable, but in practice its probability is almost nil. The energy required by the reconquest of the empire and Russia's desire to avoid a showdown with the U.S. in the "far abroad" would seem to preclude an Iranian-Russian alignment against Turkey that would go as far as military confrontation, though there might be tactical alliances, such as in Azerbaijan, in support of Aliyev against Elchibey's supporters. Attacking Iran, with Turkish support, might at first glance look attractive to Russia, since such an action could easily be "sold" in the West as democratic (and Christian) Russia's contribution to the fight against "Islamic fundamentalism." But Russia's own enormous domestic problems and the costs of taking on a nation of 63 million people would ultimately make such an endeavor too risky for Russia, and might also bring it into conflict with the West if the West suspected that Russia's attack of Iran were aimed at the oil fields. Moreover, Turkey's general inclination against risk-taking militates against Turkish collaboration with Russia in a major operation against Iran.

The situation in Transcaucasia could change dramatically if Russia became incapable of maintaining its presence in the region. In this case, the potential conflicts described in the preceding analysis would become more relevant to the Transcaucasus. Similarly, if Russia decided to truly disentangle itself from its empire and unilaterally withdrew, it might create a power vacuum in the region. Developments would, however, depend on the nature of the Russian retreat. If Russia withdrew from the Transcaucasus in good order and remained a great power, it would continue, by virtue of its mass and history, to cast a long shadow over the Transcaucasus, and deter Turks and Iranians from intervention there. On the other hand, if

Russia collapsed in anarchy, Turks and Iranians would find it easier to extend their influence in the region, thus possibly increasing tensions between Ankara and Tehran.

Notes

[1]For the Ottoman Empire and Ataturk's revolution, see Bernard Lewis, *The Emergence of Modern Turkey* (London: Oxford University Press, 1968). Turkey's Kurdish problem and the political instability in the post-World War II period (leading to a coup d'état as recently as 1980) show that it has yet to reach West European standards of stability and development. Still, its performance remains superior to that of other Moslem nations.

[2]Turkey did have the advantage that Europeanization had already made significant advances in the Ottoman period. One could argue that Algerian or Malay elites, for example, were similarly westernized, but they became so in a colonized context rather than from the policies of a native government.

[3]Kjell Engelbrekt, RFE/RL Daily Report, no. 103, 1 June 1994, 4.

[4]See Thomas B. Allen, "Turkey Struggles for Balance," *National Geographic* 185 (May 1994): 18-19, on prostitutes and "suitcase" traders from the former Soviet Union.

[5]The European Free Trade Association (EFTA) comprises Iceland, Norway, Sweden, Finland, Austria, and Switzerland. Austria, Finland, and Sweden are scheduled to accede to EU membership on 1 January 1995 as planned.

[6]Organization for Economic Cooperation and Development, whose members include the nations of Western Europe, North America, Japan, Australia, and New Zealand.

[7]Economist Intelligence Unit, *EIU Country Report* (Turkey), 1st quarter 1994, 3, 25.

[8]Economist Intelligence Unit, *EIU Country Report* (Turkey), 1st quarter 1994, 3.

[9]The Economist Publications, *The World in 1994* (London: 1993), 84, 90. Estimates are from 1994.

[10]"The Clash of Civilizations?," *Foreign Affairs* (Summer 1993): 42.

[11]Graham Fuller, "Turkey's New Eastern Orientation," in *Turkey's New Geopolitics,* ed. Graham Fuller and Ian Lesser (Boulder, CO: Westview Press, 1993), 81; Paul Henze, *Turkey and Georgia* (Santa Monica, CA: Rand, 1992); and Henze, *The Transcaucasus in Transition*

(Santa Monica, CA: Rand, 1991), 19-20.

[12]For background information on Azerbaijan, see Audrey Altstadt, *The Azerbaijani Turks* (Stanford, CA: Hoover Institution Press, 1992). On Turkey's relations with independent Azerbaijan, see Graham Fuller, *Turkey Faces East: New Orientations Towards the Middle East and the Old Soviet Union* (Santa Monica, CA: Rand, 1992), Shireen Hunter, "The Muslim Republics" (*Washington Quarterly*, Summer 1992), "Turkey," *The Economist*, 10 July 1993, 43, 46, Henze, *The Transcaucasus in Transition,* 18, and "The Transcaucasus," *The Economist*, 24 July 1993, 55-56.

[13]Fuller, *Turkey Faces East,* 52-53, and "Turkey's New," 78-79; and Paul Henze, "Turkey," in *Turkey's New Geopolitics*, 23.

[14]See articles in *Yeni Gunaydin,* 9 Dec. 1993, and *Ozgur Gundem,* 20 Dec. 1993, in FBIS-WEU-93-249, 27 Dec. 1993, 39-41; and *Tercuman,* 17 Nov. 1993, in FBIS-WEU-93-226, 26 Nov. 1993, 52.

[15]See Stéphane Yerasimos, "Caucase: le retour de la Russie," *Politique Etrangère,* Spring 1994.

[16]*Krasnaya Zveda* (Red Star), 27 Apr. 1993, 3, in FBIS-SOV-93-080, 1-2. See Fuller, "Turkey," in *Turkey's New Geopolitics*, 78 for prediction of World War III, 86 for Turks in Russia, and 87 for the Turkish role in the ex-SSRs. See *Rossiyskaya Gazeta,* 24 July 1993, first. ed., 6, in FBIS-SOV-93-141, 26 July 1993, 78-79, for discrediting of the Azerbaijan government by the US, Turkey, and Elchibey. For Col. Viktor Kostenyuk's argument that Turkey's strategy incorporates the concept of military assistance to Moslem states of the FSU, see *Krasnaya Zveda,* 24 Nov. 1993, 3, in JPRS-UMA-94-002, 5 Jan. 1994, 34-37.

[17]See Philip Robins, "Between Sentiment and Self-Esteem," *Middle East Journal* 47 (Autumn 1993): 596, *Milliyet,* 11 Sept. 1993, 15, in FBIS-WEU-93-178, 16 Sept. 1993, 73. A Georgian government official told the authors on 16 September 1993 in Washington, DC, that Turkey prefers a Russian presence on its border to stabilize the situation. See also *Milliyet,* 1 Sept. 1993, 19, in FBIS-WEU-93-176, 14 Sept. 1993, 64-65; *Sabah,* 12 Sept. 1993, 11, in FBIS-WEU-93-178, 16 Sept. 1993, 72, and Yerasimos, "Caucase."

[18]See articles in *Aydinlik,* 5 Sept. 1993, 11, in FBIS-SOV-93-172, 8 Sept. 1993, 91; and 13 Jan 1994, 3, in FBIS-SOV-94-011, 18 Jan. 1994, 53-54. See also *Oxford Analytica Daily Brief,* 13 Apr. 1993, article #3, as well as articles in *Hurriyet,* 23 Dec. 1993, in FBIS-WEU-93-249, 30 Dec. 1993, 28, and *Turkish Daily News*, 28 Jan. 1994, 1, 8, in FBIS-WEU-94-021, 1 Feb. 1994, 38-39.

[19]See *Statesman's Year-Book 1959,* ed. John Paxton (London: St. Martin's Press, 1959), 235-6, and *Statesman's Year-Book 1983-84,* ed.

John Paxton (London: St. Martin's Press, 1983), 235 for Cyprus treaties.

[20]Laurent Lamote, "Iran's Foreign Policy and Internal Crises," in *Iran's Strategic Intentions and Capabilities* ed. Patrick Clawson (Washington, DC: National Defense University—INSS, 1994), 17-18.

[21]The Islamist victory in Sudan and successes in Algeria are of little relevance to Iran's security environment in the northern Gulf.

[22]Reza Khan led a coup d'etat in 1921, became premier in 1923, and upon becoming monarch in 1925 assumed the title of Reza Shah (emperor).

[23]The Peacock throne is the Persian throne, originally taken from India during a raiding party by an Iranian ruler.

[24]For the Islamic revolution, see Graham E. Fuller, *The "Center of the Universe": The Geopolitics of Iran* (Boulder, CO: Westview Press, 1991), Shireen T. Hunter, *Iran after Khomeini* (New York: Praeger, 1992), *Imam Khomeini's Last Will* (Washington, DC: Embassy of Algeria, Interest Section of the Islamic Republic of Iran, 1989), Olivier Roy, "L'Iran," Defense nationale, Oct. 1992. Roy Mottahedeh, *The Mantle of the Prophet* (New York: Simon and Schuster, 1985) provides insights into the revolution and Iranian society.

[25]See Elie Kedourie, *Islam and the Modern World* (New York: Holt, Rinehart and Winston, 1981), chapter 3. Except for the brief Mahdi rule in the Sudan, Khomeini's revolution was unprecedented in contemporary Islam.

[26]Hunter, *Iran and the World,* 37.

[27]*The Last Will of Khomeini,* 15, 19, Cheryl Bernard and Zalmay Khalizad, *The Government of God: Iran's Islamic Republic* (New York: Columbia University Press, 1988), 153, and Mottahedeh, 189-190.

[28]Mottahedeh, 164.

[29]See Patrick Clawson, "Alternative Foreign Policy Views Among the Iranian Policy Elite," in *Iran's Strategic Intentions,* 45-46.

[30]See Fuller, *"Center of the Universe,"* 125.

[31]Economist Intelligence Unit, *EIU Country Report* (Iran), 1st quarter 1994, 5.

[32]Economist Intelligence Unit, *EIU Country Report* (Iran), 1st quarter 1994, 3.

[33]Clawson, introduction to *Iran's Strategic Intentions,* 2-3.

[34]Economist Intelligence Unit, *EIU Country Report* (Iran), 1st quarter 1994, 3. ($14.2 billion is the latest statistic.)

[35]Sources vary considerably on the numbers.

[36]Clawson, introduction to *Iran's Strategic Intentions*, 2.

[37]Olivier Roy, "Ethnie et politique en Asie centrale," *REMMM* 59-60 (1991):1-2, 33.

[38]Such influence from north to south predated the creation of the Soviet state: the Hummet socialist party in Baku was the root of the Iranian communist party, the Tudeh.

[39]Rouhollah K. Ramazani, *Iran's Foreign Policy 1941-73* (Charlottesville, VA: University Press of Virginia, 1975), 400.

[40]See Fuller, *"Center of the Universe,"* 17, and Hunter, *Iran after Khomeini,* 140. *In Islam and the West* (New York: Oxford University Press, 1993), 173, Bernard Lewis states that nationalism is clearly strong in Turkey, relatively strong in Iran, and weaker in the Arab world.

[41]Roland Dannreuther, *Creating New States in Central Asia* (London: IISS, 1994), 62-63.

[42]See Anthony G. Shirley (pseudonym), "Not Fanatics, Not Friends," *Atlantic Monthly,* Dec. 1993, 104-112; "Iran," *The Economist,* 12 Feb. 1994, 40-42; and "Iran," *The Economist,* 25 June 1994, 43-44.

[43]Fuller, *"Center of the Universe,"* 165-6.

[44]See article in *Milliyet,* 1 Sept. 1993, 19, in FBIS-WEU-93-176, 14 Sept. 1993, 64-65.

[45]Stephen Foye, RFE/RL Daily Report, no. 147, 4 Aug. 1993, 3. See also Patrick Clawson, *Iran's Challenge to the West: How, When, and Why* (Washington, DC: The Washington Institute for New East Policy, 1993), xii; Moscow Ostankino TV 1st channel, 2000 GMT 4 June 1993, in FBIS-SOV-93-107, 86, and Moscow Radio Rossii 0900 GMT, 20 July 1993, in FBIS-SOV-93-139, 22 July 1993, 3.

[46]Session on Turkish-Iranian relations, U.S. Institute of Peace conference ("A Reluctant Neighbor: Analyzing Turkey's Role in the Middle East"), Washington, DC, 1 June 1994.

[47]Andrew Mango, *Turkey: The Challenge of a New Role* (Westport, CT: Praeger, 1994), 37 (estimates vary greatly).

[48]International Institute for Strategic Studies, *The Military Balance 1993-1994* (London: Brassey's, 1993), 62.

[49]"Turkey's Kurds," *The Economist,* 11 June 1994, 27-28, and "Draft Extended Again," *Jane's Defence Weekly,* 30 July 1994, 5.

[50]See articles in (Vienna) *Kurier,* 3 Oct. 1993, 5, in FBIS-WEU-930190, 4 Oct. 1993, 54; and *Turkish Daily News,* 7 Sept. 1993, 7, in FBIS-WEU-93-176, 14 Sept. 1993, 64-65. See also Henri J. Barkey, "Turkey's Kurdish Dilemma," *Survival* 35 (Winter 1993-94): 53-57.

[51]See *Ankara Daily News,* in FBIS-WEU-93-190, 4 Oct. 1993, 56, on Turks' starting Kurdish broadcasts to northern Iraq; *Hurriyet,* 30 Aug. 1993, 23, in FBIS-WEU-93-179, 17 Sept. 1993, 43, on talks between anti-PKK Kurds and Turkey in northern Iraq; and *Aydinlik,* 10 Sept. 1993, 6, in FBIS-WEU-93-178, 16 Sept. 1993, 72, on Turk activity in northern Iraq. See also Ankara TRT TV 2120 GMT, 6 April 1994, in FBIS-WEU-

94-067, 7 April 1994, 38.

[52]Martin van Bruinessen, "Kurdish Society, Ethnicity, Nationalism and Refugee Problems," in *The Kurds: A Contemporary Overview,* ed. Philip G. Kreyenbroek and Stefan Sperl (London: Routledge, 1992), 35-38, and Philip Robins, *Turkey and the Middle East* (London: Pinter Publishers, 1991), 8.

[53]See Kelly Couturier, "Turkey Makes Move to Limit Kurdish Autonomy Inside Iraq," *Washington Post,* 1 October 1994, A18.

[54]*The Military Balance 1993-1994,* 116.

[55]On the call by National Action Party leader Alpaslan Turkes for special status for Iraqi Turcomans, see Ankara TRT TV, 12 Oct. 1993, 1800 GMT, in FBIS-WEU-93-196, 13 Oct. 1993, 174.

[56]*Middle East Reporter,* 6 June 1992, 8-10, *New York Times,* 25 Oct. 1992, sec. 1, 15, and *Hurriyet,* 12 Oct. 1993, 17, in FBIS-WEU-93-198, 5 Oct. 1993, 74-75.

[57]*Hurriyet,* 10 Nov. 1993, 20, in FBIS-WEU-93-218, 15 Nov. 1993, 20. See also Yerasimos, "Caucase."

[58]*Christian Science Monitor,* 11 Feb. 1993, 6, Economist Intelligence Unit, *EIU Country Report* (Iran), 2nd quarter 1993, 11, and Khalid Duran, "Rivalries Over the New Muslim Countries," *Aussenpolitik,* 1992, 377. See also Dept. of State, *Patterns of Global Terrorism* (Washington, DC: April 1994), 23, *Washington Post,* 13 Mar. 1993, A14, *New York Times,* 18 Mar. 1993, A8, *New York Times,* 21 Dec. 1992, A10.

[59]Garath Smyth reports Iranian irritation over the Kurdistan Democratic Party of Iran's using northern Iraqi bases against Iran in "Tehran's vendetta hits the Kurds hard," *Financial Times,* 13 Oct. 1993, 6.

[60]For PKK training in Syria (and Iran, Armenia, and Iraq), see Ankara TRT TV, 4 Nov. 1993, 1100 GMT, in FBIS-WEU-93-213, 56-57. For Bekka Valley as the site of PKK bases, see *Turkiye,* 30 Jan. 1994, 6, in FBIS-WEU-04-023, 3 Feb. 1994, 37-38. Syria-PKK links were discussed at an off-the-record seminar with a Turkish official, Washington DC, January 1994.

[61]Natasha Beschorner, "Le rôle de l'eau dans la politique régionale de la Turquie," *Monde arabe Maghreb Machrek,* no. 138, Oct.-Dec. 1992, 48.

[62]Fuller, *"Center of the Universe,"* 173-74.

[63]The Turkish press showed concern, though not hysteria, over Iranian incursions into Azerbaijan. See FBIS-WEU-93-171, 7 Sept. 1993, 45-47.

[64]Iran's sensitivity about its Turkic population and the lack of

integration of the Turkmen minority was discussed at the session on Turkish-Iranian relations, U.S. Institute of Peace conference ("A Reluctant Neighbor: Analyzing Turkey's Role in the Middle East"), Washington, DC, 1 June 1994.

[65]Fuller, *"Center of the Universe,"* 193.

[66]See John Murray Brown, "Europe links questioned," *Financial Times,* 15 April 1994, 1.

[67]Fuller, *"Center of the Universe,"* 203. See Robins, *Turkey and the Middle East,* 55-56, on Iranian insults to Ataturk's memory.

[68]See Fuller, *"Center of the Universe,"* 20-21, on paranoia in Iran. See also Shirley, "Not Fanatics," 107, Ervand Abrahamian, *Khomeinism: Essays on the Islamic Republic* (Berkeley, CA: University of California Press, 1993), chapter 5, and Dannreuther, *Creating New States,* 62-63.

[69]*Turkish Probe,* 25 Mar. 1994, 8-9, in FBIS-WEU-94-066, 6 Apr. 1994, 38-40; *Turkish Daily News,* 1 Apr. 1994, 2, in FBIS-WEU-94-065, 5 Apr. 1994, 43; Itar Tass 1750 GMT, 5 Apr. 1994 and TRT TV Ankara 2100 GMT, 5 Apr. 1994, in FBIS-SOV-94-066, 6 Apr. 1994, 46. See also Clawson, "Alternative Foreign Policy Views," 44-45.

FIVE

Conclusion

The conclusion of this study is that Central Asia and the Transcaucasus were coming under a new Russian hegemony, if not yet imperial control, by late 1994. No outside regional powers were competing seriously with Russia for influence in either region. Iran was remarkably hesitant to assume a significant role. Turkey, after initial fanfares in Central Asia and some direct assistance to Azerbaijan, retreated to a restrained posture. China pursued a modest diplomacy of engagement, as did several other regional states. CIS states within both regions sought to attract US, West European, and East Asian economic and diplomatic attention but achieved only modest results. Thus both regions were left to deal with Russia as best they could. Simultaneously, Russia gave the maintenance of political and economic stability lower priority than regaining hegemony. Internal factors in individual states, of course, contributed to differing degrees of stability in both regions.

To conclude this study, it is best to look at three developments that affect both regions' future: internal affairs, Russia's role, and the role of countries outside the CIS.

Domestic Sources of Stability and Instability

The most stable states in Central Asia and the Transcaucasus proved to be dictatorships. Turkmenistan, Uzbekistan, and Kazakhstan experienced remarkably little instability in 1992-94. Kyrgyzstan was also stable, but its inchoate democracy owed its survival less to inherent internal strength than to the shelter provided from Russian meddling by neighboring dictators who did not want

violence among ethnic groups they shared in common with Kyrgyzstan. All other states—Tajikistan, Azerbaijan, Armenia, and Georgia—were deeply involved in war and domestic violence.

Modest democratic development occurred only in Armenia and
Kyrgyzstan. Armenia's ethnic homogeneity, high educational level,
and strong sense of national identity give it a better social basis for
democratic development than any other state in either region. Its
government administration penetrated virtually all sectors of society,
effectively recruiting soldiers for the war with Azerbaijan and maintaining an elected regime. At the same time, democratic development faced serious obstacles in Armenia. The country's economy
fell into ruin from natural disasters, war, and embargoes. Its dependency on Russia in its war with Azerbaijan made it vulnerable to
Russian military influence, especially since it permitted the indefinite
stationing of Russian troops in Armenia and Russian control of its
border with Turkey. Finally, Armenia's reluctance to seek a rapprochement with Turkey impeded economic and democratic development
by forcing it to depend on Russia and to maintain a siege mentality.

Kyrgyzstan's democracy was much more tenuous. The country
had neither a strong sense of modern nationalism nor an ethnically
homogenous society. The Kyrgyz created a democratic government
when, taking advantage of Gorbachev's perestroika, they ousted the
old communist leadership through elections and brought to the presidency Akayev, a man genuinely committed to democracy. Yet the
old Soviet bureaucrats retained sufficient influence in the parliament
and the state apparatus to slow down reforms that might have sunk
the roots of democracy into Kyrgyz soil. If the Russian military truly
desired, it could create serious disorder in Kyrgyzstan by stirring up
Uzbeks and Russians living there. The one such effort, in the Fergana
Valley, was squelched only because the Uzbek dictator, Karimov,
helped Akayev repress it. Were Kazakhstan and Uzbekistan to lose
their independence from Russia entirely, Kyrgyzstan could not survive for long as a democracy or even as a sovereign country.

Social and economic bifurcation in countries throughout Central
Asia and the Transcaucasus makes them subject to popular discontent and is thus another source of instability. All countries in both
regions inherited broad masses of impoverished people, concentrated
in rural areas but also present in cities. The ruling elites and much of

the intelligentsia form a small and relatively privileged upper stratum. In the short period of independence local national elites have grabbed even more privileges and material benefits, mostly at the expense of Russian and other Slavic minorities, further reinforcing the divide. The first three years of the CIS have been too short a period for this economic and social bifurcation to prompt destabilizing popular actions against the upper stratum. Although institutions for opposition through popular mobilization existed, they were suppressed in the dictatorships, irrelevant in the war-torn states, and partly co-opted in Kyrgyzstan. The situation could change suddenly, however. For example, the rapid increase in visible inequalities caused by a new class of wealthy "businessmen" who patronize expensive establishments and drive fancy cars could generate tremendous resentment among the poor. Islamic cultural and religious institutions could eventually become the major vehicles for protest actions, although by late 1994 they had not yet done so to a significant degree. This kind of bifurcation has, of course, been common in most postcolonial states and other Third World regimes, occasionally giving rise to revolutions and wide-scale disorders.

Fragmented societies in all countries in the regions save Armenia increase the likelihood of unstable governments and civil war. Fragmentation in this context refers to vertical fissures in society and among political elites. Stalin, as the commissar for nationalities in the 1920s, intentionally drew boundaries among the republics in both regions that split ethnically homogenous territories and lumped together groups and territories that were not socially integrated. The old Soviet institutions permitted enforced political integration and the avoidance of instability. With the passing of Soviet power, however, these vertical fissures began to come into play. Where the local communist elites remained in control of the old institutions, i.e., in Turkmenistan, Uzbekistan, and Kazakhstan, they kept the lid on fragmentation. (This explains in part why the dictatorships showed the greatest stability.) In all other countries but Kyrgyzstan, fragmentation was exploited either by Russia or by local elites, producing civil war and violence.

This does not mean that ethnicity has been the cause of instability and violence but rather that it has been a condition instigators exploit to produce violence. Ethnic distinctions, one form of fragmentation, do not in themselves cause violence and civil war; in the Kyrgyz city of Osh, for instance, local citizens had difficulty distinguishing between Kyrgyz and Uzbeks although they themselves were of these two ethnic groups. Ethnicity, then, has been used to impose mutual antagonisms and hostilities on groups within a society. The Soviet nationalities policies made advancement within the republican bureaucracies and other institutions dependent on nationality. This policy increased awareness of nationality (even when the nationality was an implicit invention of Soviet policy makers) and laid the ground for ethnic conflict and rivalry in the late 1980s and 1990s. In many instances, there were preexisting ethnic tensions, but the combination of Soviet map drawing (such as the Nagorno-Karabakh oblast within the Azeri SSR) and nationality policy helped to worsen matters.

On the economic front, transitions toward market systems were proceeding slowly or not at all in both regions. War and civil violence were so extensive in 1992-94 in the Transcaucasus that policies for transitions to a market system were largely nonexistent. Certainly a large degree of de facto shifting to private-sector economic activities occurred, but no country attempted policies as bold as Russia's 1992 effort to liberalize prices and stabilize the currency.

In Central Asia, the old communist elites who held power and maintained order spent as much effort postponing genuine economic reform as pursuing it. Being tossed out of the Russian ruble zone forced them to take reform more seriously, but they continued to hold on to large statist industrial sectors and most of the collectivized agriculture. What sometimes passed as "privatization" was merely the transfer of state property to the control of individual incumbents in the regimes. This pattern, of course, is not unlike the distribution of ownership in Third World dictatorships.

Some analysts and government officials thought that hydrocarbons and other minerals would provide a fast track toward economic development. Turkmenistan, Kazakhstan, and Azerbaijan have sought to alleviate their economic plight largely through export of oil and gas to Western buyers. The example of rich oil-producing states in the Middle East caught their eye, and President Niyazov of Turkmenistan specifically cited Kuwait as his model. Kyrgyzstan developed more modest hopes for exporting gold from its rich mountainous areas, where gold ore is reportedly abundant. But oil, gas, and other high-value mineral exports will not solve the economic problems of any of these states.

The first flaw in such an economic strategy is that none of these countries has proven oil and gas reserves equal to those in the Persian Gulf states. Thus their oil and gas exporting potential is limited. Moreover, the populations of Kazakhstan and Azerbaijan are much larger than those of the richer Persian Gulf oil producers, limiting the extent to which they could follow the pattern of Kuwait, the sheikdoms, and Saudi Arabia.

Second, pipelines for transporting oil and gas to Western markets either pass through Russia or must be built through Iran and Turkey. Russia has shown no intention of letting these countries' oil and gas pass through its pipelines without extracting a huge percentage of the profits, and the availability of Western capital for constructing pipelines through Iran and Turkey is problematic.

Third, the record of economic development has not been impressive in other countries that tried to thrive on oil exports, e.g., Algeria, Nigeria, and pre-Salinas Mexico.[1] Their large inflows of capital from oil sales merely sustained statist economies, unproductive investments in other economic sectors, and corruption of government officials. Thus even if the obstacles to transporting oil and gas were overcome, the resulting inflows of capital would in fact discourage aggressive policies of transition to market economics in these CIS countries. This would only intensify the pattern of social and economic bifurcation, creating the potential for major political upheavals.

Given these internal realities, how are the political systems of these nations likely to evolve? The local dictatorships in Central Asia look somewhat like Baathist states,[2] in which an old Communist-Party apparatus is used to maintain one-party rule under the command of a forceful autocrat. Under these dictators, a partially privatized economy, with a large state sector and crony capitalism, is likely to develop. On the other hand, the Central Asian regimes could very well fail to achieve this degree of stability. The weak militaries, feeble economies, high birth rates, and fragmented societies could make it impossible to establish a relatively strong state, especially in light of probable Russian interference. As a result, civil wars, or a gradual collapse of the state, could well be the fate of some of these republics.

In the Transcaucasus, Armenia may evolve into a sort of fortress democracy, under Moscow's "protection." Georgia's central government has already lost de facto control over three regions, Ajaria, Abkhazia, and South Ossetia. Its chances of stable political development are, at present, quite limited, given its history of civil conflict and the inability of the regime to establish itself firmly. Azerbaijan will probably have to acknowledge the humiliating loss of Nagorno-Karabakh, and its politics will be complicated by this defeat and the massive refugee inflow, amounting to one seventh of the population, that the Armenians unleashed.

Russia and the CIS as Influences on Stability

Despite Moscow's claim that it was acting as "peacemaker," it was becoming obvious by 1994 that Russian military involvement has increased violence and sustained civil war in both regions. Tajikistan and Nagorno-Karabakh would have been torn by violence in any case, but Russian military involvement in both places increased violence in several instances and perhaps even prevented a settlement between Baku and Yerevan. The Russian Motor Rifle Division in Dushanbe was never neutral in the Tajik civil war, especially in 1992 when a Tajik officer commanded it. Later, under Russian command, its record is ambiguous at best. At times it appears to have been exploited by various Tajik parties to the war, and it never pursued a policy of trying to limit the conflict and force the warring clans to negotiate. Nor is the record of Russian Border Troops any better. They proved wholly unable to close the border, and they were possibly involved in drug trafficking as well, thereby contributing to turmoil in Tajikistan.

In Georgia, the Russian military clearly raised the level of violence dramatically in Abkhazia, leading to the slaughter of large numbers of Georgians as well as the creation of masses of refugees. To be sure, had the Russian military stayed out, violence would still have occurred. Gamsakhurdia had insured that. Yet the indigenous forces—militias, ethnic minorities, and various Georgian official forces—were simply too incompetent to produce the levels of warfare brought about by the Russian military. To a lesser degree, the same is true for Azerbaijan.

All the new republics are rendered more vulnerable to Russian intervention by the shortage of local ethnic officer cadres. At this stage, they face a long-term dependency on Russian military officers and officer-training schools. Armenia inherited a large number of officers from the Soviet military who are ethnically Armenian, but all the other republics had little more than token representation in the ethnic makeup of the Soviet officer corps. Officer corps cannot be trained overnight under the best of circumstances. That means that all the Central Asian states as well as Georgia and Azerbaijan must depend heavily on Russian officers, not just for a short period of transition but for at least a decade. That much time is needed to train a generation of indigenous officers in sufficient numbers to staff the senior command and staff ranks, including the local ministries of defense. Moreover, most of that new generation will be trained in Russian military schools.

The political significance of this dependency on Russia is greater than generally recognized. All countries of both regions, including Armenia, also rely on Russian supplies of weapons, equipment, and various kinds of technical military support. That itself is a huge dependency, but in principle it could be shifted quickly from Russia to some other advanced military power; China, India, Turkey, Britain, or France might fill the gap if Russia withdrew these forms of military support. They could not, however, replace Russian officers and officer schools on short notice, unless they were willing to send thousands of their own officers to lead local armies, an improbable proposition.

Military dependency, especially on Russian officers, was the most important lever Moscow exercised in reasserting control over Central Asia and the Transcaucasus. And it will be the most important for retaining control during the next several years. No country, except possibly Armenia, can break this grip on its own, and Armenia's policies toward Turkey and Azerbaijan virtually ensure its continuing reliance on Moscow. Had Georgia inherited a competent and large cadre of officers, it might well have defeated the Abkhazian separatists and expelled Russian troops from all of Georgia. Azerbaijan could have done the same. While Turkmenistan and Uzbekistan have temporarily come to terms with the Russian military, their longer-term sovereignty will depend on their capacity to create indigenous and competent militaries and internal security forces. The same is true for Kazakhstan, but its prospects are much poorer because of the unusually large Russian population there and the important military facilities in the country that remain under Russian military control with Kazakh agreement. Tajikistan is a separate case, so seriously fragmented internally that even as a Russian colony it is unlikely to regain stability. The instructive analogies with Soviet involvement in Afghanistan have been noticed by some political leaders in Moscow.

Russian military intervention has been directed from Moscow with the aim of reasserting Russian influence in the "near abroad." Russian economic policy towards the former republics has been mixed in its impact, breaking traditional economic linkages in some sectors, sustaining dependencies on Moscow in others. Russia erratically pursued two incompatible economic policies toward the CIS in 1992-94. The market-reform faction headed by Yegor Gaidar and Boris Fedorov contributed to the breakup of the ruble zone within the CIS. At the same time, many of the old command economy bureaucrats, particularly those in military industries, struggled to maintain linkages with firms in most of the CIS countries, hoping that eventually a CIS economic union would save much of the old system. These institutional conservatives in Russia received much support from their counterparts in most of the CIS countries, particularly in Kazakhstan and Uzbekistan but even in Ukraine. The result of these two different policy approaches was increasing economic disorder in Central Asia, as the conservatives obstructed progress by the reformers and the reformers made return to the old economic system more and more difficult, perhaps impossible. In the Transcaucasus, the degree of economic chaos was far greater, leaving all three countries in that region without effective currencies, with near subsistence-level incomes, and dependent on Russian energy supplies.

Other Russian economic behavior contributed to the economic chaos and retarded progress in new economic development projects. Russia's efforts to force Azeri and Central Asian oil and gas exporters to use only Russian pipelines blocked exports, held up foreign capital investments, and created uncertainty among foreign businessmen about how to proceed. Another such disruptive Russian practice was the threat to cut off energy supplies, which it in some cases implemented. Some energy deliveries to Georgia and Armenia were denied, at times because of recipients' failure to pay their accumulated energy bills, but in some instances the cutoffs were purely political strong-arm tactics.

Expecting efficient and smooth economic policymaking in the CIS, of course, would be naive. In the best circumstances the breakup of the old Soviet command system was bound to produce friction, contradictory policies, and chaotic results. Yet Russian economic behavior toward the CIS, although seldom effectively controlled under one general policy, was inspired at times by ill intentions—the desire to restore the empire, to force submission by other CIS states, and sometimes simply to deny them profitable international trade. Russian official claims of seeking to improve economic relations in the CIS and facilitate economic transition and recovery, therefore, should be viewed with skepticism. A few may be valid, but the actual record of economic practice makes many of Russia's actions appear hostile and destructive. Admittedly, the behavior of other CIS states was seldom inspired wholly by virtuous intent or policy consistency, but few could match Russian behavior in trying to exercise economic leverage to undermine others' political sovereignty. The big exception in Russia was the Gaidar government's attempt to push through market reforms. Imperfect as they were, ineffective though their implementation may have been, they did undercut almost all CIS leaders and ministerial officials who wanted to restore the old Soviet economic system. Such reforms, of course, compelled all other CIS states to make reforms of their own and to begin to break many of the Soviet command economy linkages with Moscow and one another.

Overall, Russian efforts to restore military control over Central Asia and the Transcaucasus under the CIS banner were surprisingly successful by the winter of 1993-94. By the summer of 1992, the CIS looked moribund, especially in its military institutional developments. By the summer of 1993, even the Russian defense ministry was opposing Marshal Shaposhnikov's efforts to create a unified CIS armed forces. As a vehicle for reasserting Moscow's military hegemony, the CIS looked like a miserable failure. In fact, however, only Moscow's initial strategy toward the CIS had failed. Its second strategy, creating a collective security treaty within the CIS and building networks of bilateral military agreements on a country-by-country basis, was succeeding. Even the obstreperous holdouts, Georgia and

Azerbaijan, had been forced to cooperate with Moscow's military plans for the CIS.

Ukraine and Moldova, of course, persisted in their opposition to CIS military arrangements. Ukraine is now key, and whether Russian "divide and rule" tactics will eventually break Ukraine is the most critical issue for determining the future character of the CIS. It is also an issue beyond this study, but it is essential to note it as a caveat when calling Russian military policy toward the CIS a success.

Russian reassertion in the "near abroad" could still be derailed by developments in Russia. Sustained economic reform and a stronger democratic legislative process in that country could break the imperial policy toward Central Asia and the Transcaucasus. The costs of maintaining the Russian military in both regions, and of controlling the entire southern border of the former Soviet Union, are not trivial. The numbers of troops involved in the conflicts in Tajikistan and the Transcaucasus were in the scores of thousands in 1992-94, and those serving in Kazakhstan, Turkmenistan, Uzbekistan, and Kyrgyzstan make the total much higher. The relatively high pay for contract soldiers, who provide most of the rank and file for Russian units in the conflict areas, increases the burden on the Russian military budget. Russian military officials have pushed the costs onto the host countries to the degree possible in bilateral treaties and agreements. Upkeep of installations, for example, is shared or carried entirely by the host country. And local youths are recruited to serve in Russian Border Troop units in Georgia and Armenia, and probably in most other countries as well. Notwithstanding these techniques of cost shifting, Russia is still left with the major financial burden for its military.

At the same time, the Russian government has less unchecked discretion to allocate resources to military programs than the Soviet government had. The public lobbying in the spring of 1994 to limit the defense budget reflects the considerable narrowing of that discretion. After General Grachev demanded first R80 trillion, then R87 trillion, the government proposed only R37.1 trillion to the State Duma in the budget. Only R40 trillion was authorized after strong lobbying by defense officials and particularly military industrial managers. They were up against other strong claimants on the state budget, namely the miners' unions and the collective farm bureaucracy.

To the degree that the parliament gains control of the purse strings and allocations are finally determined by the legislative process, strong forces are likely to oppose the financial burden of Russian military control of Central Asia and the Transcaucasus. In addition, the more dependent the Russian government becomes on taxation for its fiscal resources within an expanding market sector, the greater will be the potential political resistance to the costs of a new empire. In 1994, however, the Russian president retained ways to bypass the parliament in allocating funds to the military. He had decree powers with the force of law, which could be used to direct fiscal allocations "off-line." That is, President Yeltsin could simply issue a decree authorizing more funds for the defense ministry without the Duma's permission.

Using that authority could have two effects. First, it could merely increase the budget deficit, causing greater inflationary pressures. Second, it might cause funds to be raised from increased taxation. Although the latter possibility is unlikely in light of the regime's limited capacity to impose effective taxation, it would certainly cause a political reaction, including outspoken criticism in the parliament. In the debates taking place in spring of 1994, parliamentary deputies who understood the implications of a large military budget for taxation and inflation raised their voices about such a budget's ill effects. Neither increased taxation nor rising inflation would be desirable for Yeltsin and the government.

Will democratization within Russia proceed rapidly enough to restrain that country's imperial policies? One can only speculate. Certainly democratization did not slow down those policies during 1992-94. Yet it is about the only potential source of resistance to Russian imperialism. As a few Russian observers noted in 1993 and 1994, it had become clear in 1993 that neither the West nor any other outside power would offer more than token resistance to Russia's imperial policies. Earlier, expecting strong Western reactions, Russian leaders had proceeded with caution. Caution was no longer essential in late 1993.[3] The only constraints that might now operate on Russian imperialism are domestic resistance to the costs of imperialist policies and resistance from other CIS countries.

Other External Influences

With the opening of Central Asia and the Transcaucasus to the outside world, the region's relations with countries to its south, from Turkey to China, became an issue. As eight new players joined the diplomatic game, new alignments throughout central Eurasia became possible. So far, however, no foreign actor has displaced Russia as the dominant influence on the region.

In spite of all the talk about the emergence of a new Turkic community, no states in either region except Azerbaijan made strong attempts to build ties to Turkey. Turkish policies of offering cooperation met a positive response from Elchibey's government in Azerbaijan. Turkey provided military assistance training and modest help in the war with Armenia. In the spring of 1993, Azerbaijan encouraged outside mediation of the dispute of Nagorno-Karabakh in which Turkey was a participant.

Nowhere else, however, did such ties develop. The secular Central Asian regimes cited Turkey's example with favor, and a flurry of diplomacy occurred through much of 1992, but little of lasting substance followed. Turkey could not provide the capital investments and business ties to world markets on the scale sought by those states. Moreover, geographic separation discouraged their expansion of the initial openings to Turkey.

If these new nations did not seek out Turkey, neither did they look toward Iran for guidance or assistance. In fact, no states in either region tried to build strong ties to Iran except Turkmenistan. Contrary to expectations, Iran did not try to rush into Central Asia and Azerbaijan; nor did any CIS countries rush toward Iran. Linguistic and cultural linkages to Tajikistan brought early and optimistic diplomatic relations with Iran, but the changing Tajik regimes, fearful as they claimed to be of radical Islam on their own territory, had to be suspicious of Tehran. For its part, Iran pursued cautious and correct relations with these CIS countries.

Turkmenistan's interest in Iran, however, is different from that of the other former Soviet republics. President Niyazov desperately needs pipelines to the West for exporting oil and gas, and these lines have to cross Iranian territory if they are to avoid Russian control. What form Turkmenistan's relations with Iran will ultimately take was not clear by late 1994, but both countries have objective interests in cooperation. Perhaps the largest obstacle to Niyazov's success is the United States' policy to isolate and oppose economic ties with Iran. This discourages Western oil companies from making the capital investments needed to build the pipelines across Iran.

More to the east, China showed only moderate interest in Central Asia. A fairly aggressive Chinese diplomacy might have been expected in Central Asia after the dissolution of the USSR, but it did not occur. Beijing normalized relations with the two states on its western frontier, Kazakhstan and Kyrgyzstan, and it encouraged expanded trade. Otherwise, China kept a discreet reserve toward Central Asia, broken slightly by Prime Minister Li Peng's visit to the region in early 1994. Chinese caution is probably to be explained by the desire to avoid an early return to open competition with Russia in Central and East Asia.

Seeking sources of capital and investment, Central Asian countries made their strongest foreign policy bids to the Western industrial states and international financial institutions. They tried to attract business interests from Western Europe, North America, and Japan and also appealed to the World Bank and the International Monetary Fund (IMF). Whether their focus on the West will continue, of course, depends on what response they get. While the IMF, the World Bank, and a few business firms (e.g., Chevron Corporation) have responded, neither Washington nor Western European capitals have shown a comparable diplomatic and strategic interest in the region. Thus the Central Asian states have been left with little or no counterweight to Russian influence under the CIS banner.

In the Transcaucasus, the three new countries have been unable to attract any significant outside assistance, economic or diplomatic. Given the violence and civil wars in the region, the absence of outside economic interest is not surprising. To be sure, Azerbaijan attracted interest in its oil deposits as well as Turkish diplomatic interest and military assistance. The Russian reaction, however, quickly dashed the prospects for sustaining those ties. The author of those ties, Elchibey, was extremely pro-Turkish, but his victorious opponent, Gaidar Aliyev, was also attracted to the potential profits from oil exports. In the spring and summer of 1994, as he strove to reopen some of those economic deals, he met strong opposition from

Moscow. The Russian foreign ministry even protested to Great Britain that the British Petroleum-Azeri exploration offshore in the Caspian Sea would endanger the ecosystem![4]

Islam, as a political ideology rather than a religion, is also an outside influence with the potential to significantly affect the Central Asian and Azerbaijani Moslems. By 1994, however, foreign Islamic influence had not been significant. Economic failure, growing inequality, and an ideological vacuum might have made Islamic radicals significant factors in the politics of the region. But Islamic politics will be primarily endogenous (as has been the case in the Moslem world from Algeria to Indonesia) rather than exogenous.

Overall, Russian influence will be a major determinant of political development in both regions. In 1993-94 they were returning to colonial status under Moscow. If that trend is sustained, then both regions will face a long period similar to that faced by the West European imperial colonies in the first half of this century. Russian rule will prevent major regional wars within and among these states. At the same time Moscow will cultivate political fragmentation and violence as a tactic in a "divide and rule" strategy.

If Russia steps back from this imperial role, then political instability may well increase in both regions. And in many ways they could be worse off free of Russian hegemony, especially in their capacity to maintain order, and none would create a durable democracy, Kyrgyzstan's example notwithstanding. On the other hand, an end to Russian manipulations in the Transcaucasus might facilitate peace settlements sponsored by the international community. It would also leave Russia better off, without empire's costly military burdens and its retarding effect on liberal political development within Russia.

In sum, Central Asia and the Transcaucasus appear to be in a long period of transition, one marked by periodic violence, cultural and social turmoil, and the existence of dictatorships that provide stability between such upheavals. The fate of both regions will be closely tied to politics in Russia, depending as it does on whether Russian imperial impulses subside or regain new energy. The return to a "Great Game" between Russia and a Western power over these regions appears unlikely. The United States is the single Western power up to such a game, and it hardly appears inclined to accept the challenge (although such a game in Central Asia between Russia and China is not to be ruled out later in the 1990s.) Nor is such a game in the Transcaucasus likely. The dangers of a three-way game— involving Russia, Iran, and Turkey—appear well understood in Ankara and Tehran, and neither regime shows an inclination to compete. Rather each appears more concerned with how to avoid war with the other. Competition in the Transcaucasus would help neither party. Yet the Armenian-Azeri conflict has the potential to drag Iran or Turkey or both into such a competition.

Commonwealth or Empire?

It is possible to imagine three plausible scenarios for the future of Russia. The first is a new Russian imperialism, which already shows signs of emerging in Central Asia and the Transcaucasus. Largely the consequence of Russia's military policy toward these regions, it is far from mature and stable. Yet its institutional basis has evolved fairly steadily since the summer of 1993, unlike economic and political institutional relations. Interparliamentary and intergovernmental ties under the CIS have been active, but they have not enjoyed the kind of institutionalization seen in the military and security sectors where Russian hegemony is easier to exercise.

A second scenario involves a successful transition to a market economy and stable democracy in Russia. That would complete the destruction of the old Soviet economic linkages between Russia and both regions, and it would probably engender genuine Russian respect for the political sovereignty of the regions' states. In such dramatically new circumstances, the CIS could become a community of closely linked trading states with considerable coordination of their security policies. That development, of course, would depend on similar liberal economic and political transitions in the states of the two regions, a highly improbable outcome. It need not occur quickly, however, and a democratic Russia might be able to lead these states toward that goal over a number of decades, allowing them time to gain confidence in their own sovereignty, carry out their own internal reforms, and recognize that a commonwealth relationship with Russia was in their own best interests.

If this scenario were to occur, there are no indications thus far that Russia would have to fear outside powers' moving in to fill the vacuum created by its disengagement during a long period of transition and readjustment. Nor are there signs that either region would go its own way and align itself with a power hostile to Russia or become a bastion of Islamic radicalism deeply hostile to Russia. Possibly China could become a serious competitor in Central Asia, but that does not look likely in the 1990s as China deals with its own internal problems and concerns itself with Japan and with the United States' presence in East Asia.

A third scenario is that Russia could linger for a long time in a state of great internal turmoil, in which corruption so weakened its military and security institutions that they could not sustain Russian hegemony in Central Asia and the Transcaucasus. The states in both regions would remain mired in similar domestic turmoil, some experiencing periodic civil strife, some acting as highly oppressive dictatorships. Border disputes and shifts might occur, leading to wars that might involve Russia with Kazakhstan and with parts of Georgia in the Caucasus. Factions in Russia could ally with factions within states in both regions, adding to the political disorder. Conceivably, this scenario could last for several years, perhaps a decade or more.

The first scenario could eventually turn into the third scenario, as a new imperialism proved beyond Russia's ability to sustain indefinitely. And the second scenario might occur in Russia while the third emerged in either or both of the two regions in question. A democratic Russia, in this event, would probably try to wall itself off from both Central Asia and the Transcaucasus in security affairs. Yet the large Slavic populations in these regions would make such a move difficult unless substantial portions of them migrate back to Russia, Ukraine, and Belarus. In all events, Russia's entanglement with Central Asia and the Transcaucasus remains deep and will not diminish quickly unless Russian leaders agree to disengage and then aggressively pursue that course.

It may be too much to say that the fate of Russia's democracy depends on disengagement from these regions, but its prospects for democracy would surely improve if it were to disengage. Other parts of the CIS, most notably Ukraine, also bear heavily on the fate of Russian domestic political development. A stable Ukraine making even modest progress in a liberal economic and political transition would help push the CIS toward becoming a genuine commonwealth instead of an empire. Still, Russia's relationship with Central Asia and the Transcaucasus will remain an important influence on its domestic political development and a major determinant in answering the question "commonwealth or empire?"

Notes

[1]Mexico made remarkable progress under President Salinas, but this was the result of a more effective economic policy rather than of oil wealth, which did not prevent Mexico from sliding into a severe debt crisis in the early 1980s.

[2]The Baath Party is an Arab nationalist party whose rival wings rule Syria and Iraq. Baathist techniques of rule share much with the techniques used by Leninist parties.

[3]Andranik Migranyan made this point publicly about Russian involvement in the Transdniester region in particular, and a Russian diplomat made the same point in a discussion with one of the authors in early 1994, saying that even the Baltic republics would probably be brought into the Russian empire. Russian foreign minister Andrei Kozyrev traveled and spoke endlessly in the West in 1993-94, both denying that Russia was following an imperial policy and justifying it. He used his liberal credentials to help sell his ambiguous message. See for example Therese Raphael, "Russia: The New Imperialism," *The Wall Street Journal,* 22 June 1994.

[4]RFE/RL Daily Report, no. 107, 8 June 1994. The transparent hypocrisy of the Russian opposition was further evident in the attempt to have the Caspian designated a "lake" instead of a "sea," thereby making irrelevant offshore economic rights as defined in the law of the sea.

Bibliography

I. The Former Soviet Union

The USSR

Alexiev, Alex, *Soviet Nationalities in German Wartime Strategy 1941-1945*. Santa Monica, CA: Rand, 1992.

Bremmer, Ian, and Ray Taras, *Nations and Politics in the Soviet Successor States*. Cambridge: Cambridge University Press, 1993.

Carrere d'Encause, Helene, *L'URSS de la Revolution á la mort de Staline 1917-1953*. Paris: Le Seuil, 1993.
Carrere d'Encause, Helene, *L'Empire eclaté*. Paris: Flamarion, 1978.

Conquest, Robert, ed., *The Last Empire: Nationality and the Soviet Future*. Stanford, CA: Hoover Institution Press, 1986.

Denber, Rachel, ed., *The Soviet Nationality Reader: The Disintegration in Context*. Boulder, CO: Westview Press, 1992.

Hajda, Lubomyr, and Mark Beissinger, eds., *The Nationalities Factor in Soviet Politics and Society*. Boulder, CO: Westview Press, 1990.

Hauner, Milan, *What is Asia to Us: Russia's Asian Heartland Yesterday and Today*. Boston: Unwin Hyman, 1990.

Motyl, Alexander J., *Thinking Theoretically About Soviet Nationalities*. New York: Columbia University Press, 1992.

Nahaylo, Bohdan, and Victor Swoboda, *Soviet Disunion: A History of the Nationalities Problem in the USSR*. New York: Free Press, 1989.

The Russian Federation

Arbatov, Alexei G., "Russia's Foreign Policy Alternatives." *International Security*, Fall 1993 (Vol 18:2).

Bodie, William C., "Threats from the Former USSR." *Orbis*, Fall 1993 (Vol 37:4).

Dannreuther, Roland, "Russia, Central Asia and the Persian Gulf." *Survival*, Winter 1993-94 (Vol 35:4).

Hill, Fiona, *Report on Ethnic Conflict in the Russian Federation and Transcaucasia*. Cambridge, MA: Harvard University, John F. Kennedy School of Government, 1993.

Hill, Fiona, and Pamela Jewett, *"Back in the USSR."* Cambridge, MA: Harvard University, John F. Kennedy School of Government, 1994.

Yeltsin, Boris, *The Struggle for Russia*. New York: Random House, 1994.

Central Asia

Akiner, Shirin, *Central Asia: New Arc of Crisis?* London: Royal United Services Institute for Defense Studies, 1993.

Allworth, Edward A., *Central Asia: 120 Years of Russian Rule*. Durham, NC: Duke University Press, 1989.

Allworth, Edward A., *The Modern Uzbeks: A Cultural History*. Stanford, CA: Hoover Institution Press, 1990.

Allworth, Edward A., ed., *The Nationality Question in Soviet Central Asia*. New York: Praeger Publishers, 1973.

Becker, Seymour, *Russia's Protectorates in Central Asia: Bukhara and Khiva, 1865-1924*. Cambridge, MA: Harvard University Press, 1968.

Black, Cyril E., et al., *The Modernization of Inner Asia*. Armonk, NY: M.E. Sharpe Inc, 1991.

Canfield, Robert L., ed., *Turko-Persia in Historical Perspective*, Cambridge: Cambridge University Press, 1991.

Critchlow, James, *Nationalism in Uzbekistan: A Soviet Republic's Road to Sovereignty*. Boulder, CO: Westview Press, 1991.

Fierman, William, ed., *Soviet Central Asia: The Failed Transformation*. Boulder, CO: Westview Press, 1991.

Fuller, Graham E., "The Emergence of Central Asia." *Foreign Policy*, Spring 1990.

Fuller, Graham E., *Central Asia: The New Geopolitics*. Santa Monica, CA: Rand, 1992.

Goble, Paul, "Running Aground in Central Asia." *CEO International Strategies*, June/July 1993.

Grousset, René, *L'Empire des Steppes: Attila, Gengis-Khan, Tamerlan*. Paris: Payot, 1939.

Holdsworth, Mary, *Turkestan in the Nineteenth Century: A Brief History of the Khanates of Bukhara, Kokand and Khiva*. Oxford: Central Asian Research Center, 1959.

Krader, Lawrence, *Peoples of Central Asia* (Uralic and Altaic Series, vol. 26). Bloomington, IN: Indiana University Publications, 1966.

Mandelbaum, Michael, ed., *Central Asia and the World: Kazakhstan, Uzbekistan, Tajikistan, Kyrgyzstan, and Turkmenistan*. New York: The Council on Foreign Relations, 1994.

Olcott, Martha Brill, *The Kazakhs*. Stanford, CA: Hoover Institution Press, 1987.

Pierce, Richard, *Russia in Central Asia 1867-1917*. Berkeley, CA: University of California Press, 1960.

Richards, Alan, "Political Economy Review of Kazakhstan." Washington, D.C.: Chemonics, 1994 (unpublished paper).

Rumer, Boris Z., *Soviet Central Asia: "A Tragic Experiment."* Winchester, MA: Unwin Hyman, Inc., 1990.

Shashenkov, Maxim, *Security Issues of the Ex-Soviet Central Asian Republics*. London: Brassey's, 1992.

Wheeler, Geoffrey, *The Modern History of Soviet Central Asia*. New York: Frederick A. Praeger, Publishers, 1964.

Transcaucasia

Altstadt, Audrey L., *The Azerbaijani Turks: Power and Identity Under Russian Rule*. Stanford, CA: Hoover Institution Press, 1992.

Henze, Paul B., *The Transcaucasus in Transition*. Santa Monica, CA: Rand Corporation, 1991.

Henze, Paul B., *Turkey and Georgia: Expanding Relations*. Santa Monica, CA: Rand Corporation, 1992.

Kazemzadeh, Firuz, *The Struggle for Transcaucasia*. New York: Philosophical Library, 1951.

Suny, Ronald Grigor, *Looking Toward Ararat: Armenia in Modern History*. Bloomington and Indianapolis, IN: Indiana University Press, 1993.

Suny, Ronald Grigor, *Armenia in the Twentieth Century*. Chico, CA: Scholars Press, 1983.

Suny, Ronald Grigor, *The Making of the Georgian Nation*. Bloomington, IN: Indiana University Press, 1988.

Suny, Ronald Grigor, *Transcaucasia: Nationalism and Social Change*. Ann Arbor, MI: University of Michigan, 1983.

Yerasimos, Stéphane, "Caucase: le retour de la Russie." *Politique étrangère* (Spring 1994).

The North Caucasus

Blank, Stephen, "The Formation of the Soviet North Caucasus, 1918-24." *Central Asian Survey* (12:1) 1993.

Broxup, Marie Bennigsen, *The North Caucasus barrier: the Russian advance towards the Muslim World*. New York: St. Martin's Press, 1992.

II. Outside Countries

China

Barfield, Thomas J., *The Perilous Frontier: Nomadic Empires and China*. Cambridge, MA: Basil Blackwell, 1989.

Barnett, A. Doak, *China and the Major Powers in East Asia*. Washington, D.C.: The Brookings Institution, 1977.

Benson, Linda, and Ingvar Svanberg, eds., *The Kazaks of China: Essays on an Ethnic Minority*. Uppsala: Almqvist & Wiksell International, 1988.

Chen, King C., *The Foreign Policy of China*. Roseland. NJ: East-West Who ? Inc. Publishers, 1972.

Fairbank, John King, *The Great Chinese Revolution: 1800-1985*. New York: Harper & Row, 1986.

Fairbank, John King, ed., *The Chinese World Order: Traditional China's Foreign Relations*. Cambridge, MA: Harvard University Press, 1968.

Fairbank, John K., Edwin O. Reischauer, and Albert M. Craig, *East Asia: Tradition & Transformation* (Revised Edition). Boston, MA: Houghton Mifflin Company, 1989.

Forbes, Andrew D. W., *Warlords and Muslims in Chinese Central-Asia—A Political-History of Republican Sinkiang, 1911-1949*. New York: Cambridge University Press, 1986.

Kao, Ting Tsz, *The Chinese Frontiers*. Aurora IL: Chinese Scholarly Publishing Company, 1980.

Maltor, Isabelle, and Dongfang Ouyang, "Nouvelle donne régionale pour le Xinjiang." *Le Monde Diplomatique*, November 1993.

Mancall, Mark, *China at the Center: 300 Years of Foreign Policy*. New York: The Free Press, 1984.

Odom, William E., *Trial After Triumph: East Asia After the Cold War*. Indianapolis, IN: Hudson Institute, 1992.

Schwartz, Benjamin, *China's Cultural Values*. Tempe, AZ: Arizona State University, 1985.

Segal, Gerald, "China's Changing Shape." *Foreign Affairs*, May-June 1994 (Vol 73:3)

Spence, Jonathan D., *The Search for Modern China*. New York: W. W. Norton & Co., 1990.

Worden, Robert L., et al., *China: A Country Study*. Washington, D.C.: U.S. Government Printing Office, 1988.

Turkey

Abramowitz, Morton I., "Dateline Ankara: Turkey After Ozal." *Foreign Policy*, Summer 1993.

Alpay, Sahin, "Turkey in 2020." *Cumhuriyet*, March-April 1991.

Barkey, Henri J., "Turkish-American Relations in the Post-War Era." *Orient* 33 (1992) 3.

Beschorner, Natasha, *Water and Instability in the Middle East*. London: Brassey's, 1992.

Birand, Mehmet Ali, *Shirts of Steel: An Anatomy of the Turkish Armed Forces*. London: I. B. Tauris & Co. Ltd, 1991.

Blank, Stephen J., et al., *Turkey's Strategic Position at the Crossroads of World Affairs*. Carlisle Barracks, PA: SSI U.S. Army War College, 1993.

Davidson, Roderic H., ed., *Essays in Ottoman and Turkish History, 1774-1923*. Austin, TX: University of Texas Press, 1990.

Fromkin, David, *A Peace To End All Peace: Creating the Modern Middle East 1914-1922*. New York: Henry Holt and Company, 1989.

Fuller, Graham E., *Turkey Faces East: New Orientations Towards the Middle East and the Old Soviet Union*. Santa Monica, CA: Rand, 1992.

Fuller, Graham E., and Ian O. Lesser, eds., *Turkey's New Geopolitics: From the Balkans to Western China*. Boulder, CO: Westview Press, 1993.

Georgeon, Francois, "De Mossoul à Kirkouk la Turquie et la question du Kurdistan irakien." *Monde arabe Maghreb et Marchrek*, April-June 1991, no. 132.
Lewis, Bernard, *The Emergence of Modern Turkey*. London: Oxford University Press, 1968.

Lewis, Geoffrey L., *Turkey*. New York: Frederick A. Praeger, 1965.

Pitman, Paul M., *Turkey: A Country Study*. Washington, D.C.: Superintendent of Documents, US GPO, 1988.

Robins, Philip, "Between Sentiment and Self-Interest: Turkey's Policy toward Azerbaijan and the Central Asian States." *The Middle East Journal*, Autumn 1993 (Vol. 47:4).

The Kurdish issue

Chaliand, Gerard, ed., *A People Without A Country: The Kurds and Kurdistan*. London: Zed Press, 1980.

Entessar, Nader, *Kurdish Ethnonationalism*. Boulder, CO: Westview Press, 1992.

Gunter, Michael M., *The Kurds in Turkey: A Political Dilemma*. Boulder, CO: Westview Press, 1990.

Gunter, Michael M., *The Kurds of Iraq: Tragedy and Hope*. New York: St. Martin's Press, 1992.

Kreyenbroek, Philip G., and Stefan Speri, *The Kurds: A Contemporary Overview*. London: Routledge, 1992.

Iran

Abrahamian, Ervand, *Khomeinism: Essays on the Islamic Republic*. Berkeley, CA: University of California Press, 1993.

Abrahamian, Ervand, *Iran Between Two Revolutions*. Princeton, NJ: Princeton University Press, 1982.

Ajami, Fouad, *The Vanished Imam*. Ithaca, NY: Cornell University Press, 1986.

Amirahmadi, Hooshang, and Nader Entessar, *Iran and the Arab World*. New York: St. Martin's Press, 1993.

Amirahmadi, Hooshang, and Nader Entessar, eds., *Reconstruction and Regional Diplomacy in the Persian Gulf*. London: Routledge, 1992.

Arjomand, Said Amir, *The Turban and the Crown: The Islamic Revolution in Iran*. New York: Oxford University Press, 1988.

Atkin, Muriel, *Russia and Iran, 1780-1828*. Minneapolis, MN: University of Minnesota Press, 1980.

Bakhash, Shaul, *The Reign of the Ayatollahs*. New York: Basic Books, 1984.

Bernard, Cheryl, and Zalmay Khalilzad, *The Government of God— Iran's Islamic Republic*. New York: Columbia University Press, 1984.

Chubin, Shahram, *Iran's National Security Policy: Intentions, Capabilities, and Impact*. Washington, D.C.: The Carnegie Endowment for International Peace, 1994.

Clawson, Patrick, *Iran's Challenge to the West: How, When and Why*. Washington, D.C.: The Washington Institute for Near East Policy, 1993.

Clawson, Patrick, ed., *Iran's Strategic Intentions and Capabilities*. Washington, D.C.: National Defense University (INSS), 1994.

Embassy of Algeria, Interest Section of Iran, *Imam Khomeini's Last Will and Testament*. Washington DC: Embassy of the Democratic Republic of Algeria, Interest Section of the Islamic Republic of Iran, 1989.

Fuller, Graham E., *The "Center of the Universe:" The Geopolitics of Iran*. Boulder, CO: Westview Press, 1991.

Hunter, Shireen T., *Iran and the World: Continuity in a Revolutionary Decade*. Bloomington, IN: Indiana University Press, 1990.

Hunter, Shireen T., *Iran after Khomeini*. New York: Praeger, 1992.

Kamrava, Mehran, *The Political History of Modern Iran: From Tribalism to Theocracy*. Westport, CT: Praeger, 1992.

Keddie, Nikki R., *Roots of Revolution: An Interpretive History of Modern Iran*. New Haven, CT: Yale University Press, 1981.

Kedourie, Elie, and Sylvia G. Haim, eds., *Towards a Modern Iran: Studies in Thought, Politics and Society*. London: Frank Cass & Co., 1980.

Kemp, Geoffrey, *Forever Enemies? American Policy and the Islamic Republic of Iran*. Washington, D.C.: The Carnegie Endowment for International Peace, 1994.

Mertz, Helen Chapin, *Iran: A Country Study*. Washington, D.C.: Superintendent of Documents, U.S. GPO, 1989.

Mottahedeh, Roy, *The Mantle of the Prophet*. New York: Simon and Schuster, 1985.

Norton, Augustus R., *Amal and the Shi'a*. Austin, TX: University of Texas Press, 1987.

Ramazani, Rouhollah K., *Iran's Foreign Policy, 1941-1973: A Study of Foreign Policy in Modernizing Nations*. Charlottesville, VA: University Press of Virginia, 1975.

Ramazani, Rouhollah K., *The Foreign Policy of Iran: A Developing Nation in World Affairs, 1500-1941*. Charlottesville, VA: University Press of Virginia, 1966.

Zonis, Marvin, and Daniel Brumberg, *Khomeini, the Islamic Republic of Iran, and the Arab World*. Cambridge, MA: Center for Middle Eastern Studies, Harvard University, 1987.

Zonis, Marvin, *The Political Elite of Iran*. Princeton, NJ: Princeton University Press, 1971.

Afghanistan

Banuazizi, Ali, and Myra Weiner, eds., *The State, Religion and Ethnic Politics, Afghanistan, Iran and Pakistan*. Syracuse, NY: Syracuse University Press, 1986

Bradsher, Henry S., *Afghanistan and the Soviet Union*, Durham, NC: Duke Press Policy Studies, 1983.

Brigot, André, and Roy Olivier, *The War in Afghanistan*. New York, Harvester-Wheatsheaf, 1988.
Dupree, Louis, *Afghanistan*. Princeton, NJ: Princeton University Press, 1973

Fuller, Graham E., *Islamic Fundamentalism in Afghanistan: Its Character and Prospects*. Santa Monica, CA: Rand, 1991

Harrison, Selig S., *In Afghanistan's Shadow: Baluch Nationalism and Soviet Temptations*. New York: Carnegie Endowment for International Peace, 1981.

Hauner, Milan, and Robert L. Canfield, eds., *Afghanistan and the Soviet Union: Collision and Transformation*. Boulder, CO: Westview Press, 1989

Khalilzad, Zalmay, "The Politics of Ethnicity in Southwest Asia: Political Development or Political Decay." *Political Science Quarterly*, vol. 99, no. 4 (1984).

Maley, William, and Fazel Haq Saikal, *Political Order in Post-Communist Afghanistan*. Boulder, CO: Lynne Reinner Publishers, 1992.

Nyrop, Richard F., and Donald M. Seekins, *Afghanistan: A Country Study*. Washington, D.C.: U.S. Government Printing Office, 1986

Roy, Olivier, *L'Afghanistan: Islam et modernité politique*. Paris, Le Seuil, 1985.

The Indian subcontinent

Bhatia, H. S., ed., *Military History of British India (1607-1947)*. New Delhi: Deep & Deep Publications, 1977.

Duran, Khalid, "Rivalries Over the New Muslim Countries." *Aussenpolitik*, IV/1992.

Handa, Rohit, *Policy for India's Defence*. New Delhi: Chetana Publications, 1976.

Minault, Gail, *The Khilafat Movement*. New York: Columbia University Press, 1982.

Nyrop, Richard F., *Pakistan: A Country Study*. Washington, D.C.: U.S. Government Printing Office, 1984.

Spear, Percival, *The Oxford History of Modern India, 1740-1975*. Delhi: Oxford University Press. 1979.

Thapar, Romila, *A History of India* (volume 1). London: Penguin Books, 1990.

Tsagronis, John, *Pakistan: Prospects for Democracy*. Washington, D.C.: Hudson Institute, 1992

Wolpert, Stanley, *A New History of India*. New York: Oxford University Press, 1993.

III. Specific Issues

Crime and drugs

Labrousse, Alain, and Alain Wallon, *La Planete des drogues: Organisations criminelles, guerres et blanchiment*. Paris: Le Seuil, 1993.

Economic issues

Country Reports from the International Monetary Fund and the Economist Intelligence Unit.

Energy

Bell, Helen, et al., *The Golden Road to Oil & Gas In Central Asia*, New York: Petroleum Intelligence Weekly, April 1993.

Brady, Rose, et al., "The Scramble for Oil's Last Frontier." *Business Week,* Jan. 11, 1993, pp. 42-44.

British Petroleum, *BP Statistical Review of World Energy: June 1994*. London: The British Petroleum Company p.l.c., 1994.

British Petroleum, *BP Statistical Review of World Energy*. London: British Petroleum p.l.c., 1993.

Central Intelligence Agency (U.S.), *USSR Energy Atlas*. Central Intelligence Agency, 1985.

Energy Information Administration (U.S.), *International Energy Outlook 1993*. Washington, D.C.: U.S. Government Printing Office, 1993.

Energy Information Administration, U.S. Department of Energy, *International Energy Outlook 1994*. Washington, D.C.: Energy Information Administration, 1994.

General Accounting Office (U.S.), *Kazakhstan Unlikely to Be Major Source of Oil for the United States*. Washington, D.C.: General Accounting Office, 1994.

Islam

Arberry, A. J., ed., *Religion in the Middle East*, vols. 1 and 2. Cambridge: Cambridge University Press, 1969.

Atkin, Muriel, *The Subtlest Battle: Islam in Soviet Tajikistan*. Philadelphia. PA: Foreign Policy Research Institute, 1989.

Bennigsen, Alexandre, et al., *Soviet Strategy and Islam*. London: Macmillan, 1989.

Bennigsen, Alexandre, and S. Enders Wimbush, *Muslims of the Soviet Empire*. Bloomington. IN: Indiana University Press, 1986.

Bennigsen, Alexander, "Mullahs, Mujahidin and Soviet Muslims." *Problems of Communism*, Nov-Dec 1984.

Esposito, John L., *The Islamic threat: myth or reality*. New York: Oxford University Press, 1992.

Fuller, Graham E., *Islamic Fundamentalism in the Northern Tier Countries: An Integrative View*. Santa Monica, CA: Rand, 1991.

Gross, Jo-Anne, ed., *Muslims in Central Asia: Expressions of identity and change*. Durham, NC: Duke University Press, 1992.

Guillaume, Alfred, *Islam*. New York: Penguin Books, 1978.

Kedourie, Elie, *Islam in the Modern World*. Holt, Rinehart and Winston: New York, 1981.

Kepel, Gilles, *Le Prophete et Pharaon*. Paris: La Decouverte, 1984.

Lewis, Bernard, "The Enemies of God." *New York Review of Books*, 25 March 1993.

Lewis, Bernard, *Islam and the West*. New York: Oxford University Press, 1993.

Mitchell, Richard P., *The Society of the Muslim Brothers*. London: Oxford University Press, 1969.

Political development

Codevilla, Angelo, "Is Pinochet the Model?" *Foreign Affairs*, Nov-Dec 1993 (Vol 72:5).

Dahl, Robert A., *Polyarchy: Participation and Opposition*. New Haven, CT: Yale University Press, 1971.

Huntington, Samuel P., *Political Order in Changing Societies*. New Haven, CT: Yale University Press, 1968.

Huntington, Samuel P., *The Third Wave: Democratization in the Late Twentieth Century*. Norman, OK, and London: University of Oklahoma Press, 1991.

Machiavelli, Niccolo, *The Prince*. New York: Alfred Knopf, 1992.

Migdal, Joel S., *Strong Societies and Weak States: State-Society Relations and State Capabilities in the Third World*. Princeton, NJ: Princeton University Press, 1988.

Naim, Moses, *Paper Tigers and Minotaurs*. Washington, D.C.: Carnegie Endowment for International Peace, 1993.

Odom, William E., *On Internal War: American and Soviet Approaches to Third World Clients and Insurgents*. Durham, NC: Duke University Press, 1992.

Olson, Mancur, *The Rise and Decline of Nations: Economic Growth, Stagnation, and Social Rigidities*. New Haven, CT: Yale University Press, 1982.

IV. Periodicals

Foreign Broadcast Information Service, *Daily Report: West Europe* and *Daily Report: Central Eurasia*.

Radio Free Europe/Radio Liberty, *Daily Report* and *Research Reports*.

Journal articles from *Central Asia Monitor*, *Central Asian Survey*,

Demokratsyia, Foreign Affairs, Foreign Policy, International Security, Jane's Defence Weekly, Orbis, Survival.

Articles from weekly publications (*The Economist, Far Eastern Economic Review*) and dailies (*Financial Times, Le Monde, New York Times, Washington Post*).

Index

About the Authors

Lieutenant General William E. Odom, U.S. Army (Ret.), is Director of National Security Studies for Hudson Institute and an adjunct professor at Yale University. General Odom served as Director of the U.S. National Security Agency from 1985 to 1988, and from 1981 to 1985 he was Assistant Chief of Staff for Intelligence, the Army's senior intelligence officer.

From 1977 to 1981, General Odom was a senior member of the National Security Council staff and military assistant to the President's Assistant for National Security Affairs, Zbigniew Brzezinski. He graduated from the United States Military Academy in 1954, received an M.A. in political science from Columbia University in 1962, and received a Ph.D. from Columbia University in 1970.

His publications include four books—*The Soviet Volunteers*; *On Internal War*; *Trial After Triumph: East Asia After the Cold War*; and *America's Military Revolution: Strategy and Structure After the Cold War*.

Robert Dujarric is a research fellow in the Washington, D.C., office of Hudson Institute. He specializes in research on international security issues. From 1989 to 1993, he worked for Goldman Sachs International in London. Previously, he was an investment banker with the First Boston Corporation in New York and a consultant to the Investment Banking Department at First Boston (Asia) Limited in Tokyo.

He holds a master's degree in public and private management from Yale University and a bachelor's degree in government from

Harvard University. He is the author of *Hudson Briefing Paper* No. 160, "Russia and the 'Islamic' Threat," and *Hudson Briefing Paper* No. 169, "America and Europe: The Risks of Isolationism."

About Hudson Institute

Hudson Institute is a private, not-for-profit research organization founded in 1961 by the late Herman Kahn. Hudson analyzes and makes recommendations about public policy for business and government executives, as well as for the public at large. The institute does not advocate an express ideology or political position. However, more than thirty years of work on the most important issues of the day has forged a viewpoint that embodies skepticism about the conventional wisdom, optimism about solving problems, a commitment to free institutions and individual responsibility, an appreciation of the crucial role of technology in achieving progress, and an abiding respect for the importance of values, culture, and religion in human affairs.

Since 1984, Hudson has been headquartered in Indianapolis, Indiana. It also maintains offices in Washington, D.C.; Madison, Wisconsin; Montreal, Canada; and Brussels, Belgium.